Up the Down Dollar

No one who cares about the condition of his bank account or the health of the nation's economy can afford to ignore UP THE DOWN DOLLAR. Author Edward Meadows, a trained economist and Associate Editor of *Fortune* magazine, explains in clear and rousing language why the American economy is so bedeviled by inflation and recurrent unemployment. Writing from a broad social and political perspective, Meadows uncovers the basic conflict between our democratic ideal and the economic reality of our large-scale technology. The result of this clash is nothing less than inflation. And contrary to the views of mainstream economists and White House advisers, Meadows believes the government's policies are completely powerless to abolish this inflation.

As Meadows explores this theme, he takes the reader on a colorful, forthright tour of our current economy, exposing along the way sundry economic charlatans in Washington and on Wall Street. Meadows manages to turn what is often a dull subject into a lively and relevant discussion accessible to the lay reader. UP THE DOWN DOLLAR is essential reading for anyone who wants to understand the complex realities behind today's headlines.

Up the Down Dollar

A REALIST'S GUIDE TO
THE MARKETPLACE

Edward Meadows

ANCHOR PRESS/DOUBLEDAY
Garden City, New York
1980

ISBN 0-385-15144-6
Library of Congress Catalog Card Number 79-7203

Copyright © 1980 by Edward Meadows

To Mr. and Mrs. E. M. Meadows,
Mamie, Pam, Diane, little Pam,
Brian, Rosie, Sally, and Missy

Contents

1

The Roots of Dissent

THE YEARS AFTER World War II witnessed the flowering of American technological magic on a scale that had never been seen before and is not likely to be seen again in this century. By the time the 1960s rolled around, American wealth had become so abundant, so assured, that its very munificence unleashed at last the cultural and political contradictions that had laid hidden deep in the cracks of the giant technological machine. In the 1970s the bills all came due. In the 1980s they must be paid.

American technology grew to a truly large scale during World War II, when industry was called on to produce tanks, bombers, and big ships, en masse. It was during the war that airplane manufacturers like Douglas and Boeing first developed the kind of large-scale manufacturing that could produce thousands of warplanes a year. To keep the immense facilities working after the war, the aircraft makers needed bigger and more expensive planes to construct, so they went full-scale into production of jet passenger planes. American steel, aluminum, shipbuilding, auto, and chemical companies had also accelerated into high gear for war production, with the biggest operations concentrated among relatively few firms. (The government had placed a third of its orders with only ten companies, among them General Motors, Chrysler Corporation, and B. F. Goodrich. In all, defense contracts went to only a familiar handful of the nation's manufacturing companies.)

When the war ended, the United States was endowed

with the world's most advanced technology of production. Big assembly lines were poised, ready now to supply the world with consumer goods instead of arms. The United States could not have been put in a better position. All of Europe and much of Asia were in ruins. The United States, in contrast, was just awakening to what Henry Luce called the American Century. Not only would our huge factories supply the needs of the world, but if the rest of the world, ravaged by war, didn't have the cash to buy American, we would supply the wherewithal via the Marshall Plan.

At home, it had been feared that when the war ended and the defense orders stopped, massive layoffs would create another depression just like the one that had caused economic stagnation in the years before World War II was declared. But the criers of doom had forgotten that many who stayed at home during the war had accumulated large savings accounts because there were few consumer goods to buy. Not only that, but foreigners had deposited more than half the world's gold supply in the United States for safekeeping. After the war, Americans went on a wild spending spree. Cars were bought up so fast they disappeared from the showrooms. Tires were not to be had. Refrigerators and washing machines sold like hot cakes, as did suburban tract homes.

American industry had its hands full. Every businessman's dream had come true, for the great postwar demand, at home and overseas, fed industry with profits through which to expand the technological structure. It was the golden age of corporate business enterprise. Productivity was rising, individual incomes were increasing, and inflation was only an occasional, minor problem. In those innocent days, an inflation rate of 3 percent was intolerably high. Between 1946 and 1960 after-inflation Gross National Product soared in the United States. Measured in 1972 dollars, it went from $477 billion in 1946 to $737 billion in 1960. It was a dramatic tour de force.

Compared to the bustle of the war era and the postwar spending boom, the 1950s were mild and prosperous years, during which the nation was building up the new technology and applying it to a host of inventions—many of which had been created before or during World War II but put off because of lack of money or foresight. Television was one such innovation. The computer was another. A third was the jet airliner. Edwin Land came up with the Polaroid camera and Chester Carlson developed the Xerox machine.

The 1960s were palpably more energetic years, during which gentle prosperity turned into the ebullient rush of boom times. Who can forget the go-go conglomerate empires of business "geniuses" such as James Joseph Ling, who built a paper house of stock deals—a house that collapsed by 1970, with $70 million in losses that year? Or the investment funds that soared with growth stocks like Xerox and Polaroid, and promised to make thousands of small investors rich?

Yet to those of us who came of college age in the 1960s, the business boom was unremarkable. It was something in the background, hardly to be noticed. After all, we had no memories of depression or wartime sacrifice. Our short memories recalled only the bland but reasonably comfortable 1950s of our childhood, symbolized by the avuncular caricature of President Dwight D. Eisenhower. For many of us, it was a time when our families were steadily moving up the income ladder, buying bigger homes and bigger cars, partaking of what we assumed to be the normal and God-given state of American prosperity. To have money became the expected state of things. The getting of it became a trivial problem, even a boring one.

The politics of the epoch followed naturally from the assumption of eternal affluence. For if middle-class comfort was the norm, then clearly aberrations from the norm were unnatural and therefore caused by some greater force. If ghettos contained many thousands of desperately poor people in an era of limitless wealth, we reasoned that someone must have willfully oppressed these people. Why would they want to do this? Since many of the American poor were dark-skinned, racism was the easy answer.

Notice what we were doing. We were simply applying the same logic that had sped the United States to its technological and managerial miracle. Jean-Jacques Servan-Schreiber, writing in 1967, remarked that American supremacy was based on nothing more nor less than "the use and systematic perfection of all the instruments of reason." Our conclusions were identical to those reached by logicians many years earlier, during the French Revolution, when it was imagined that men could sit around a table and reason their way out of any problem. The ultimate induction of French revolutionary thought was that man is perfectible. Its corollary is that, if man is perfectible by nature, then it must necessarily be external, evil forces that keep him from reaching his perfect state. Our job, then, was to find these forces, identify them, and destroy them.

The first and easiest target was the old South, blatantly racist and a ready whipping boy for the nation's awakening righteous indignation. Of course, it wasn't as simple as that. A Mississippi sheriff would openly display his contempt for blacks in front of network news cameras, but the average cabdriver in Queens was just as much of a racist. White liberal freedom marchers could demonstrate against racism in Alabama, but they returned to lily-white suburbs on Long Island. As the decade wore on, it became evident that if the South was the most obviously racist section of the nation, it was also, paradoxically, the region that had the closest ties to the black culture and the one that finally offered blacks the most opportunities. By the middle of the 1970s, far more southern neighborhoods and schools were integrated than their counterparts in the North and Middle West. Black people, fed up with the hypocrisy of white northern liberals so bloated with moral superiority that they were blind to their own racism, began moving back to the South. If there is a black middle class today, it will be found there.

Racism couldn't be directly tied to corporate magnates. Most large corporations were quick to establish affirmative action programs, even if they hired only pretty black receptionists. But the seemingly racist war in Vietnam could in part be laid at the doorstep of big business. The Pentagon had become a sort of giant corporate headquarters, run by Robert McNamara, fomer president of the Ford Motor Company and now President Kennedy's Secretary of Defense. The Vietnamese war gave an extra push to the 1960s business boom. Hundreds of small companies grew fat on government war contracts. The most modern electronic and chemical technology of postwar America was used to murder Vietnamese. "Smart" bombs and napalm improved army "kill ratios." The "kill ratios" were themselves a product of modern corporate management science, an application of quantitative techniques learned at MIT.

If large-scale technocratic corporatism is by nature bloodless and scientific, representing bureaucracy in the service of corporate greed, the war in Vietnam offered a ghastly illustration of its perversion through the profit motive. Yellowskinned "gooks" were to be killed with new technology in order to make Southeast Asia safe for American business and political interests. The fact that corporate executives were as repelled by the anti-war views of the emerging young as were Pentagon officials and White House aides made the division clear. We saw the military-industrial complex, first identified by President Eisenhower on leaving office, as the very soul of American-industry-at-war. It was not a war to defend the nation's boundaries from aggression. It was a war to bludgeon into submission Third World peoples who had threatened to upset the geopolitical designs of American diplomatic thinkers. These thinkers devoutly believed that a Communist Vietnam would mean a Communist Southeast Asia, therefore a Communist Asia, and soon a

Communist world. The Domino Theory, however, was an abstraction imposed by Western minds on a war which, as we found out later, had its true origin in centuries of antagonism between Asian tribes.

As if this weren't sufficient cause to alienate a generation of the pampered young, our political leaders seemed to relish political styles that made them appear ugly and alien to the ideals of the American democracy. President Johnson's patent deviousness and, after him, President Nixon's paranoia did nothing to boost the credibility of their causes. Both men were caught in a policy commitment—to bomb Vietnam into oblivion—that divided the nation irreparably.

Enter the counterculture, with marijuana as its hallmark and peace as its ideology. Slovenly dress styles, anarchistic instincts, and sexual freedom characterized a young people's culture that legitimized vague grievances and offered some nonconformity to conform to. The anti-racism and anti-war and anti-business sentiments were credible enough, and so was a general sympathy with the loudly proclaimed oppression of Third World peoples, as they called themselves— Chicanos in California and Orientals in Boston and Indians in Arizona. Everyone, it seemed, had a claim of oppression to exercise. But it didn't do to examine closely exactly what the "oppression" consisted of, or exactly who the oppressor was. The assumption seemed to be that anyone who wasn't rich and upper-middle-class was ipso facto being oppressed, and that anyone who became rich and upper-middle-class also became an oppressor.

And fashion was on the side of the "oppressed." One might be awfully bored with slogans like "Free Huey Newton" (the Black Panther who was accused of murder). One might have found the stiff revolutionary harangues in underground newspapers unpalatable. But if one wanted to have fun and get girls, it was best to wear the hair long and keep a few extra joints in the shirt pocket. Street demonstrations had their political purposes, but for many they were primarily social occasions. Who in his right mind cared to march down the Washington Mall and assemble at the Washington Monument just to hear some ideologue emit dull rhetoric that everybody had heard a hundred times before? The fun was in sitting on the White House lawn, with President Nixon inside, smoking a joint of marijuana with friends. The fun was later consorting with a pretty blue-jeaned blonde who, in the spirit of the times, gave easily of herself. Freedom seemed to mean sexual freedom, too. But most of all, the new music was fun, especially if it was diffused through a thick cloud of marijuana smoke, as it always was. Style was what really counted. And this was true even for the handful of counterculture media stars, people like Abbie Hoffman and Jerry Rubin. For though these people steeped themselves in revolutionary rhetoric and gave every appearance, in network television interviews, of deadly earnestness, it has subsequently been revealed, in the inevitable biographies and autobiographies of the 1960s, that these so-called revolutionaries really wanted to become movie stars all along. Or at least rock stars. Or, if nothing better, media stars, which they did become. What they were really "into" was self-aggrandizement.

The counterculture manifested a number of sharp contradictions. *Rolling Stone* magazine, a San Francisco music periodical that for a time became the bible of the hippie culture, preached the usual peace and brotherhood, but its writers were most unegalitarian elitists. Their *modus operandi* was to spend an evening in the company of some rock star, who fed them, gave them dope, and let them ride along in the limo. As payment, the *Rolling Stone* writer told his audience how great it was to hang out with the heavy rock star, and what a genius this rock star happened to be, and by inference how clever the writer was to have been so favored by the star. The *Rolling Stone* writer kept himself ahead of the masses by describing whatever was truly chic in the past tense, so that by the time his readers found out, it was already passé.

The movement was united, however, in giving free vent to any brand of dissent. If blacks were already deemed oppressed, soon homosexuals were declaring their oppression, and wealthy white middle-class women decided they too should be counted among the oppressed. Backpackers became militant environmentalists. Pet owners marched for animals' rights. Ladylike home economists metamorphosed into sharp-tongued consumer advocates, ready to sue every corporation in the *Fortune* 500. Their voices were amplified in the echo chambers of the national media. For media correspondents were anxious to be as fashionable as the hippest rock musician or women's liberationist. Journalism, after all, is full of bright, aggressive people who often come from lowly roots and who use their clout to climb social ladders. *Time* magazine writers hung Mao posters on the walls of their cubicles, and CBS reporters bought rustic farms where they could commune with the natural environment. The media's sympathies lay with the hip culture.

For most of post-Vietnam, post-Watergate, post-OPEC America, the upheaval of the 1960s is a faint, often unpleasant memory of discontent—which is ironic since it was also a time of great prosperity for the nation, and a boom time for Wall Street. But the spirit of the 1960s seemed to have been dashed by the OPEC price rise and the recession that followed, which sobered the young with the worry once again of how to make money in the real world. In affluent Washington, however, the spirit of the counterculture lives on. The more militant children of the 1960s protest movement, alienated as they were from corporate America, prepared themselves for public service, for doing good, and a large number ended up as government bureaucrats.

Visit any government agency today and you will find the keepers of the public interest, circa 1968. The agency chief may be a traditional sort, even a former corporate executive.

But down in the regulatory trenches, where the detailed rules are written, sit former flower children, some still sporting their beards and, occasionally, beads. The Environmental Protection Agency, the Consumer Product Safety Commission, the Federal Trade Commission, the Occupational Safety and Health Administration, and a dozen more bureaucracies are staffed with children of the 1960s, there to express their distrust of private enterprise through specific rules and regulations restricting the power of corporations. If they can't topple the private economy, at least they can strangle it with regulations. That is what's called working within the system. (Magazines even sprang up to cater to this group. The "new" *Esquire* magazine, for instance, advertised itself in 1978 as a periodical for the 1960s counter-culture type who has now joined the "new, better Establishment.")

It is curious, though, that by the late 1970s the spirit of the nation at large had turned nearly 180 degrees away from the pretensions of the 1960s ethic. The new style is haute disco culture and, beyond that, right-wing working-class punk rock. At Studio 54 on Manhattan's West Side, one gets little sense of deep social consciousness at work as one watches long-haired models undulating in their Marcia Trinder slit dresses, with jewelry by Kenneth Jay Lane, shoes by Charles Jourdan, hair by Benjamin of Benjamin Salon, and $300 worth of cocaine in their purses. Hairy imitation-proletarian revolutionaries are out; sleek wealth is in. Or, as Argentinian entertainer Nacha Guevara is quoted as saying, in *Interview* magazine, "I give much importance to dressing because I think it's really a way of communicating many things. It's a part of economics. It reveals the division of the classes." Here is a princess of the high disco social circuit speaking in tones calculated to send 1960s radicals screaming for blood—and speaking in the very journal of the new style, Andy Warhol's *Interview*, a magazine full of large photographs dripping with expensive chic and intimate delineations of the lives of designated Beautiful People. *Interview* is the very obverse of *Rolling Stone*. If *Interview* has any politics at all, they are the politics of the upper-middle-class social conservative, à la Guevara.

Moods have changed dramatically everywhere except in Washington, where young bureaucrats, protected by civil service tenure, form a permanent government, immune to presidential administrations and mere public opinion. They are, instead, guided by the private voices of their own ideology. Some, including Michael Pertschuk, chairman of the Federal Trade Commission, have openly proclaimed their intention to use regulation for broad social ends, to redirect the very nature of American society. This is a frightening prospect. A group of unelected bureaucrats, above the political pressures that constrain members of Congress and Presidents, seeks to tell us how to live. These bureaucrats have counterparts in the Kremlin, but nowhere else in America.

Yet it's misleading to say that our social consciousness was not changed during the 1960s. The national psyche did come to accept the need for restraints, for racial justice and safe consumer products, for a safe environment and a curb to untrammeled economic power. If the 1960s changed anything, they pushed attitudes toward what might be called social enlightenment. But when does a pro-environmental sentiment become an anti-business sentiment? For after all, by the early 1970s, even big industrialists saw the need to cut pollution. In February of 1970 *Fortune* magazine came out with a special issue on the environment, in which the need for a cleanup was expressed clearly and specifically. That issue of the magazine was subsequently used as a basic working paper in the formation of the Environmental Protection Agency. The very bastion of business consciousness had given concrete impetus to the novel idea that the environment, and by extension all the detritus of modern technological enterprise, could be cleaned up at little cost to society.

That early optimism has evaporated, however, for we have learned all too well that the stringent conditions of post-OPEC, post-EPA America have landed us in a thick mud of economic stagnation. A maddening concatenation of new forces has resulted in a basic inflation rate that would have been unheard-of only a few years ago, when, as in the 1960s, it was thought that anything above 3 percent inflation a year would involve society in violent clashes.

A decade after that *Fortune* article, it's getting so you have to take out a mortgage to buy a steak at the grocery store, and a full tank of gasoline costs as much as a weekend used to cost. Meanwhile, the fifty-dollar raise you got was just enough to kick you into a higher income tax bracket, which means you have to pay more to Uncle Sam even though you can buy less today than you could a year ago with less pay. Then you pick up the morning paper and see that, amid all the turmoil, oil company profits are at record levels again and some giant corporation has just merged with another corporate monolith. You get the sneaking suspicion that you and everybody else are being had by big business. And the President can't seem to do anything about it at all.

But sit down to dinner with an average corporate executive and you'll get an entirely different story, though one no less sad. The executive squawks about how government regulation is costing him so much that he can't earn a profit anymore, and about how the government paper work is driving his accountants crazy. He also says American workers don't want to work these days, and even if they did, the government keeps raising the minimum wage and Social Security taxes and unemployment compensation so it's too expensive for him to hire more workers anyway; instead, it's cheaper to buy a new machine, even though the fuel bill will be swollen. All in all, he thinks the government is harassing him. He really gets angry when populist politicians go on television and blame businessmen for all the country's ills.

Which story is closer to the truth? The problem is that both stories ring true. Each reflects a different perspective on the crisis that threatens modern America. When the consumer complains about inflation and the businessman complains about the higher costs imposed on him, both are really talking about the same thing. The higher prices result when the businessman passes on his higher costs to his customers so he can earn the same profit as before. But what causes his higher costs? They go up because of numerous political decisions made in Washington and in state capitols and in the palaces of petroleum princes.

What has happened is that the rules of business have changed, right in the middle of the game. OPEC oil ministers decided that businesses could no longer get away with cheap energy costs. Environmentalists decided that businesses could no longer, at no cost to themselves, spew their industrial wastes into the nation's air and water. And politicians decided that big corporations, no matter how efficient they may be, wield so much power that they are incompatible with democratic ideals and must be cut down to size.

Consider an industrialist who, in 1960, decided to construct a paper mill. His problem was to figure out the best combination of workers and machines that would produce paper cheaply enough so that he could charge the going prices for paper and still earn a margin of profit—say 10 percent. In 1960, he knew that labor was relatively expensive because in America labor has always been relatively scarce, and because the government taxes labor much more than it taxes machines. He also knew fuel was dirt-cheap. So, given the state of papermaking technology, the industrialist told his engineers to design a plant using as much machinery as possible and as few workers as possible. He emphasized the latter because friends already in the paper business kept telling him how tough the paperworkers' union was.

But in 1960, what the industrialist didn't know was that some fifteen years after his plant was designed and built, OPEC would send the price of fuel through the ceiling, and the Environmental Protection Agency would force him to buy millions of dollars' worth of pollution abatement equipment. At the same time, the Occupational Safety and Health Administration would force him to rewire his whole plant to replace the two-wire electric outlets with three-wire plugs, and OSHA would demand that he buy toilet seats that conformed to OSHA regulations. Meanwhile, the industrialist had to hire a staff of lawyers, accountants, and clerks just to deal with the paper work forced on his company by the Federal Trade Commission, the Securities and Exchange Commission, the Equal Employment Opportunity Commission, the Council on Wage and Price Stability, and the staffs of congressmen who were writing bills to break up the paper industry.

If the paper manufacturer had had a crystal ball in 1960, he might have decided to build a plant that would take all the imposed costs into account. Not being in possession of a crystal ball, however, the industrialist reacted to each higher expense by raising his prices the same amount, so that he could keep the 10 percent margin of profit. The only trouble with this is that when the paper business is in a slump, as it often is, he can't get the kind of prices he needs to maintain his profit margin. So profits fall and the price of his common stock takes a dive and soon the board of directors is rumored to be actively looking for a new chief executive. The industrialist wonders if the company shouldn't diversify out of the papermaking business by buying a smaller company in another line. The future isn't very promising for paper manufacturing, since energy costs and regulatory costs keep going up. Besides, the Justice Department is launching a splashy new investigation of concentration in the paper industry.

Newspaper and **book** publishers blame paper companies for the higher cost of newspapers and books.

The consumer of paper products—you and I—isn't privy to the worries of the paper manufacturer and, frankly, doesn't care too much about his problems. The consumer has a problem of his own: how to continue buying paper products and all the other products that keep rising in price. The answer, of course, is to get more money. One way is to use more credit cards and bank loans, if the government has made credit cheap. But that's just a temporary solution. The only satisfactory way to cope is to get a pay raise. Unfortunately, the payroll is also a business expense, and when it increases, business tries to pass that higher cost along, too, in higher prices, so that when everyone gets higher wages, inflation soon goes up by about the same amount and everyone is back where he started.

There are several possible ways out of this dilemma. If business sacrificed its profits, then prices wouldn't have to go up as much as they do. But how can business give up profits? Profits are what makes the economy grow. These profits are what is left over after all taxes and expenses, including salaries, are paid. Part of the profits is paid out to stockholders to keep them content. (One in six Americans is a corporate stockholder, and nearly half are housewives, retirees, or the unemployed.) The profits that are left over after stockholders get their cut are kept in the company. They can be used to expand factories or build new ones or buy other companies. This spending by companies is what keeps the private economy growing.

Of course, profits are thought by some polemists to be obscene. But on the most personal level, do Americans really prefer that businesses should earn low profits, or no profits? One doubts it. I always wish Time, Inc., my employer, to make the fattest possible profits. I fervently hope Doubleday will earn riches from this book. I also hope my favorite radio station, WNEW-FM, will continue to do well, so that it will keep the same progressive new-wave rock format I enjoy. Frankly, I want everybody who does me a service to make a profit, whether it's Max's Kansas City, where I sometimes go to hear music, or the news dealer on the corner of Fifty-seventh Street and Lexington Avenue who sells me the Sunday *Times* late Saturday night. Profits are good.

Even from afar, profits are good. Think of Johnny Carson, the longtime regular host of "The Tonight Show." Carson is an absolute monopolist; his appearance on that show has brought NBC 17 percent of the company's entire pretax profits. So Carson gets a paycheck of at least $3 million a year. Yet did anyone cry out that Carson was a dirty monopolist and the possessor of obscene profits? Most Americans only admire Carson's accomplishments. If some crusading senator had suggested putting Carson in jail under the antitrust laws, he would have been laughed out of Washington. Not even Ralph Nader dared complain. (Ralph has appeared on the show with Carson several times.)

Let us assume, then, that profits are necessary. What if we instead got consumers to sacrifice their higher incomes? That would solve inflation as easily as eliminating profits. But who is willing to accept a lower standard of living? We expect not merely to keep up with inflation but to do better with every passing year. It's the American Way, isn't it? Ever since World War II, that's the way the American people have progressed. Until the 1970s, of course, the raises in pay were accompanied by increases in the amount of work produced, and therefore the higher income wasn't inflationary. We were paid more, but we produced more, and employers could recoup the higher payroll costs from the sales of the extra output we produced. Our output increased because Americans were moving from unproductive hand labor on farms to productive work in factories, and because efficient machines were being used more and more.

It is obviously unsatisfactory to ask businesses to give up profits or to ask consumers to give up their living standards.

Then maybe we could strip away the new, higher costs of doing business, and restore American industry to the good old days of bustling growth. Here we come to the heart of the crisis we face. It is that many of these new costs represent our earnest efforts to come to terms with the deep contradictions that arise when a large-scale technocratic state tries to coexist with the ideals of American democracy. These contradictions had remained dormant inside the great technological machine ever since World War II. In the heady decades of business growth, everyone just assumed that energy was cheap and abundant, that foul industrial fumes simply disappeared, and that giant corporations were harmless marvels of industrial efficiency. But OPEC decided to teach us a thing or two about the true value of petroleum energy. Medical researchers armed environmentalists with studies indicating that pollution from petroleum-burning engines could cause cancer, as could a host of technological artifacts. Congress discovered that large corporations had political power as well as financial power, a state of affairs contrary to Jeffersonian views of a democracy in which power is distributed among the people.

Only lately have we begun to realize what has happened. Modern technology, the fountain of our wealth, flourishes under a system of inexpensive energy and free pollution. As it flourishes, it calls forth large-scale enterprise, for reasons that will be duly explained. The modern corporation comes along to manage these large-scale operations. It does a good job of it, but at the same time these corporations inevitably become big, centralized concentrations of power that are incompatible with the ideals of democracy.

The problem presented by the needs of big technology is compounded by a hidden contradiction within democracy itself. With or without large-scale technology, the democratic imperative to build an egalitarian society gives rise to bureaucratic government institutions which enforce equality among the American people, but which also centralize government power in ever-larger authoritarian agencies. De Tocqueville foresaw that this would occur, and he wondered if democracy could survive this concentration of government power.

Now, if we have powerful corporate bureaucracies and powerful government bureaucracies, what is the result? Naturally, the two powers fight each other. Corporate bureaucracies throw their money around Washington to get government subsidies from friendly members of Congress. Government bureaucracies turn themselves into nonelected lawmakers, judges, and juries and regulate the corporate bureaucracy to death. The American people are caught in the crossfire, for the fallout from the battle is inflation and ultimately higher unemployment. Every subsidy given to industry is paid for out of your taxes. Every regulation forced on industry is paid for out of your spending money, as prices go up to cover the cost of complying with the regulation.

So when you hear White House advisers talk about how they can stop inflation by getting Congress to raise taxes or lower the federal budget, or by asking the Federal Reserve to tighten credit, or by slapping on wage and price controls, you know these officials are missing the point. They can't cure the basic inflation rate by any of those traditional measures. Yes, they can slow inflation a little bit, for a short time, or they can make it worse. But there's no way to stop it without addressing the fundamental crisis of modern technology.

And whether inflation caused by the technological crisis came before or after inflation caused by government policies is unimportant. The fact is that government-created inflation has existed since Roman times. In modern postwar America, it has exacerbated an already existing problem. Government inflation-pumping is done for political reasons. Often the public has demanded that the government inflate the money supply to relieve it of its temporary impoverishment. We all love money, don't we? The trouble is that when the government pumps more cash into the economy to compensate for higher prices, the extra cash pushes prices even higher and begets a demand for more money, which further pushes inflation upward, ad infinitum. No one wants to sacrifice, naturally enough, and the government becomes the agency of relief, until the inflation bubble bursts and a dire recession follows.

To solve the inflation problem, it is first necessary to resolve technology's crisis. When that is done, then moderate, stable government economic policies will be able to keep inflation within decent bounds, so long as politicians resist the temptation to use the government's money-creating machine as a vote-getting mechanism. But presidential advisers are only human. How can they handle a crisis that seems to call for drastic action beyond the powers of a President? Perhaps the solution is to reinvent present technology, or scrap it for a new sort of technology; the only alternative is to give up democratic ideals as outmoded.

There are some hints that the nation is moving toward a reinvention of present technology. In 1979, for example, President Carter proposed a $142 billion program to escalate development of alternative energy, and a plan to redesign cars so that by the year 2000 they'll get up to fifty miles per gallon without air pollution. This could work, as far as it goes. Yet it won't go far enough, because no amount of tinkering will eliminate the need for corporate and governmental bigness. On the contrary, huge crash programs will call for even larger scale, and for the bending of environmental and worker safety regulations. In other words, retooling won't get at the very basic difficulty of technocratic corporate and government bureaucracy.

It is possible that in the decades to come we will be saved by the evolution of a new sort of technology, one that uses very little fuel, is clean, quiet, small-scale, and cheap. This new technology will be based on some profound developments under way in the semiconductor industry. The trouble is that the new technology can't replace all our present technology. Making paper, for instance, will remain largely a crude, dirty mechanical-chemical process regardless of refinements in electronic mechanisms. Yes, replacement of newspapers and personal letters by electronic messages read on television screens will decrease the need for paper, and such changes could take the pressure off the physical and social environment. But this new technology will take years to develop into its full potential, and we cannot predict just what that potential will be.

Yet wouldn't it be rather less of a headache if we just accepted rule by huge centralized bureaucracies, whether corporate or governmental or a merger of both? After all, have not even the "neoconservatives" among us come to acknowledge the reality of the welfare state? If we went ahead and agreed on a democratic socialist form of government, then nationalized corporate bureaucracies could blend with government bureaucracies and become a harmonious unity. Planners and paper shufflers would then run the nation in the name of the people. The government would have no trouble imposing anti-pollution regulations because it would own the corporations. Nor would the government have to worry about inflationary rules and regulations because it would control all prices, except those that arose in the inevitable black markets. A sufficient national police force could wipe out the black markets.

This, clearly, is the most unpalatable scenario possible to most of us. It would represent the crushing failure of the world's greatest and richest democracy. It would put an end to perhaps the most ambitious social experiment in the world's history. It would mean the end of individual freedom and a regression to darker times when freedom was only for the select few, the rulers of the authoritarian state.

But this or any other specter of sweeping change is hardly realistic. In real life, things change slowly and haphazardly. Ideals are compromised and contradictions are accommodated. Surely we can muddle through the coming years without huge catastrophes, monstrous depressions, or apocalyptic wars. Surely the pragmatism of the American people will moderate the force of principles in deep conflict with each other. Time is, after all, the great healer, and evolution the mechanism for adapting to new conditions.

Yet danger is present. The danger is in not recognizing the nature of our problems. It is all too easy for demagogues to blame inflation and unemployment on big business or big government. The liberal senator says we'll be cured of our woes if we break up all the big evil corporations. The conservative senator claims that if we just cut taxes and eliminate the Environmental Protection Agency, then we can turn back the clock to the days when business was America's business and growth was unrestrained. Well, neither solution will work. The situation is too complex. No matter how appealing it may be to return to a past era of small business or small government, that is all but absurd, for the cost of going back would be unimaginably expensive. The only possible course is to go forward, into uncharted waters. We've always managed to navigate them before. In the chapters that follow, perhaps we can glimpse the outlines of a map to guide us through the decades of conflict and confrontation that await our entry into the twenty-first century.

2

Technology's Nature

TECHNOLOGY HAS its marvels. Such a technological behemoth as the Concorde supersonic jetliner resembles a large, sleek creature from another world. Shaped like a twenty-first-century dinosaur, the jet testifies to the decades of research and high technology that went into its construction. It also gives intimations of more fabulous technological birds to come, their well-sculptured aluminum bodies wired with the mysterious sinews of even more advanced technology, so that they may soar higher, faster, and farther. It hardly seems possible that mundane humans in drab factories built these machines. The total looks much greater than the sum of its parts. The machine possesses its own dignity—its spirit, so to speak.

In truth, however, a big corporate enterprise manufactures the Concorde piece by piece, on assembly lines and in machine shops. (In this case the Concorde is built by a consortium of British and French companies, while the American Congress voted to ban the new technology of the supersonic transport because of its contribution to pollution.) The Concorde is produced in a large-scale process, by which the detailed work of specialists comes together only at the final stages, when the skeleton of the airplane is supplied with electronic organs and metal blood vessels. As is the case with any other manufactured good, the plane is the end result of an ordered process: i.e., the reasoned application of knowledge, which is the process of technology. To grasp its imperatives, one can think backwards, so to speak, from the finished product to the thousands of small parts that at one time lay spread out on factory floors to be assembled. One can go further back, to the foundries and machine shops and electronics plants that made the individual parts. One can then go even further back, to the research laboratories that invented the technical processes by which the many parts were perfected. And if persistent, one will go yet further back, to the scientist's blackboard, on which logic and hunch led to one insight and then another and another and finally to a theory about how to do something useful.

John Kenneth Galbraith gives a credible exposition of the elements of the technological imperative in his book *The New Industrial State,* and since his exposition is as good as any, we might as well defer to it. Galbraith's exposition gives some meaning to the backward-looking exercise just described. Using the example of automobile manufacture, he points out that while there's no way to bring organized knowledge to bear on the production of the automobile as a whole entity, still knowledge can be applied to the production of each part. A simpleminded point? Think about it. Metallurgy, notes Galbraith, is used in the design of the car's cooling system. But in strict technical terms, the metallurgical knowledge is applied only to the special steels used in the cooling system. And when we get down to the actual engineering details, we see that the metallurgical technique concerns itself not with the steels as a whole but only with such interesting characteristics as steel tensile strength, which are important for certain uses of special steels.

As a closer example, consider this very book and the structure of its arguments. It tries to progress by delineating a theme, then by exploring the theme's sources and its sundry effects by breaking economic institutions down into their working parts, and then by studying the mechanisms by which these parts work. When we have finished this analysis, we can put the pieces back together and draw some interesting conclusions from the insights thus opened to us.

This is the way of logic—the way it must work, whether applied to ideas or to the manufacture of automobiles or Concordes. (Thus we can find the real roots of industrialism germinating in the philosophy of Descartes.)

Galbraith, not unlike some economists of quite opposite ideology, sees that one consequence of technology and its division of labor is "an increasing span of time [that] separates the beginning from the completion of any task"—which means that the more extensively technology is applied, or the further back in the production process it is applied, the longer will be the time needed to produce the thing. Consider the unlikely example of the guitar. Now, a Martin acoustic guitar is a fine thing, but it is made from wood, and its technology is centuries old. The production process takes a limited time. But compare it with a sophisticated electric guitar, such as the Gibson Recording guitar that wails, screams, and sings so beautifully in live rock concerts. That guitar needed the application of advanced acoustical and electronic technology in its design, and thus the production involves more investment in time. Or in the application of knowledge to thought, consider that a newspaper article, being brief and often superficial, takes a day, at most a week, to produce. An article in *Fortune* usually requires a minimum of three weeks to three months or more. A book may take years to finish.

Another direct consequence of technology listed by Galbraith is the increase in financial investment required for the lengthier production. Time costs money because production must be sustained even while no money is coming in, and because it costs money to borrow money in the interim. (For this reason alone, success brings mighty problems to small businesses. If an umbrella manufacturer gets orders to double his delivery of umbrellas next month, where's he going to get the huge sums needed in the meantime to buy new machines and hire extra workers? The stores that ordered the umbrellas won't advance him the money until he's proved himself, if then. His bank might or it might not.) But Galbraith is talking about an increase in investment that's above and beyond that needed to expand production; he means the amount called for by the increased application of technology.

The third consequence Galbraith calls attention to is the fact that the heavy application of technical knowledge and the resultant commitment of time and money leads a company on a fixed, inflexible course. The firm is pinned down to one production plan, and any abortion of its course precipitates serious losses. Again I come to the example closest at hand: this book. Doubleday committed itself to publishing it back in September of 1978. From the time the manuscript was turned in last May, nine months passed before the book could reach your hands. If the world had changed catastrophically in the meantime, so much so that everything said here was no longer valid, Doubleday would be in for a loss that couldn't easily be avoided once the manuscript went into production.

Fourth on the list is the consequence that technology requires specialists of all types who can apply their knowledge to the endeavor of production; and fifth, that it also requires organization to manage the coordination of multitudinous special tasks. So here we find the raison d'être, born of technology, for the modern corporation—and more specifically, as we shall see, for the *large* modern corporation, if we add up all the consequences that Galbraith has elucidated. The time and money and commitment, specialization of manpower, and need for organization all create a necessity for a big corporation that can finance and oversee the sophisticated processes involved in the application of knowledge to production.

Galbraith adds the need for planning as a sixth technological necessity, and this need is obvious. He places it, however, at the epicenter of his economic scheme, in which large corporations together form his "planning system," which is apart from the "market system" and which operates on different rules. The paradigm is useful, but we will follow our own route to a different destination. For now, we'll take careful notice of how the imperatives of technology must concretely manifest themselves inside the corporation and outside it.

The technological imperatives appear in the guise of what are called *economies of large scale,* which themselves come in many varieties. The principle is simplicity itself, deriving from the consequences of applied knowledge given us by Galbraith. In brief, when products are manufactured on a big scale, they become much cheaper to produce. Isn't this impossible? No; the products become cheaper in *per-unit cost,* not in the overall cost of the operation. This happens because the most efficient machinery and equipment comes in large chunks. Let me frame the idea in an example. On summer Sunday afternoons, I often enjoy strolling among the colorful wares, oddments, delicacies, and curios of the typical Manhattan street festival. My favorite stands are those vending old-fashioned engraved printing plates from ancient newspaper shops in New England. These plates have all sorts of designs and lettering, from the bygone days of handset printing. I use them to decorate letterheads and envelopes. To use them in this way is somewhat laborious, but cheap. For the operation I need a rubber roller, which must first be washed. I need a piece of Plexiglas on which to apply printer's ink. Then I must experiment several times to get the right impression, by pressing my hands down on the plate with varying force. Often I do it wrong and have to try again. All in all, the whole thing is messy and time-consuming. Suppose, then, I were to invest $250 in a small letterpress, the smallest manufactured. It would be far cheaper to print each letter, at least in terms of time. But of course I wouldn't buy a press just for the occasional letterhead. If I were to buy a press at all, it would be too expensive for occasional use. There is no low-technology press of good quality. In order, therefore, to make a substantial saving in the per-unit cost of printing my letterheads and envelopes, I must increase the scale of my operation, because only by so doing will I be able to justify financially the expense of the press.

What is true of the letterpress is true of most manufacturing machines. Small is inefficient, because a small producer can't exploit the lower cost of production schemes using specialized machines. This contradicts many romantic notions of the 1960s which suggested that we all employ ourselves with quaint nineteenth-century equipment bought from the *Whole Earth Catalog*. But bigness in manufacturing has enabled us to raise our living standards. The exploitation of economies of large scale has brought us everything from cheap shoes to autos that everyone can afford. Compare the price of a Rolls-Royce at $25,000 and that of a Ford at $7,000. The Rolls-Royce involves much small-scale manual labor in a fairly small and inefficient factory. Think of the custom cars made in California, where automobiles are icons. Attractive as they may be to some tastes, these autos cost upward of $40,000 at the least, because they're made by hand in glorified garages.

What economies of large scale permit is the most extensive *division of labor* in production. Here is an ancient and honored idea. Adam Smith popularized it when he described the making of pins. He noted that one man could produce a single pin a day if he went through all the various smithing operations himself, stopping to change tools, pausing to remember the next task, and interrupting the train of his work to switch over. But Smith compared this inefficient worker to a group of workers, each of whom took up a different piece of the work. One formed rough pins from molten steel. Another spent the day smoothing and finishing the rough pins. Another attached the heads to the pins. Yet another inspected the finished ones and put them in wooden boxes for shipment to market. Together they could manufacture one thousand pins a day rather than the handful that could be made by four workers, each doing the entire operation by himself. Why the difference? Because the specialized worker quickly becomes proficient at his job. (Remember those television films of factory workers who screw nuts or sort oranges at lightning speed?) The specialist has no need to waste time switching from one task to another and learns the necessities of his particular task so well that he can often devise aids to help him and/or machines do part or all of it (though this might throw him out of a job).

The natural child of the division of labor was the modern assembly line, instituted on a large scale by Henry Ford at his auto plant. This was the ultimate in organization of specialized work; a skeletal product passes down the line, and every specialist adds his bit to it. The assembly line has been and still is the conduit of industrial prosperity. In the auto industry and in others, the machines have been modernized, often evolving from mechanical power to electronic technology; but for processes such as papermaking they are still as crudely mechanical as they were in the last century. Whether mechanical or electronic, however, no more efficient form of mass production has ever been devised. Of course, the assembly line adds a fair measure of human degradation. The work it offers is dull and monotonous, no matter how high the pay. Labor unions sprang up to extract some needed concessions from early industrialists, who thought nothing of having children and women work eighteen hours a day for pennies of pay. But there are today more than a few assembly line workers who announce that they enjoy the work—the very mindlessness of it, the lack of responsibility for dealing with other people, the separation such a job allows between work and pleasure. Let it be said that no assembly line worker has to carry his work home with him, as lawyers or professors or writers must. If we are to believe the copious literature of industrial unrest, however, the majority of assembly line workers abhor their labors.

In certain manufacturing operations whereby things are "processed" into other things by means other than assembly (or disassembly, as in the case of meat-packing plants), we get a different kind of large-scale economy. Take as an example the oil refinery, which drinks raw crude oil and then digests it in huge distillation columns. (These separate out the heating oil, gasoline, kerosene, naphtha, and so on, depending on the temperature at which each of the successively lighter petroleum derivatives condenses from gas to liquid.) For this kind of manufacturing process, and for chemical production, glass manufacturing, and the smelting of crude ores, economies of large scale are expressed in what industrial engineers call the *two-thirds rule*, whereby the cost of a processing unit, with all its tanks and pipes and valves, rises to the two-thirds power of the size of the unit. This is so since the output of such a chemical processing unit tends to be proportional to the volume of the unit. Now assume we have a petroleum refining plant with an output capacity of 6,000 gallons of gasoline a day. Using the two-thirds rule, we find that doubling capacity, to 12,000 gallons a day, will increase our costs by 39 percent, and tripling it, to 18,000 gallons, will result in costs that are up 106 percent. Let me restate the result: a 100 percent increase in capacity causes production costs to go up only 39 percent, and a 200 percent rise in capacity causes costs to go up only 106 percent. So it's quite correct that it becomes cheaper to be bigger. If no economies of large scale were embodied in these manufacturing processes, then a 100 percent increase in capacity would add at least 100 percent more to production costs, and a 200 percent rise in output capacity would cost 200 percent more. And if we were speaking of the rare manufacturing process that offers "diseconomies" of large scale, then a 100 percent increase in capacity would cost more than 100 percent extra. This would hold true, for instance, in the manufacture of rare hand-painted porcelains, where the training of a new master (to double production) would be a long and expensive process.

We have spoken of economies of large scale in the dimension of space, but there are also economies that function in the dimension of time. One is the phenomenon of the *learning curve*. As time passes, workers on a new production line become more experienced; there is hence less downtime in the factory, fewer poorly made products that have to be thrown away, and generally faster production—all as a consequence of on-the-job experience. This is quite crucial for efficient production. It is said that part of the ability of the Japanese to sell their goods at lower prices than most nations is simply that Japanese factories produce fewer special, customized products and more standardized ones that permit workers on the assembly lines to learn their tasks thoroughly. For consider that every time there is a change in a product's design or a change in the design of the assembly line, a costly break-in period will ensue while the employees learn new methods and get the bugs out of new machines. So the learning curve shows a declining slope on a horizontal axis of output and a vertical axis of cost. Or it can show a curve climbing upward on a horizontal axis of time with a vertical axis of products made. Either way, the message is that as time passes or as production accumulates (which is the same thing) costs decline and thus efficiency in production rises.

There is a case where neither economies of time nor those of space are practical. It occurs when a product is bulky and expensive to transport to its markets. The cement industry offers the quintessential example. What if one huge cement plant operated in central Pennsylvania and supplied cement to the whole nation? No matter how large and advantageous the economies of large scale captured by this big cement plant, the savings could not possibly compensate for the costs of shipping heavy, hard-to-manage cement across great

distances. Thus any city of modest size has one or more cement plants, so that the cement is close to wherever it will
be poured and transport expenses are kept to a viable level.

Similarly, home construction is not amenable to large-
scale economies of the assembly line, because construction is
dependent upon the weather in many parts of the nation. If
a company adopted huge pieces of equipment for automated
home building, it could not afford to keep these expensive
machines idle during the long winter months. There are,
however, some efforts to automate housing construction.
Companies like Centrex and Ryan Homes have pioneered in
making prefabricated walls and even bathroom units in factories. (It's true that some entire homes are also built in
plants, but these have a reputation for flimsiness and are
sold mostly to the rural poor of the South, where nature sel-
dom enforces the need for strong, weatherproof construction.)

Similar to economies of large scale are notions of *vertical
and horizontal integration.* The best way to understand
these is to ponder the theory put forward by R. H. Coase in
1937 to explain the emergence of the business firm. Imagine
a set of concentric circles, with a retail vendor of pies in the
center ring. In the next circle is the wholesaler of pies. In
the ring outside of his is the baker. In the ring outside of his
is the miller. In the ring outside of his is the farmer. The pie
seller offers his pies to the public. He performs only that
simple function: to sell pies he has previously (but, one
hopes, not too previously) bought. It is, he feels, a satisfactory arrangement, as long as the wholesale price of the
pies stays stable and as long as he's sure of getting his daily
delivery of pies. But, alas, there comes a week when he has
no pies to sell because the baker's delivery truck was
wrecked. By the next week, when the truck has been re-
paired, the wholesale price of pies has risen 10 percent. So
the pie seller must add 10 percent to his retail price just to
stay even. His customers, of course, don't like it, and a few

stop buying pies. The pie seller, traumatized by this double shock of interrupted supply and raised price, considers that if he undertook to bake pies himself, at least he could be sure of his supply of them, and, even better, would no longer have to pay the wholesaler's premium. He ventures to set up a pie-baking plant. What he is doing is to internalize an operation that was previously external to his business. He is moving to a wider ring of the circle. Rather than contract with the wholesaler in the open market, the pie seller gets a secure supply and lowers costs by making his own. He might extend the internalization by going so far as to mill his own flour, or even to grow his grain and plant his own fruit orchard. This is called *upstream* vertical integration. It isn't dictated by large-scale economies of the technical variety, but it does cut costs and ensure a safe supply of raw materials (wholesale goods, in the case of the seller-cum-baker). And if a wheat farmer moved into the milling of his wheat and the baking of the resultant flour and even the selling of the bread products, then he would be vertically integrating *downstream* for the purpose of better controlling his market and avoiding the sharp practices of the wholesalers and dealers who used to buy wheat from him before he manufactured his own baked goods.

Vertical integration need not be anticompetitive. Indeed, it usually isn't so, unless one company in an industry can gain so large a cost advantage over its rivals by integrating that it beats them out of their market shares. Even this isn't really anticompetitive; it's only smart business—nothing untoward here. What does tend to be untoward, certainly in the eyes of the Justice Department, is horizontal integration, whereby a company simply buys up its competitors, or buys identical businesses in other cities. Gannett Newspapers is a fitting example. It's a chain of small and medium-sized daily newspapers in one-newspaper towns scattered all over the nation. Gannett now owns scores of these papers, though none are distinguished. The effect is to bring all these news-

papers under the dominion of a single corporation, with consequences that are at best neutral, at worst anticompetitive.
The prospect is all the more threatening because newspapers still wield considerable influence. Thus some
members of Congress—notable among them is Representative Morris Udall of Arizona—would like to curb media
conglomerates.

These types of scale economies have been recognized for a
long time, but economists are only now beginning to catch
up with the reality of large corporations that produce a wide
variety of goods. Obviously, they will make use of economies that may be different from the ones exploited by single-product firms. And since single-product companies are
getting to be a rarity, let's look at multi-product economies,
as described by Professors Robert Willig and John Panzer of
Princeton. They've coined the term *economies of scope* for
posterity; it refers to the situation that exists when a company finds it cheaper to produce two or more products at
the same time than it does to produce just one. It may be
that if a corporation makes, say, television receivers, it could
be less expensive to add on the production of car stereos
than it would be to go into the production of car stereos
alone. So what? The company is already making TV receivers; isn't the comparison irrelevant? Not if one already
established firm makes a wide range of electronic products
including car stereos. For then if you wanted to start up a
company that would produce only car stereos, you'd have to
face the prospect of competing with this firm, which can
make car stereos more cheaply with its economies of scope.
Therefore, you would have to consider going into production to make more than just car stereos. In other words, it's
going to be harder than you thought to go into the car
stereo business. In fact, you'll have to go into the electronics
business if you expect to compete on an even basis with the
big electronics corporations already in the field. And if the
economies of scope are great, then you'll have to produce a

wide line of electronics products before your production costs will be low enough for you to compete with your rivals, and that can be very expensive. So the larger the economies of scope in an industry, the harder it is for a corporation to enter the business, because that corporation will have to go in massively, producing a wide assortment of products. This turns out to be true in the breakfast cereal industry, where it is cheaper to make a dozen different brands of cereals than to make only one, and that is what the cereal giants—General Mills, General Foods, and so on—do. They have been sent to court for alleged antitrust violations.

Economies of scope usually derive from the cheapness of using the same raw materials on several assembly lines and using the same parts—electronic parts, for example—in a number of products. These economies of scope are a major type among those available to conglomerates.

The logic of technology that leads to large-scale efficiency is something Thomas Jefferson and Adam Smith never took into account. But Karl Marx accommodated the tendency toward bigness in his theory. He made the growth toward economic concentration the centerpiece of his vision of the future, though he saw capitalist greed as the prime mover rather than the mechanical requirements of large-scale production. No theoretician of this century has been able to reconcile the need for technological bigness with the need for human-scale smallness in society. Perhaps it is because those who revile large-scale enterprise ignorantly ascribe its bigness to metaphysical evil forces—or, even worse, because those who do understand the logic of large-scale technology have been too quick to accept, without question or qualification, its manifold implications.

3

When Bigger Is Better

UNINFORMED APOLOGISTS for business often invoke technical economies of large scale to explain away all manner of monopoly abuse. They carelessly leap to the conclusion that since existing economies of large scale do enhance the efficiency of technological enterprise, then the unbridled development of corporate bigness must be encouraged; i.e., the bigger the better. Well, it isn't necessarily so. Merely on the technical level, big-scale efficiencies go only so far, and in some industries even moderate large-scale economies are nonexistent. The dressmaking business, for instance, can get on quite well in a small shop, as the work depends more on labor than on machines.

Economists use the phrase *minimal optimal scale* to indicate the smallest size of an industrial plant that's still large enough to capture all the economies of large scale inherent in the technology used. When minimal optimal scale is studied closely, the invariable conclusion is that technological economies of large scale certainly exist but aren't so pervasive as to account for the heavy concentration found in many American industries. But this conclusion loses considerable weight when it is understood that nontechnological economies of large scale become nearly as important as technological ones in a world of large corporate bureaucracies. Ironically but not surprisingly, heavy government regulation and inflation only increase the advantages accruing to big organizations.

There are managerial economies of scale whereby a number of corporate divisions can be administered by a central headquarters as cheaply as can a single division. Here we think of the costs of management and paper work as overhead—costs that have nothing directly to do with production (production costs being those of the raw materials plus labor and machinery use). The fixed overhead costs are necessary even if we have only one plant running an assembly line. But if we can "spread" the costs of management and administration over several product divisions, then the per-product cost of this overhead will become much cheaper. The same will be true if we produce a large amount of a single product. In this case, as the number of products increases, the per-unit cost of overhead declines. Suppose we're making watches. We turn out 100 a month, and the cost-per-month of management and administration is $500. Then we'll have to include $5.00 in the price of each watch to cover these expenses. But if we produce 500 watches, then we need only charge $1.00 per watch to cover overhead, and with 5,000 watches a month, the cost becomes a mere dime per watch. (By so simple a principle, applied not only to overhead costs but also to direct production costs, do we get mass-produced products vastly less expensive than those which could be had in the days of handiwork.)

Economies of distribution are available to companies that use central warehouses and computerized shipping methods. There are also economies of large-scale selling in which it's cheaper to market a number of products simultaneously; the sales catalog is a prime example. Likewise for economies of promotion; it is more efficient to run an ad for six products than for one, and the more time one buys on network television, for instance, the cheaper the unit of time gets. Since the 1970s it has dawned on a number of corporate executives that there are cost-saving economies of large scale built into pollution control; an industrialist is better off centralizing all his electrostatic air precipitators and smokestacks and water filtration systems. And it turns out that in many an industrial process the cleanest wastes come from the largest-scale production equipment—perhaps because it is better designed.

Beyond these practical, often physical reasons for corporate bigness, there's another motive for a huge corporation to operate above the scale needed for technological economies. It is simply that large corporations often reap certain advantages from their size alone. AT&T, for example, has no difficulty in raising many millions of dollars practically overnight. The company is well established and its stock sells widely at a high price. From a banker's perspective, AT&T is a large, solid, trustworthy company; it doesn't pose the risk that a small, unknown company would. Both bankers and stockholders have some faith in the ability of such a huge corporation to pay its debts and make money. It has a strong advantage in the market for credit. The same is true of most large corporations, because by the time they become so large they have usually been around for a good long time and established a successful reputation. Often their brand name is a household word—Xerox, Kleenex, Frigidaire, or Ford.

Consider the advantage Time, Inc., for example, has over a small magazine publisher. If Time wants to start a new magazine (which it does periodically) it has the money to spend years in market research, polling the populace to see if they'd read the magazine. The company then has the money to produce a test edition and see how it flies. If Time decides to go ahead and publish, then it has the long-established company name, dating from the 1920s, to back up the product. It also has a well-established advertising and distribution system through which to market the magazine, and long-established contacts with television networks and newspapers to help with publicity. Most important, Time has the sheer wealth to take a loss on the new magazine for years, until it begins to catch on and finally make money. *Sports Illustrated* started publication in 1954 but didn't

make any money for years. Now, of course, it's well established and makes loads of cash. Time even has the
wealth to sustain the loss of all the money invested in a new
magazine if it fails absolutely. (In fact, a few years ago
Time tried a new magazine titled *Woman,* and it flopped.)
The company will still prosper. In stark contrast, the small
independent publisher will be wiped out if his magazine
doesn't sell; and, lacking access to efficient marketing or
publicity, his magazine is very likely to go under after
briefly struggling to find its market along with dozens of
other new publications. It's no surprise that the failure rate
for new magazines is more than 80 percent. Only a fat company like Time, Inc., can beat the odds—first by doing the
kind of expensive research necessary to ensure that there's a
market, and then by having the financial prowess to stay
with it.

Businessmen are forever alert to new ways of improving
their prospects. Their inventiveness has given rise to yet another form of economic prowess that confers further advantages of large scale and economic concentration. It is
known as the *corporate joint venture.* A joint venture is em-
barked on when, for instance, a multibillion-dollar chemical
company arranges with a small photographic firm to jointly
develop a new kind of film the small company has invented.
Or an American oil company enters into an agreement with
an Argentinian firm to supply the latter with top-quality petroleum drilling equipment in exchange for a percentage of
the oil. Or two medium-sized airplane manufacturers collab-
orate to produce a jumbo jet that will be competitive with a
Boeing. A joint venture can simply confer the advantages of
merger where two companies are just living together rather
than entering the holy matrimony of formal merger. Or, at
the other end of the spectrum, a joint venture can be in essence a cartel.

The advantages come in many forms. The joint venture is
a cheap way for one company to acquire the improved tech-

nology owned and pioneered by another. It's also a good
way for a small company to have its new invention developed, manufactured, and marketed without the tremendous
expenditure and risk involved in undertaking it alone. A
joint-venture combination can give two or more corporations the ability to crash an oligopoly market that would be
closed to any single company other than those already dom-
inating the market. It can make one group of corporations
the most powerful force in a once-competitive market. A
joint venture allows its participants to reap the afore-
mentioned economies of scope, especially in the cost of dis-
tributing products, in the provision of capital, in the operation of similar technologies, and in combined research and
development. All these economies can allow a joint-venture
combination to knock down the barriers to entry in an oligopoly market.

The dark side is that all this can lessen competition. This
may in fact be the intent of many corporate joint ventures,
especially "horizontal" ones involving corporations that sell
the same kinds of goods in the same markets. A joint venture might deny important raw materials to its competitors.
It might be in a position simply to take the market away
from all uncombined competitors. In any case, the joint venture is very likely to increase oligopoly in the national economy; in the international economy the possibilities are
mind-boggling. Imagine a half-dozen auto companies
around the world joining to exercise the kind of economic
power that OPEC exercises in petroleum. Though accomplished in the guise of a joint venture, this would be no less
than an international cartel, which there are no laws to in-
hibit.

Our tax laws encourage corporate joint ventures, since the
two companies can treat their shared gains as capital gains
rather than income. The capital gains tax is lower than the
corporate income tax. What, then, discourages joint ventures? Not much, except the possibility that they may go

sour. If one partner starts losing bundles of money, the other will become pretty uncomfortable with the arrangement. Even in the smoothest of joint ventures it's not easy to keep accurate records, to determine whether both companies are shouldering their fair share of the expenses and risks. It may be just as hard to keep straight which partner is getting what share of the profits. These can be decided disadvantages, since joint ventures are at best loose marriages, in which either partner can walk out the door on the slightest whim. They are more fragile than cartels, which are usually cemented by formal agreements and provided with some mechanism—a trade association, for instance—to enforce them.

Inflation encourages joint ventures and every other sort of corporate conglomeration. During a long season of inflation, the only thing a businessman can count on is that prices will be escalating. If he begins construction of a new factory, he has no way of knowing what the cost overruns will be. And if the inflation is followed by a recession, as it usually is, then by the time the factory is built there may be no customers for its products. So the inflationary impulse is to buy factories rather than build them. This adds nothing to the health of the economy. For in buying another company, businesses are merely transferring ownership titles. They are not spending money that will increase the Gross National Product. They are not creating new jobs, as they would do if they opted to build. Instead, the added conglomeration further concentrates economic power.

Advantages of big scale aren't the only source of monopoly power. Companies can obtain it by making their goods or service unique. This entails a curious irony. If we are to have a perfectly competitive economy, there will be no monopoly power, and therefore no *product differentiation*. Thus all tubes of toothpaste sold at retail would be of exactly the same color, issued in the same kind of tube, with the same spare lettering saying only "toothpaste." There

could be absolutely no advertising, no distinguishing characteristics. Otherwise we get product differentiation, and
therefore some monopoly power. This would make for quite
a dull world. Even today, in mass-produced America you see
far fewer varieties of any product than you're likely to see in
Europe. (New York City is the exception, with its heavy European influences.) When you see a commercial on television and the slick-haired announcer is immortalizing the
special "whiteness power" of a toothpaste, you know the
manufacturer is trying to promulgate the notion that its
toothpaste is different from all the rest, which only clean
teeth. The assumption is that you'll be willing to pay more
for this "different" product. Advertising is thus the vehicle
by which corporations emphasize the uniqueness of their
goods. Its end is to extract monopoly power, power that
allows the company to charge a higher price than it could in
a competitive market. Of course, since not all the people can
be fooled all the time, companies have to make an effort to
actually "differentiate" their product. Hence the multi-
plicity of million-dollar automobile style changes, and the
large research and development departments that spend
millions formulating new mystery ingredients that supposedly enhance the potency of deodorant tampons and
headache powders.

If all this superficial product differentiation costs money,
both for cosmetic changes and for advertising, then it should
not surprise you that you're paying higher prices. This fact
isn't lost on a few entrepreneurs. In the suburbs of Long Island and Minneapolis and Gainesville, new no-frills grocery
stores have opened in recent years, stripped of the usual
Muzak, the baggers, and the huge frozen-food sections. Instead they are little more than warehouses, dimly lit, with
boxes of food lined up on the floor—and customers bring
their own grocery bags. The only serious inconvenience is
the lack of fresh meats and frozen foods. But the food
shoppers pay only three quarters of what they'd have to pay

in a regular grocery store, and plenty of customers find the deal attractive.

We get into the question of a manipulative cycle here. Automobiles make the best example. The car style changes do cost a great deal of money, and it also costs a lot to advertise them. Both costs are reflected in the price of the new car. Are car buyers therefore paying for their own exploitation? Is this not a social waste? (If you say yes, then you are imposing your aesthetics on the whole population. Perhaps there are legions out there who all but live for the flattened hood, the cocked fender, the red vinyl see-through dash panel.)

Quite apart from the technological, managerial, and physical excuses for large corporate enterprise, the government unwittingly boosts corporate concentration directly through inheritance and capital gains taxes. While capital gains taxes are high, estate taxes are higher, seizing three quarters of large estates. The heirs of a family business may have to borrow millions just to pay the taxes on their inheritance. And if it's a small, closely held company—as is most often the case—the stock of the company is not likely to have a ready market so its market price may be unknown, and it may be impossible to unload the stuff. If the heirs want to sell some of the stock to pay the huge inheritance taxes, they must depend on the uncharitable whim of the Internal Revenue Service in estimating a value for the stock and thus their tax liability.

Is there any way to judge whether a corporation is too big? Members of Congress and economists regularly attempt it. Senator Edward Kennedy has chosen size alone as his criterion—companies worth $2 billion or more would be prohibited from merging, as would companies having $2 billion a year in sales. But this or any other touchstone is arbitrary. The tendency of modern technological enterprise is toward bigness, toward the concentration of power. It is reason, not evil conspiracy, that drives the forces of concentration. But reason in fact leads everyone to wish to be a pure monopolist. I devoutly wish that this book would prove a monopoly of sorts—that it would become one of a kind and enjoy sales second only to those of the Bible. Economic concentration is profitable and comfortable and eminently reasonable—for the practicing monopolist. In the twentieth century the eternal advantages of large size have received their impetus from the development of modern technology and the economy of mass-produced consumer goods.

4

The Double-edged Sword

NOT UNLIKE the spider who murders her lover, technology can destroy the very bigness it creates. For it is by technological innovation that new products arise to steal the market from existing ones—the electronic calculator versus the slide rule and the adding machine, for instance. Inventors can design new production processes that make conventional ones obsolete almost overnight, thus destroying the raison d'être of huge factory complexes. Small street-fighting companies can outwit their big monopolistic brothers through technological brilliance.

The only impediments to healthy technological competition are time and government protection of entrenched monopolies. The process of technical innovations is slowed, however, during inflation, because creative inventors are dependent on risk capital, on gambling money, which dries up when the inflation rate promises to stay high, thus scaring investors. Taxes on capital gains make venture capital scarcer, for investors prefer to evade a possible capital gain that will be heavily taxed. In a broader sense, the creation of new industries and companies and the destruction of old ones occur by degrees, over years, though the rapid pace of new inventions in electronics, for example, shortens the lifespan for slow-moving firms that fail to keep a team of talented researchers constantly busy in their laboratories.

One group of economic scholars has argued that monopoly power encourages innovation. A few, among them Galbraith, argue that it is essential. The hypothesis they espouse is, very simply, that large monopolistic firms have the "protected profits" to invest in the creation or development of a new product. Being monopolies, they can take a beating without mortal damage, as in the example already mentioned of *Sports Illustrated.* On the other side is a group of economists who say that the opposite is true—that big monopolies become lazy and content with their lucre, and therefore don't bother to innovate. Why should they? They already have the cream of the marketplace. Even if one of their more unruly scientists were to perfect a radically new and cheaper product (or way to make a product), the monopoly would, according to this hypothesis, suppress the invention so as to continue using its existing machinery.

The trouble with the latter argument is that a lazy monopoly becomes a vulnerable monopoly except when it's protected from competition by the government. Technological innovation and invention are the agents of change in the economic sphere and are not confined within the walls of the monopoly corporation. A man in his garage can and often does invent a better mousetrap or television receiver. He can start a new company to sell it, and if he's successful he'll steal the market from the sleeping giant. It happens all the time.

As to the effect of monopoly on innovation, it is best seen in the results of studies which show that inventions—whether of new products or of new ways of making existing products—characteristically come from small companies. Often they are the work of a talented engineer heading his own firm after being fired by a large corporation for his eccentricity.

The large and hierarchical research and development labs that typify the big corporation are anything but conducive to creative breakthroughs. Yet large companies *do* have the advantage when developing an invention into a marketable commodity. It takes millions to refine and develop the capabilities of, say, integrated electronic circuits for home and commercial use. The first integrated circuits were transistor circuits, reduced photographically (and lately by X ray) to microscopic dimensions and etched on silicon wafers. They were used to make calculators that cost in the range of sixty dollars or more. Now, of course, the technology has advanced far enough that calculators are a "mature" product, quite cheap—and the integrated circuit has gone on to greater glory in minicomputers, industrial processing machines, and a huge variety of special applications. This is being done by the big semiconductor companies, like Texas Instruments and National Semiconductor; it is where they can use their expertise and financial clout. But the small backyard garage operations will continue to produce many of the most important inventions. Galbraith says that this will no longer be the case because all the simple inventions have already been invented, but I doubt the accuracy of his assertion. When the railroad train was invented, pundits thought there was nothing left to invent. During the 1939 World Trade Fair in New York, the New York *Times* scoffed at the brand-new television technology on display. The *Times* saw it as an expensive but useless curio. Even if television became widespread, the newspaper said, Americans would never sit still in their living rooms long enough to watch it. One could compile a thick catalog of such predictions concerning the potentialities of new technologies.

A dramatic example of how technology creates new devices and thereby destroys existing ones is right now unfolding before the eyes of those who care to notice. Advanced cable television threatens the preeminence of network broadcast television. The wealthy commercial television networks face an inevitable technological threat, because the logic of cable television is so compelling that it will force change. It isn't possible to know exactly what the change will be, or how greatly it will cripple the existing broadcast television networks. But there is justifiable fear on Sixth Av-

enue in New York, where the three big networks are headquartered.

The networks are artificial monopolies, created when the
government wrote its regulations governing television airwaves. The theory which dictated these rules was that the
electromagnetic spectrum of television and radio broadcast
frequencies is limited by physics, so that there are only a
few frequencies in the range of efficient television transmission. That was the theory, but in fact there have always
been many more frequencies than the government wished to
release for commercial broadcast use. Whole bands of television frequencies are reserved for occasional military and
government use. In effect, they are going to waste. Nevertheless, the regulation of television is based on this precept.
But it doesn't stop there, for in the early 1950s, when television was still in its infancy, the Federal Communications
Commission, which oversees broadcasting, decided rather
arbitrarily that not more than three very-high-frequency television frequencies suitable for network use would be allocated to each city in the United States, except for a few very
large metropolises, which got more. The effect of this ruling
was immediate. The old Dumont television network
promptly went out of business for want of enough local television stations that could broadcast its programs.

The FCC regulation thus ordained three commercial networks, and until this day there are only three. Why? You
must understand that very-high-frequency television trans-
mitting is the only practical technology for *broadcast* television. For years after its misguided ruling, the FCC has
tried to promote ultra-high-frequency broadcasting to provide more diversity. But the technological fact remains that
broadcasting in the ultra-high frequencies is much less
efficient. It requires more costly transmitters and antennas
and power to attain half the range of very-high-frequency
transmission. The FCC ploy has never succeeded, and UHF
stations are still marginal operations with marginal audi-

ences and therefore marginal profits. But alas, in the 1960s a new television transmission technology arose: cable television. The idea began in the hills of Pennsylvania where people couldn't pick up television signals from stations in Pittsburgh or Philadelphia. Some clever entrepreneur decided to build a big antenna to receive the distant signals, then amplify them and send them out through wires attached to the home television sets of people willing to pay him ten dollars a month. This really wasn't a technological breakthrough. All he was doing was using some very old-fashioned technology as a way to organize the transmission of television signals in unfavorable circumstances. But the implications of cable television technology became evident almost immediately; one could envision an improved system of communication with breathtaking potential.

Consider advanced cable television technology: now that the engineers have gone to work on it, we have cable systems capable of sending up to 100 television channels into the home, through the old-fashioned wire or via the new fiber optics of laser technology. We have two-way capability, so that the viewer can talk back, using the home television set and push-button telephone as a computer terminal. The system can be connected by satellite to a multitude of other local cable systems. Thus we see a home communications system vastly more sophisticated than the passive crudity of broadcast television. Cable viewers at home can order groceries, pay bills, cast a vote, and have access to a computerized data bank such as that of the Library of Congress. When they tire of talking back in one way or another, they may flip past dozens of channels to find the entertainment that suits them.

Now we must pause to ponder one salient aspect. With twenty or thirty or forty commercial cable television channels—the number limited only by the size of the cable market and the collective tastes of viewers—how can any network charge the million-dollar-a-minute advertising rates

that have prevailed for so long on network television? They
can't. The networks figured this out long ago, and they have
fought cable television from its inception. Their first com-
plaint was that since cable television systems merely transmitted programs that were being broadcast on the commercial channels, they should pay a royalty fee. The matter was
taken to court and in the end the cablecasters won. The
owners of movie theater chains also tried to stop cable TV
companies from showing first-run movies, since they feared
this could ultimately ruin their business. After many court
battles, the cable companies won this one, too. The television networks, in league with their friends and promoters at
the Federal Communications Commission, tried every ploy
to delay the spread of cable television. Though they finally
lost the battle, they did succeed in delaying its introduction
by twenty years, so that now the state of the cable industry
is still roughly twenty years behind its technology.

In 1974 the White House promulgated a new, radical set
of regulations for advanced cable television, stipulating that
its operators would have no control over the content of the
material sent over their systems. They were not to be censors. More than that, they must provide public access channels for use by anyone of any political or moral or cultural
persuasion. Part of the beauty of cable television is that, as
it's not broadcast over the airwaves (and therefore the leg-
endary little old lady in Dubuque wouldn't be able to tune in
a cable channel inadvertently), there is no need to restrict
either language or scenario. Nudity and profanity were considered permissible, because those who rented cable service
presumably did so with some knowledge of what they're
paying for. The Nixon administration formulated these
rules, not out of any love for free speech, but simply because
it was frustrated by what it saw as the liberal bias expressed
throughout the commercial networks. It wanted to create a
forum in which conservative opinion would not be stifled by
a prejudiced authority. In order to do that, it had perforce

to design rules permitting the free expression of any opinion. In 1979 the Supreme Court abrogated these regulations, but local governments still exercise the authority to maintain public access rules.

Perhaps the most highly developed cable TV system in the United States is Manhattan Cable TV in New York. It's a marvel to watch. There isn't yet two-way communication of the sort I alluded to, but there is a large variety of unusual and interesting programming—programming that would never have a wisp of a chance of being seen on commercial television, either network or local. First of all, there are twenty-six channels. One offers pay movies; one lists the news, another the stock market reports. There is a separate channel for sports news, and one that does comparison shopping for you. Another displays weather meters. A dozen others provide the standard American television fare in English but also Spanish, Japanese, Greek, Korean, and Yiddish programs. Now we come to the public access channels, where each night at midnight you may turn to "Midnight Blue" and see nude women and men in sundry poses and predicaments, brought to you by the editors of *Screw* magazine. But it's not the only pornography; on any night after 8 P.M. you're likely to see a variety, from some low amateur sleaze to more refined productions of professional pornographers. I, however, prefer a show called "If I Can't Dance You Can Keep Your Revolution." It's hosted by Coca Crystal, a pretty Manhattanite, a survivor of the 1960s counterculture who sits at her place smoking marijuana, saying what she pleases, and presiding over a menagerie of unusual, often bizarre, performers. Expletives aren't deleted. In fact, nothing is.

You may complain that nudity and dope-smoking should not be allowed on television. With due respect, you have no right to dictate what I shall see or hear or think. The Constitution permits me the right to indulge myself. Cable television gives that right its full meaning. Soon enough, I expect

Coca Crystal to go from being a hand-to-mouth Manhattan television phenomenon to some species of stardom as financiers awaken to the possibilities of cable television. The pioneers of cable programming like Coca need only have patience. Already most television broadcasting corporations have seen the handwriting on the wall and invested in cable television. Does this mean broadcasters will merely create new monopolies within cable television? To find the answer, we must look at how economies of large scale apply to cable television, as opposed to the way they apply to television networks.

A local cable television system is a *natural* monopoly in a way that a local television station is not. At its headquarters is all the apparatus to receive and process signals from broadcasting stations, plus facilities for telecasting motion pictures, and the all-important studios for public access programming. From this headquarters emanates a large underground network of cables that feeds into every apartment and office building that has contracted to receive cable television. Now, what would be the purpose in having two or three cable operations competing for the same area of service? Remember that the cable operator is forbidden by law to censor what goes over his cable wires. If we had three cable systems fighting for the same territory, the city of New York would have to have three separate but identical cable systems wired underneath the streets. One connection is enough, in the same sense that one set of water pipes is enough for any home. (If two water companies competed for the same neighborhood, each home would have to have a duplicate set of plumbing pipes, so that the homeowner could choose the company he preferred to do business with; it doesn't make sense.) Cable television, like plumbing, telephone service, or electricity, constitutes a "natural" monopoly at the local level.

The local broadcast television station has no such claim to a unique interconnection. There could easily be one or a hundred local TV stations on the air competing with each other. The only economies of scale in television occur in networking; one central organization can undertake expensive program productions that no single local TV station could hope to mount. But this advantage does not call forth any natural monopoly; there could in theory as easily be fifty television networks as three, though in actuality the number of any such networks would be limited by how many the market could support. That there are only three commercial networks is due to a governmental decision and has nothing to do with market forces.

Therefore, even if the television networks did buy up every local cable system in the United States, they would still not have a license to create a new hegemony of television fare. There will indeed be economies to be gained by networking, most likely via satellite. But with up to 100 television channels to be seen on cable, and with local laws forcing the cable operator into the most passive of roles, we can stay fairly sure that no lowest common denominator will persist, governed by a handful of producers and censors in New York and Hollywood. Even without regulations, the presence of so many channels and the obvious public utility characteristic of cable television systems will mitigate network dominance. Eventually the swollen monopoly profits of the traditional three television networks will disappear as their advertising revenues are diluted over scores of television channels. This will happen even in the unlikely event that most viewers prefer to watch the eternal flow of sitcoms on the network channels. (But what about the social consequences of advanced cable television? Could we become a nation of recluses, satisfying our every wish through the cable's circuits? It's always possible, but people haven't abandoned movie theaters, nightclubs, and sports stadiums since the advent of television. We are not yet so docile as to be completely overwhelmed by any technological convenience.)

The forces thus operating in television can also be traced in the development of the minicomputer to destroy IBM's long large-computer monopoly. Let us note what Joseph Schumpeter said in *Can Capitalism Survive?* (1947) about the march of capitalism: "The fundamental impulse that sets and keeps the capitalist engine in motion comes from the new consumers' goods, the new methods of production or transportation, the new markets, the new forms of industrial organization that capitalist enterprise creates." Schumpeter even went so far as to say that capitalism's history is a history of revolutions, wherein "industrial mutations" constantly revolutionize the economic structure from within. He named the process "Creative Destruction." We must ask whether within such a process there is still a residual proclivity for largeness to endure—largeness in any form that cheats consumers, squeezes independent producers, and corrupts the government. It would seem, on a little introspection, that this is surely the case.

Schumpeter was an adherent of Nikolai Kondratieff, the Russian economist who in the 1920s invented the long-wave economic theory, also known as the Kondratieff Wave Theory. He said a long economic slump can come about when a new technology is invented and the old technology it will replace must be used up. When it is used up and finally scrapped, there begins a long wave of prosperity, as the major new technology—of, say, railroads, airplanes, or television—is installed, and as an economic and social infrastructure is built up around the new technology. In the case of airplanes, for instance, this infrastructure would take the form of airports, airlines, airplane manufacturers, government regulatory commissions, increased interdependence between cities connected by airline service, and so on, ad infinitum, through all the economic, political, and cultural ramifications of the new technology. It is from the building of this infrastructure that the wave of prosperity derives. Long-wave buffs see them lasting about fifty years, followed by fifty years of decline. Some theorists, such as Jay Forrester at the Massachusetts Institute of Technology, believe the United States is at the end of a long wave of prosperity fed by the technology boom following World War II. (It's interesting that Kondratieff won a vacation in the cold wastes of Siberia for his advocacy of the long-wave theory, because it predicts that capitalism would be reborn, from technology's womb, after its periodic declines; this was counter to orthodox Marxism.)

Some studies have predicted that even if all companies were of equal size to begin with, and were served equal shares of the market, they would, over the course of decades, converge to a position where a few large firms dominate the market. The scholars who conducted these studies can only offer one explanation for this result: plain luck. Some companies strike it rich with a brilliant advertising campaign that engraves their slogan upon the American consciousness ("Things Go Better with Coke," "Ford Has a Better Idea," "Avis Tries Harder"). Other companies pay the same millions to their advertising agencies and are supplied with hokum that disgusts even the most undiscriminating television viewer. One company hires a wise chief executive; another, one who has all the right Ivy League credentials and a hollow place where his mind should be. A company like Kaiser Aluminum has the opportunity to buy an aluminum plant dirt cheap after the Second World War, when the government has finished with it. One firm has two research scientists who invent transistors, as did J. Bardeen and W. H. Brattain at Bell Laboratories in 1948. Another company employs a fellow whose genius supplied us with the infamous Edsel, the greatest automotive lemon of all time (though it's a prime collector's item today). The combinations and permutations are endless.

Is this movement toward bigness the central result of modern capitalism, as Marx proclaimed? He saw the process leading inevitably to the dead end where all power would come to rest in a very few hands, perhaps a half-dozen trillion-dollar conglomerates, all of them so automated in their production processes and their administration that alongside their monstrous riches would exist a monstrous pool of the permanently unemployed. But it is Schumpeter's "Creative Destruction" which prevents the final galactic stage of gargantuan capitalism. The system is slowly dynamic. Marx's scenario implies a static state that has never existed, and so his prediction has never been fulfilled.

5

The Conglomerate Octopus

IN THE BOOM YEARS of the late 1960s we were regaled with tales of the *Wunderkind* conglomerators—modern corporate adventurers such as James Ling, who built empires on the back of envelopes, manipulating stock deals and borrowing money with money already borrowed. Conglomerates emerged as powerful new forms of enterprise that spread their tentacles in all directions and behaved in ways not fully understood by the more traditional corporate managers. Conglomerators moved all over the corporate landscape, assembling companies that made movies and baked bread and owned banks, too—and they were not at all hesitant to sell divisions as quickly as they acquired new ones.

Though its evolution seems recent, the conglomerate has roots reaching back to the start of this century. For instance, Joseph P. Kennedy was one of the first of the big-time conglomerators (which is quite ironic in view of his son Teddy's adamant stance against mergers). Kennedy had the best instincts of a conglomerator. He was, in the words of a friend, a man with "a passion for facts," who displayed no messy sentiments but did possess a great sense of timing. Thus disposed, Kennedy melded investment banking, movie theater ownership, whiskey manufacturing, and real estate wheeling and dealing. He made millions.

Most conglomerates arose as an effort to get around some of the difficulties of traditional management in a time of inflation and economic uncertainty. What evolved was a corporate organization resembling the spokes of a wheel. A central headquarters acts as a sort of holding company for a number of independent divisions in separate and sometimes wildly dissimilar businesses. The unique feature of conglomerates is the philosophy of management they have inspired. Conglomerate managers look on themselves as analogous to investors who manage a portfolio of stocks and bonds. The only difference is that, instead of stocks representing the assets of a company, conglomerate managers own the actual companies. But they view each company as sophisticated investors might view each stock in a portfolio. If investors prudently manage a portfolio of stocks and bonds by judicious buying and selling of the right securities, corporate conglomerate managers handle their "portfolio" of subsidiaries by doing the same, by buying smaller companies that become divisions, and by selling old divisions that have turned into "dogs." The first rule of a wise manager is, naturally, to invest in sound enterprises. The second is to spread risk among a variety of assets. If a stockholder buys the common stock of a high-technology "growth" company, one with good prospects for the sale of its products and a rapid growth in profits, then this investment probably entails a risk. Suppose you invest in the stock of a small San Francisco electronics firm that has a patent on a new laser television system that won't be on the market for five years. You, along with the company's executives, are betting that no competitor will beat your company to it, and that the public will pay for the unproven new invention. It's a large gamble. The way to cover yourself is to invest an equal amount in some perennially stable stock, such as that of AT&T, which is substantially a monopoly in the telephone industry.

If you have invested in the stock of a corporation that builds suburban homes, you know very well that its business depends on the availability of home mortgage money—and that mortgage money is the first category of credit to dry up in a business downturn. So, to avoid a cycle in which your home-building stock plunges every time business is bad, you might also invest in a relatively recession-proof company, such as a chain of local newspapers. Since local newspaper advertising disseminates information essential both to retailers and to consumers, it doesn't disappear in a recession; grocery stores still run their Wednesday shopping ads, and furniture store owners want the public to know of their latest cut-rate prices.

Conglomerate managers use these same principles to husband their collections of "investments." Running a conglomerate offers the prospect of minimal risk, as a result of diversification and cheap profit growth. When you buy a going concern in a different industry, you are achieving diversity at a lower price than if you built a new plant and hired an inexperienced work force to be supervised by managers ignorant of the business. The use of existing buildings and machinery alone constitutes a substantial saving. A plant built in 1970 will have been constructed much more cheaply than one put up in 1980. Construction costs tend to be especially inflationary because plant construction is an old-fashioned piecemeal affair, done by crews of subcontractors to individual specifications. The process just isn't amenable to the assembly line's quick efficiency. And in any case construction work slows in bad weather.

Now, you may want to acquire another company with a product line related to your own. If your company offers high-quality stereo receivers, you might think of buying a small firm that makes a prestigious brand of loudspeaker. That way your company can do more business with most of its customers without trying to learn about loudspeakers, start the business from scratch, and compete with established brand names. Instead, the loudspeaker manufacturer will now operate under the umbrella of your brand, and its hitherto little-known speakers will bear your widely recognized trademark. Or you could buy up a smaller company that makes stereo receivers, but ones of lower price and commensurate quality. Then, by continuing to sell the low-priced receivers under their original brand name, you cover both ends of the market without removing the quality cachet from your own.

There could be less obvious connections between the product of the conglomerate and that of the company it wishes to buy. A potato chip maker that has a national distribution network could easily distribute paperback books to grocery store racks alongside those that hold his potato chips. A national magazine publisher could buy a men's toiletries manufacturer and place mail-order coupons for them in his magazines. A company that makes canned milk can better compete for the scarce space on grocery store shelves by offering several different brands of canned milk to the same stores, even if the prices of the cans are exactly the same. Some conglomerates let their various brands of an identical product compete with each other for sales, on the theory that by doing so they'll weaken the other competition —and even if one of their own brands loses out to another, the company reaps the same rewards. It could also be that the production technology used in a particular plant is nearly identical to that of a company the first one wants to buy. Then at least it will already be familiar with the workaday problems of production and will be better able to manage the two diverse enterprises. Perhaps it can put some of its idle machinery, if it has any, to work at the plant of the business it has bought. Another real possibility is that a company is weak in research and development, so it "buys" R&D by acquiring a company heavy with research facilities and scientists on the payroll.

Acquisitions can enable a corporation to exploit the sort of economies of scope mentioned earlier. More often the company will benefit from conglomerate economies of management; the newly formed division can be operated more cheaply than it was as an independent company because its management overhead can now be spread among a multitude of other divisions. One centralized conglomerate management will be able to replace the separate managements of the companies it has acquired. By the same reasoning, once a company is merged into a conglomerate, it may benefit from economies of information. Put simply, the new division just plugs into the centralized computer system of the corporate headquarters.

The huge financial needs of many industries might offer incentives for merger, simply because the combined financial clout of several companies can be used to get hold of millions of dollars in capital. Any one smaller firm couldn't command such power. Banks do favor larger corporations; they seem more stable and more prone to prosperity, especially if when they combine they create an oligopoly in the markets in which their products are sold.

But along with the many advantages of growth by acquisition there are some distinct disadvantages. As the number of diverse lines of business increases and the number of company divisions multiplies, the managers at headquarters may begin to show their incompetence. If ITT knows how to install satellite communications systems, it isn't so good at baking cupcakes. Good managers, of course, will recognize failure and sell off their poorly performing divisions. Yet some corporate conglomerates take over good companies, turn them into divisions, and then milk the divisions dry: by taking all the profits and reinvesting none in the division; by transferring the division's key people to other company divisions; by neglecting the sales; by failing to pay for needed maintenance expenses; or just by sapping the entrepreneurial spirit from what had been a small company happily operating on its own. In recent years the number of "unfriendly" corporate take-overs has multiplied.

As the tentacles of American conglomerates have stretched outward, they have reached across national borders. At the same time, an important number of foreign firms have brought their business over here. The new phrase to sum up the international dimension is *world-scale*—a phrase of the 1970s that speaks of manufacturing plants large enough to supply a conglomerate's global markets. But multinationals are not distinguished by their ability to export; nearly any sophisticated company can do that. Rather, these conglomerates also manufacture their products overseas. Ford assembles cars in Mexico, and Coca-Cola bottles its drink in mainland China. More than that, the big multinationals can move their manufacturing to wherever labor and raw materials are cheaper and then ship the end products to nations where the prices are highest. This is what we call *maximizing global earnings.*

By moving their operations from nation to nation, the multinationals can immediately exploit comparative foreign advantages, no matter how temporary. The multinational electronics corporations based mostly in California have had their electronic circuit chips mounted and sealed by manual labor overseas, moving their plants around to follow cheap labor costs. In the late 1970s, for instance, they favored Southeast Asia. If wages go up there, they'll move on to another part of the world. For it turns out that even after figuring the cost of shipping their electronic parts to, perhaps, Singapore for assembly and then back to the United States for incorporation in various products, the total expense is cheaper than if the entire operation were carried out here on home soil.

Now, when a multinational ships its unprocessed goods—say, electronic circuit chips fresh from the silicon ovens—from one nation to another for processing, the division in the second nation pays some "price" to the division in the first for these raw materials. But the multinational corporation can decide what "price" this will be, thus avoiding, or at least reducing, taxes. That is, when one division "sells" its output to another division for further processing, the transfer "price" of the internal sale can be marked up if the "buying" division is located in a country where the tax on profits is high. Thus the company will show less of a profit and will have to pay less in taxes. In contrast, for a nation where the income tax is lower than the usual 50 percent, the "selling" division can mark its output down when it "sells" the output to the other division. In this way, profits are transferred to the nation where the profits tax is more favorable. Similarly, a multinational conglomerate can react to the unfavorable policies of a host nation by running down its operations there and transferring them to a more pleasant business climate. The domestic firm, on the other hand, must more or less accept the proclivities of its national leaders, many of whom, through envy of wealth and power, attempt to strangle large corporations.

Are the multinational conglomerates corporate outlaws, or are they highly sophisticated businesses that have transcended petty nationalism and are guilty only of being ahead of their time? We must look at their economic and political ramifications. It is often charged that multinationals, with their global perspective, care little to boost the domestic policies of any individual nation in which they operate. It is said, for example, that the major oil companies owe their allegiance to no nation, and certainly not to the United States. (To whom do they owe allegiance? Lewis Lapham, the editor of *Harper's*, says an oil executive told him, "We get down on our knees and pray to Mecca every morning.") Presidents and prime ministers sometimes find themselves powerless to impose any economic policy on the multinational corporate divisions residing in their nations. It has also been said that the multinationals play too strong a role in the domestic policies of the host nations. One can call up the horrible example of ITT secretly contributing $1 million to get rid of leftist Salvador Allende in Chile.

Then it is added that, though multinational conglomerates theoretically sell their stock shares across the world, no international stock exchange exists. What in fact happens is that most of their stockholders live in the country where the conglomerate is headquartered. One tends to think most are located in the United States, but that is decidedly not so. Even when the dollar was strong, corporations such as Philips of Holland, Nestlé of Switzerland, British Petroleum, Nippon Steel, and many others were major international bases, with long-standing divisions in the United States.

Most Americans would be surprised to learn how many traditional "American" products have always been produced in this nation by foreign firms. Among the *Fortune* top fifty industrial companies in the world for 1978, twenty-eight were non-U.S. corporations. And in these days of the weak dollar, the United States has become a hunting ground for foreign investors who want bargains. The late 1970s saw a huge influx of foreign money to buy American companies, from the Korvettes discount chain, bought by Agache-Willot of France, to Howard Johnson restaurants, bought by the Imperial Group Ltd. of Britain. Some of the foreign companies, by the way, are state-owned in whole (like France's Renault) or in part (like Volkswagenwerk in Germany).

Many of the complaints against the nature of multinational corporations are simply unfounded. Still, it is not easy to condone their proclivity to bribe when abroad, though it is a way of life overseas. And while our honest instinct is to condemn corporate corruption, in this case we ought also to be apprised of the consequences of our moral righteousness. When Congress passed sanctions against multinational corporations that endeavored to engage in financial sordidness abroad, the European multinationals could hardly conceal their joy, because Congress was thereby handing them a nice competitive edge. A French banker was quoted in an American business magazine as saying he and his fellows felt they had died and gone to heaven when they heard how the American government was curbing the use of payoffs by American multinationals. Here our morality bears a price tag that can be measured in increments of inflation, as American companies become less competitive in the rigors of the world market.

If it is charged that the large multinationals foster monopoly and oligopoly in the nations where they operate, it is also charged, rather curiously, that from a global perspective these same multinationals have brought on a terrible state of competition that somehow threatens the world economic order. Not surprisingly, the savants who make this claim yearn for global regulation of corporations. These critics are alarmed by the vision they see of international competition without the cozy order provided by dominant companies that set prices.

In other words, these critics, while eternally complaining of oligopoly at home, attack the absence of oligopoly overseas in the world market. The global laissez-faire policy, they claim, has resulted in the "overproduction" of goods and services. They cite a surplus world capacity to produce steel and plastics and chemicals, among other things. But in reality the supposed overcapacity can only be temporary. Demand will always catch up with it eventually. Over the long haul, after all, the world population increases, and the average income rises, so there are new customers beyond the horizon.

The growth of multinational conglomerates has speeded development of the technology of international trade. Most prominent is the birth and rapid growth of the Eurocurrency market, which didn't even exist twenty-five years ago and is now worth about $500 billion. Several hundred banks serve the Euromoney market through their foreign branches, but only a handful predominate. (On the other hand, foreign banks have come in droves to American shores, where they cannot take deposits but can, like the U.S. banks' overseas branches, make loans.) The vitality of the Euromoney market is such that the top ten American banks earn up to 50 percent of their profits from these loans —loans that are outside the control of any nation's monetary authority. Periodically, political agitators see a vast conspiracy in the intercourse of the multinational conglomerates and the Eurocurrency banks, but the system has indubitably facilitated a worldwide banking system that could and most probably will become the norm of the future. Even now, recessions are mitigated in one nation by its ability to export to another part of the world unaffected by the recession. In addition to the Euromoney banking system, multinational commerce has developed its own hardware. One thinks of satellite-transmitted telephone and teletype communications; the corporate Learjet; the air cargo jet; international computer systems; and new methods of container shipping that alleviate the need for expensive dock facilities. There is also a new corporate management schooled in global business techniques.

The Euromoney-conglomerate connection inspires sinister conspiracy theories precisely because this powerful financial market is unregulated and thus beyond the grasp of government bureaucracy. Scholars of the paranoic fringe churn out learned papers reporting that American industry is tied up in a network of secret national and international control. The theory is that a handful of extremely powerful bankers run the whole nation and indeed much of the world through their control of international corporations based in the United States.

David Kotz is the latest sounder of the alarm. In a book titled *Bank Control of Large Corporations in the United States,* he sets out to prove the standard left-wing conspiracy theory by underlining the banks' holdings of a high percentage of corporate stocks and their potential influence over corporate decisions to borrow money. When a bank owns a sizable block of a corporation's stock, the argument runs, it can seduce the corporation into borrowing heavily, to the corporation's detriment. Yet if such borrowing were to the corporation's detriment, its stock would fall in value, and the bank would in turn lose money.

Kotz also asserts that banks like to sit in on management decisions. But if a corporation makes a decision the bank doesn't like, it can sell its stock in that firm. Kotz argues that if the bank owns a huge amount of the corporation's stock, selling it off all at once might have to be done at a loss, because the stock price will be depressed. Perhaps that's possible, but it is hardly enough evidence to warrant the reactionary rhetoric of Kotz and his colleagues.

Of course, there is a play of power in the relationship between a corporation's managers and its major creditors and major stockholders. What is the result? Kotz has suggested, but only suggested, that bankers may have urged corporations to merge, so as to cut down on competition and provide stable profits. One wonders if corporate managers need urging; most seem perfectly willing to merge on their own. Well then, Kotz speculates that a bank could encourage one of two corporations with which it does business to buy from or sell to the other. Or it could arrange a merger between two companies tied to the bank. Anything is possible. We might equally well concoct such a theory on the ground that mutual funds and labor union pension funds invest billions in the stock market, too.

The important question in all of this becomes whether life would be substantively different if neither banks nor any outside institutions had any indirect chance to influence corporations via stock ownership. The most likely answer is that the important decisions concerning corporate pricing, the quantity of output, and the companies acquired or sold would be no different.

6

The Petroleum Economy

GASOLINE, KEROSENE, NAPHTHA, heavy oils, natural gas—these are the life juices of technology as we know it. Combustion engines and turbine engines use petroleum fuels directly, but even electricity has been most cheaply produced by the burning of fuels distilled from crude oil. The availability of cheap, seemingly inexhaustible petroleum energy spurred businesses on to build bigger, more powerful machines that could work faster and harder than mere humans. Machines automated manufacturing production and eased life around the house. Everything from the forklift truck to the home lawn mower substituted petroleum power for muscle power. The result was that society became more productive; workers could produce more goods with less effort. And if the machines we built wasted energy, that didn't matter. Energy was cheap enough to waste. It was hardly more expensive than water from the tap, and it flowed just as freely.

The relationship between energy use and economic growth is a close one. Until the recent conservation efforts, the increase in American energy consumption closely paralleled the growth in Gross National Product. The ratio of energy consumption to GNP has been nearly one to one for the greater part of the postwar period, though lately it has fallen to about one to three, a marked improvement.

In 1973 the Organization of Petroleum Exporting Countries jacked up the price of crude oil four times, and continued to pull the price up higher and higher afterward, thereby upsetting a major assumption of the industrial nations: i.e., that petroleum-based energy would always be cheap and abundant. The assumption had allowed industrial engineers and car designers to ignore considerations of fuel economy. Suddenly, many billions of dollars' worth of complex machinery was inefficient, too expensive to operate, unless the new costs could be passed along to someone else. A number of manufacturers were able to recoup higher energy costs in higher product prices. And then consumers were able, in effect, to pass along these higher prices to the government, which eased the pain throughout the 1970s by pumping extra money into the economy. That is, when OPEC in effect slapped a huge tax on the economy, the government sought to restore our incomes to where they were before the tax. The result was inflation. That inflation is a measure of our refusal to accept the lower living standards dictated by OPEC's tax.

In the aftermath, the nation's economic growth slipped to half its pre-OPEC rate, as did that of all industrial countries. But the poor, undeveloped nations were already in bad shape at the outset of the new economic world order; they lacked the reserves of wealth to pay steep oil prices. The poor countries of Africa, Asia, and Latin America were then forced to increase their borrowings from the United States and the industrialized nations of Europe, though OPEC did lend a small amount to African Moslem nations. It is feared, with good reason, that some billions of dollars in loans made by the developed countries, especially the United States, may never be repaid because the poorest countries just get poorer—unless, like Mexico, they strike it rich with oil.

Petrodollars, which are the dollars Arab sheikhs get for their oil, have also played their part in expanding the world money supply, thus increasing inflation throughout the developed world. This happens on the Eurodollar market, which is the market for credit made available at the foreign branches of international banks. Eurocurrencies are not under the control of any monetary authority, so the Eurodollar market can flout any attempt to restrict money flows. If a company wants to borrow $1 billion to expand its operations and domestic credit is tight, the company can go to the Eurodollar market and get the cash, though it won't get a loan of sufficient maturity for its long-term needs. However, the Euromoney market has greatly helped the world economy by recycling petrodollars via Eurodollar loans to developing countries. From time to time we hear dark reports that the Eurodollar market is in imminent danger of collapsing, and that its fall would topple the world's monetary system. In 1976 an American socialist ran for President by sounding the alarm that within weeks the market would cave in. It didn't happen, and he didn't get elected.

Yet OPEC's "tax" wasn't imposed just for punitive political reasons. Since the late 1960s our use of Persian Gulf oil had increased dramatically but the after-inflation price of oil remained as low as it had been ten years earlier. A price increase was due, if only because the demand for Middle Eastern petroleum had soared. OPEC members also felt the West wanted to use up Arab oil first and then go on to wells in other lands. Middle Eastern oil princes saw crude oil being pumped feverishly out of their wells, at artificially low prices, until in a few years these nations would be left dry. Then they might revert once again to poor desert kingdoms. The fear was legitimate. OPEC potentates asked themselves why they should not raise the oil price and slow down production, which was at levels too high to sustain anyway. That way, they could bring in plenty of cash with which to build industrial economies, so that when the oil did finally run out they would have something more for subsistence than camels and date palms. If the size of the OPEC oil price increase was out of proportion to the higher demand for petroleum, that was because the new price was designed to dam the flood of Persian Gulf oil flowing into the West. And a political message was to be read between the lines, for the Arab OPEC members did not approve of our support for Israel. But the political intent of the 1973 price hike has been overrated. Actually, the most staunchly Arab nations in OPEC have been moderating forces in the oil cartel; non-Arab members such as Venezuela and Indonesia have often clamored for the most radical price increases.

The petroleum price rise served notice on the industrialized world that the age of inexhaustibility was over. In fact, it had never existed except in the blind optimism of American businessmen, steeped in the frontier mythology of forever open boundaries, of raw resources just waiting to be seized and squandered. The first hint of exhaustible resources came after World War II. President Truman's Materials Policy Commission reported in 1952 that by 1950 the United States was using some 10 percent more raw materials than it was producing, whereas the reverse had been true early in the century. The United States had once exported oil, iron ore, copper, lead, and zinc. By 1950 it had become an importer of these depleting native resources. But the report of the President's commission and the warnings of various private economists were drowned out in the roar of the great postwar industrial machine, running at full horsepower.

If OPEC sent us a warning in 1973, the warning grew into an ultimatum by 1979. For in that year OPEC instituted a new and dangerous method of oil pricing. The cartel still set a base price for petroleum but allowed each OPEC oil-producing nation to add a surcharge as it wished. This provision opened up the strong possibility of an uncontrollable upward spiral of oil prices. If any one oil-producing nation should cut back its production, the resulting shortfall in oil supplies would give OPEC members free license to tack on hefty price surcharges and thus raise the price of their crude oil beyond any limits. Shortly after OPEC announced its policy, almost all of the OPEC nations had added surcharges ranging from $1.20 to $2.50 and more a barrel of oil. They did this in response to the tight demand caused by

Iran's cutback in oil production following the rise of the Ayatollah Khomeini. But since then, OPEC nations like Kuwait, Iraq, Venezuela, and even conservative Saudi Arabia often announce their intentions to cut back oil production too, thus adding impetus to the upward escalation of oil prices. In 1979 alone, the new OPEC pricing method added another $18 billion to the United States' $40 billion annual oil import bill. And as crude oil prices increase, the prices of gasoline and home heating oil and all the things made from oil increase even more, reflecting the most expensive oil supplies.

Still worse, the OPEC price of oil is now influenced by the prices received on what's known as the *spot market*. This is the oil market centered in Rotterdam and London, where oil traders operate over the phone, selling quantities of oil for the highest bids they can get. The amount of oil sold on the spot market is minuscule, because most oil is sold under long-term contracts between the OPEC nations and the major oil companies. But recently some OPEC countries have reneged on their long-term contracts in order to sell some of their oil instead on the spot market, where prices of $20 or more a barrel were not uncommon in 1979. When spot market prices go up, soon enough the OPEC base price goes up too.

Oil prices promise to continue spiraling upward throughout the 1980s. Thus there are many voices calling for the West to break up OPEC. Some have suggested military action against the Persian Gulf nations. But Saudi Arabia and other countries have always claimed they would destroy their own oil fields in such an event. More reasoned voices have advocated a sort of cartel of Western oil-consuming nations, to prevent major industrial nations from trying to outbid each other for oil. Such a consuming cartel would presumably also be able collectively to resist the more outlandish OPEC price gouging. However, international economic and political cooperation seems too advanced, too civilized for the world in which we live today.

Throughout the 1970s the West, and especially the United States, depended on Saudi Arabia to cool the radicalism of OPEC's price hawks. Saudi Arabia had repeatedly pronounced its friendship with the United States. The conservative Saudi kingdom opposed the leftist doctrines espoused by the Soviet Union. Yet in the 1980s the role of Saudi Arabia becomes ambiguous, for the Saudis were deeply stung by the Egyptian-Israeli peace accord President Carter engineered in 1979. It gradually dawned on the U. S. State Department that, after the treaty was signed, the United States could no longer count on Saudi Arabia to hold oil prices down and generally act as our silent partner. In fact, the Saudi government, in the face of the peace treaty, began to make overtures to the Russians. America may still have friends in Riyadh, but the friendship will never be as useful as it has been.

Ever since the OPEC price increase of 1973, the American government has demonstrated its profound unwillingness to grapple with the issue of expensive energy supplied by volatile foreign powers. The issue is a political as well as an economic one. In fact, on strictly economic terms, the sensible policy would be to continue allowing the nation to increase its dependence on foreign oil, because foreign nations have what economists call a comparative advantage over us in the cheap production of oil. Yet the purely economic argument falls apart. The issue becomes one of national security. For if we still require immense volumes of crude oil to fuel the industrial economy, our cars, and, significantly, our military hardware, then it is better to have that crude produced here at home—despite the declining amounts of American underground petroleum reserves—with any shortfall to be made up by the supplies of friendly, non-OPEC nations. Thus the government has advertised a policy of energy independence. But its policy has actually encouraged dependence by artificially holding the domestic price of oil and its products below the world price, thereby subsidizing OPEC, and thereby also increasing our imports of foreign oil, which have hurt the balance-of-trade deficit and have weakened the dollar because of that deficit. Presidents have exhorted Americans to use less gasoline and heating oil, to stop "wasting" energy. But these gentlemen have ignored the simple fact that we weren't wasting fuel; we were simply using it in accord with its artificially low price. If gasoline is so cheap that I can afford to drive around in a car that gets only ten miles to each gallon, what am I wasting? When the price goes up, I will adjust my use of it to reflect the greater expense.

Failing to see that the need must precede the sacrifice, our leaders have consistently asked Americans to please turn down their thermostats and stop driving to work alone. The citizenry has ignored these calls for voluntary hardship. Only in 1979 did a President finally take the first halting steps toward an intelligent energy policy. President Carter announced that he was phasing out crude oil price controls, for the first time since they had been imposed in the early 1970s by President Nixon. (He should have decontrolled gasoline prices, too.)

This was a politically risky step, as the outraged screams of consumer groups and populist senators demonstrated. But the President's courage deserves less emphasis than is generally thought. He was forced into the decontrol decision, and even then he avoided making it until the last minute. If he hadn't acted either to end the price controls or to extend them, sudden decontrol might have plummeted the economy when the controls expired in 1981. Carter couldn't very well extend the controls, for OPEC had just posted fat new price increases of 25 percent and oil was selling in the world spot market at $20 or more a barrel. Sheikh Ahmed Zaki Yamani, the Saudi Arabian oil minister, told the United States that he had done all he could for the West, and that now it was up to us. He declared that if the United States hadn't come up with some strong policy to curb its consumption of Middle Eastern oil by the summer of 1979, large new price increases would be guaranteed.

Carter bastardized his new price decontrol policy by attempting to aim the public's outrage at the major oil companies, which stood to gain up to $15 billion a year. Carter's political game was to make these oil companies the whipping boys of expensive energy, and he encouraged a vague conspiracy theory of oil prices. He hinted that the big oil companies had benefited from OPEC's actions and might be in cahoots with Arab petroleum princes to steal from the innocent American people. So Carter proposed that the new profits from the higher oil prices be taxed almost completely away from the oil companies. Yet the idea of Carter's "windfall profits tax" made little sense. Without any new tax, more than half the oil corporations' new profits would pass into the government treasury by way of the corporate income tax, oil well royalty payments, and oil lease bonus payments. The amount left over would go in part to stockholders, but most of it would be used to explore for more oil —which is what oil company profits are supposed to be used for. But no, President Carter fell into the easy rhetoric of scorn, noting that Mobil had, in 1974, used its fat oil profits to buy the Montgomery Ward chain rather than to explore for oil. But when Mobil bought the chain, oil price controls were in full effect, making exploration for oil less profitable than other enterprises such as retailing.

The idea of price decontrol is to allow prices to function as they naturally do, to signal to producers and consumers how much a commodity is valued by society. The higher the price of a commodity, the more will be supplied and the less will be consumed, until, ideally, supply will come to match demand. But the moral flab of cheap rhetoric sent Carter and the Congress into fits of anger. The nation had once again all but failed to come to grips with the economic reality. By 1980 nearly every nation on earth was paying at least two dollars a gallon for gasoline, and many of the poorest paid considerably more. Yet America held on to the myth of cheap gasoline.

Beyond the immediate contingencies of cutting energy consumption as much as is feasible and stimulating production of safe new sources, what really counts is how we adjust over the long haul. In fact, the nation has made some adjustments. A combination of measures like the mandated fifty-five-miles-per-hour speed limit and the mandated higher fuel efficiency of American cars has helped. So has the massive import of more efficient foreign compacts, which all but dominate the American small-car market. Industry has moved to plug steam leaks and install heat exchangers in factories. Homeowners are insulating their homes. Greater savings will be forthcoming as new, more fuel-efficient factories replace old ones, as new cars replace gas guzzlers, and as new designs build energy efficiency into housing. But higher prices would greatly speed the transition.

Indeed, the President's Council on Environmental Quality last year came forth with what it called "the good news about energy." The council says the combination of increased fuel efficiency and slower American population growth means that, in the years ahead, we could possibly live as comfortably as we do today on 30 to 40 percent less energy per person. The slower birth rate means our demand for the things that energy can provide will be increasing at a slower rate. Meanwhile, claims the council, if we vastly increase the productivity of cars and home appliances and office buildings, then by the year 2000 we will be able to get on quite nicely using no more than 10 or 20 percent more energy than we do today—just enough, that is, to accommodate the increase in population. The future projected by the Council on Environmental Quality is a cheerful one, but it rests on the assumption that the nation will commit itself to mandatory energy conservation and the development of low-energy-use technology. Unfortunately, the "determined national effort" called for by the council remains a pipe dream. The American government hasn't the willpower to let freed energy prices bring forth conservation by signaling to the public the value of petroleum energy.

Other students of energy tell us that there's plenty of oil yet to be found. They say that the oil and natural-gas potential of less-developed nations is phenomenal. Mexico leads the group, with almost as much oil under its land as Saudi Arabia, according to some estimates. More possibilities may lie in wait in South America, Indochina, Canada, and Australia. It is said that half the petroleum in the earth is perhaps yet to be discovered in the underdeveloped nations. Even in the United States, the estimates of untapped oil in the ground range from 61 to 149 billion barrels; of unfound natural gas, from 322 to 655 trillion cubic feet. Finding and developing these supplies of fuel both in the United States and in underdeveloped nations could give us some breathing space, some margin of comfort for the immediate future. The World Bank has committed $5 billion to the search, but not without opposition from the major oil companies.

Yet these are still stopgap measures. The great long-range energy choice is more fundamental: Either we find some substitute energy sources to fuel our existing technology, or we build a new kind of technology. Finding substitute sources of hydrocarbons appears to be attractive. We already know how to turn coal into oil and gas, even if the technology isn't perfected. We can, if necessary, squeeze petroleum from oil shale and tar sands and convert viscous heavy oils into usable petroleum products. In 1979 President Carter called for development of all this. But there's a catch. It's true that as the cost of a barrel of oil goes up, such substitutes become more competitive; yet the accompanying technologies also become costly to install. Suppose we say that when oil is $25 a barrel, coal liquefaction becomes feasible, because it costs only $24 a barrel to produce oil from coal at today's prices. The trouble with the argument is that we aren't really talking about today's prices. For when oil has risen to $25 a barrel, the cost of the coal liquefaction machinery will also have escalated, so that when oil is $25 a barrel, we may then have to say coal liquefaction will become feasible when oil is at $28 or $30 a barrel, and so on. This ratcheting effect comes about because when the price of a barrel of oil goes up, so does the price of almost everything, starting with gasoline and heating oil and spreading to aspirin and polyester suits—both made from oil—and reaching everything produced in the economy, including the equipment that would make oil from coal.

Unless inflation can be greatly slowed—and that isn't likely, except through recession, until we have solved the energy dilemma—the reasons for using techniques such as coal liquefaction must be founded more on politics than on economics. The argument for this technology, in fact, has political and long-term economic merit. If the installation today of coal liquefaction and gasification plants would be so uneconomic that they'd need to be subsidized, once in place they could produce fuels that need not rise in price, because the United States has several centuries' worth of coal to be used. Thus the real, after-inflation price of oil and gas made from coal should stay constant. Some corporations, notably the Continental Oil Company (which owns 14 billion tons of coal), have pioneered in coal conversion technology, with little assistance from the government. These companies aren't prepared to undertake the substitute technology on a scale that's large enough to make any difference. But the government could launch a Manhattan Project to develop coal liquefaction and gasification complexes, though the very idea has outraged Washington's environmentalists, who prefer a no-growth economy.

At the same time, just burning coal causes a host of regulatory snarls. The idea is to take clean-burning coal from the Western states and to transport it to industrial and utility company boilers throughout the nation. But how? Doing it by railroad would call for several dozen 100-car trains moving through Western communities each day, a plan that doesn't please the people who live there. Besides, the pollution caused by diesel locomotives and by cars idling at railroad crossings would rankle the Environmental Protection Agency. Moving coal by pipeline would require an expensive pipeline, large quantities of water with which to flush the coal, a way to dry it out at the other end, and a method of protecting the pipeline from cold temperatures that would freeze the water inside. But that's only the beginning. What about the waste from burning coal? It has been estimated that the typical 1,000-megawatt coal-burning plant would produce nearly a million tons of ash a year, not to mention daily piles of sludge. The waste may contain enough exotic chemicals to classify it, under government regulations, as hazardous waste. Again, the EPA can hardly be expected to let this kind of thing go on. This is not to mention the possible changing of the climate through the release of carbon dioxide by burning coal.

The situation with nuclear power is similar to that of coal, only multiplied a hundred times. After the Three Mile Island nuclear media event of 1979 the industry remains in jeopardy. The trouble at that nuclear electricity-generating plant caused no immediate harm to anyone, but it nearly killed an already comatose industry. Nuclear energy remains stuck in a quagmire of uncertainty. Inept bureaucrats, stupid industry officials, and Chicken Little press coverage have unwittingly conspired to nearly eliminate nuclear power as an option. Professional scientists saw the Three Mile Island debacle as, more than anything, a massive failure of the American educational system. They viewed the outcome as more unhappy proof that the American people and journalists and even government leaders are scientific illiterates, ready to believe the wildest fantasies and incapa-

ble of making intelligent judgments concerning the risks and
benefits of modern technology. During the Three Mile Island event it became apparent that a good many people, including television network correspondents, believe that a
nuclear power plant can blow up like an atom bomb, though
any high school physics student should know that this is
simply impossible. One wonders if the American populace is
becoming collectively less scientifically literate just as American technology is becoming more advanced.

Obscured by the gaudy headlines of the nuclear scare in
1979 was a more significant energy debacle. Standard Oil of
Ohio gave up its attempt to build an oil pipeline that would
send surplus Alaskan oil from California to Texas, where it
could be refined and shipped cheaply to Midwest and Eastern consumers. The White House badly wanted the pipeline
to be built, but told company officers it was powerless
against the Washington juggernaut which, in concert with
many state regulators, had killed the pipeline project.

A White House aide asked a high official of the project
what the President could do to expedite the pipeline. The
official told him he'd have to issue an executive order that
would prohibit state and federal litigation over the pipeline.
The White House spokesman was shocked at the idea. He
immediately saw the tremendous political liabilities involved in any such attempt. "Well," said the pipeline expert,
"then we'll get no pipeline. The regulators have killed it."

But what complicated the issue was the fact that the state
of California had stopped the project and its governor, Jerry
Brown, was running against Jimmy Carter for President—
unofficially at least. Brown had lashed out at Sohio, painting
it as a greedy big oil company out to harm the interests of
the American people. And the White House figured that if
Carter offered any concrete help to Sohio, Brown would
then be able to accuse the President of aiding and abetting a
major oil company, and a foreign-owned one at that (Sohio
is part of British Petroleum). So much for the Sohio pipeline,

and the low-cost petroleum it would supply to the nation's midsection.

We possess an almost mystical enthusiasm for such soft, clean energy sources as solar power and wind power and the power of steam generated under the earth. But these technologies seem even more remote than coal technologies. They are inefficient as generators of useful energy. The best solar cell, still under development, can convert only 22 percent of the sun's energy that it receives into electrical energy. Windmills of sufficient size to supply power to a home often break apart after the first gust of strong wind. One hears wondrous claims for biomass, the fermenting of organic matter into methane gas. It is said that we could use inexhaustible corn or sugar cane crops to produce abundant synthetic gas. But it has also been calculated that if you count the amount of energy put into growing the crops—as you must—then some twenty-six acres would be needed to produce each equivalent barrel of oil. At present farmland prices, this would make each barrel more expensive by far than the most costly Arab oil. Major technical breakthroughs are needed to bring the soft-energy technologies into the realm of reality. One can guess that those breakthroughs won't come easily, because such technologies involve the extraction of usable power from raw materials with only small concentrations of energy. Matter can be turned into energy, but what's important is how much energy is compacted into the matter and how accessible it is. Coal, for example, is in some sense a source of solar energy, since coal is thought to be the substance that results when organic matter—plants and animals—is compressed and heated slowly for thousands of years. Coal, then, is a concentrate of energy. To use matter that doesn't have energy concentrated in it is bound to be less efficient. That is, the use of this diffuse energy source itself requires much energy. To take the extreme example, a scientist could no doubt get some quantum of energy from granite, but the amount of energy required to extract it would make the whole exercise absurd.

The soft-energy technologies, however, have a political appeal that is decidedly lacking for the yet dirty technologies of making gas and oil from coal or shale. Wind and sun and geothermal steam power seem so natural, so pristine. These technologies don't lend themselves to large-scale applications, say their proponents, so besides their aesthetic appeal they offer the political advantage of conforming to Jeffersonian ideals of small-scale enterprise. We are speaking here of technological democracy, as envisioned by survivors of the 1960s back-to-nature counterculture—of utopian schemes in which every home would possess its neat, homemade solar apparatus, its energy self-sufficiency. No huge oil company would be reaping its "obscene" profits anymore. Life would be as it was in the nineteenth century, and the *Whole Earth Catalog* would be every household's bible.

It is one thing to find suitable replacements for petroleum. It's quite another to create a new kind of technology that doesn't require hydrocarbon energy at all, or not very much of it. Such a new technology is possible, even probable over the long haul. It can already be seen on the distant horizon. The key to it is likely to be the very-large-scale integrated-circuit chip of the electronics industry. One day, advances in semiconductors and superconductors will be able to change radically the way we do things. We will explore the presently visible possibilities in later pages.

The federal government has proposed a massive effort to modify present technology rather than replace it. President Carter's then transportation secretary, Brock Adams, announced to Congress in 1979 that he wanted Detroit to reinvent the automobile so that the average car will get between 40 and 50 miles per gallon by the year 2000, compared to the present rate of 20 to 30 miles per gallon. Adams would like it to be a joint government-industry project, with Washington chipping in a half billion dollars each year.

But the auto makers told Adams they are having a hard enough time just meeting the current federal mileage standards, which call for an average 27.5 miles per gallon by 1985. They say that will end up costing the industry $80 billion, and the industry just isn't wealthy enough to keep spending amounts like that. Already the car companies have had to expand their engineering departments by nearly 50 percent and retool dozens of assembly lines.

But some of Adams' congressional detractors wondered if it wouldn't be a waste of effort to raise car fuel efficiency much above 27.5 miles per gallon. Rather, they said, the government ought to be pouring the money into research on alternative energy sources, as Carter proposed. They argued that when fuel mileage is increased, one runs into diminishing rewards. In other words, in a plan to go from 15 to 50 miles per gallon, by the time a car is getting 27.5 miles per gallon it has already achieved 70 percent of the energy savings to be had.

It may well be that attempting a huge new program to modify automobile technology could turn out to be a rearguard action. For if history is any guide, radical new energy-efficient technologies could be lurking around the corner ready to receive the investment that would otherwise be squandered on squeezing diminishing amounts of fuel savings from the conventional technology of the internal combustion engine. That engine, after all, is quite crude. Developed back in the latter part of the nineteenth century, it depends for its power on the controlled explosion of gasoline mist inside a cylinder. Surely we are now able to invent more sophisticated methods of converting energy into physical work. One gets a dim sense that we are now poised for some dramatic new technological departure. We exist in a period that suggests itself as a literal and figurative *fin de siècle*—a period of decadence and expectation.

When Americans had to start lining up at the gasoline stations, in mid-1979, the mood was palpably different from

that of the previous gasoline crunch during the Arab embargo days of 1973. That prior shortage had a clear cause
and a convenient foreign villain to blame: Arab OPEC was
mad about American support of warring Israel. It was that
simple, on the surface, in the easy commentaries of television anchormen. This recent shortage, it soon turned out,
was much more sinister. Its cause was hard to discover and
it promised to last, in varying degrees, for years to come. In
the first weeks of the 1979 crunch, the whole nation was
convinced it was a hoax perpetrated by the big oil companies to force up gasoline prices (though these prices were
actually controlled by the government). Congressmen called
oil executives to testify and angrily shouted them out of the
committee room. The mass news media played up the popular feeling, often without even trying to find out the source
of the shortage. Americans, furious at having been deprived
of their carefree automotive life-styles, shot each other and
stabbed pregnant women to get in front of the gasoline
lines. A talk show host got big laughs when he called for the
murder of the president of Exxon.

Of course, we didn't want to hear the real reasons for the
gasoline shortage, for the delineation of those reasons revealed the dimensions of the technological crisis and
brought it into cold reality. What had happened was that
the fall of the Shah of Iran and his replacement by an anti-
American Ayatollah of radical reactionary proclivities had
disrupted the supply of crude oil. Iranian production
dropped by several million barrels a day, and the loss eliminated the tiny margin of safety on which the world oil industry had to operate. The companies could have bought
some oil on the world spot market, where prices went up to
$50 a barrel, but the Department of Energy at first asked
the oil companies to stay out of the market, lest the United
States be accused later, when OPEC was to meet, of having
bid the price up. At the same time, the nation's stock of
heating oil for the winter was depleted and refiners needed

to switch over, producing less gas and more heating oil, to build the stocks up. Otherwise the country would freeze in the winter of 1979–80. Environmental laws had complicated the picture. First, the Environmental Protection Agency had ordered car makers to install catalytic converters, which cut down pollution but which also required unleaded gasoline—which in turn requires more crude oil to make the same amount of gas, unless refiners were permitted to use such octane-enhancing chemicals as MMT. The EPA had, however, banned those chemicals because they harm converters, too. Gasoline price controls kept profits on gasoline low enough that refiners couldn't afford to invest in expensive new equipment to make unleaded gas without such chemicals. Indeed, at the very time the problem became fully apparent, the EPA was also proposing to classify some twenty refinery wastes as "hazardous"—thus forcing refiners to divert millions of dollars from the financing of gasoline production to the financing of equipment to comply with the regulations.

The American governmental and media establishment proved incompetent to deal rationally with the gasoline shortage. President Carter and his advisers issued contradictory explanations of the problem. Meanwhile the Federal Trade Commission set out to uncover a conspiracy among the oil companies. Network television and the dailies took the conspiracy theory and ran with it. That was, after all, about as much as they had to go on. The oil companies, especially the giants, mostly refused to cooperate with the mass media in explaining to Americans why gasoline was in short supply and heating oil prices would go through the roof. Most oil company executives seemed to believe the media were themselves organized in a conspiracy to nationalize or otherwise hamper the oil industry. Some oilmen say the attitude arose from the industry's long tradition of secrecy due to its competitiveness. They have also noted that oil executives are engineers with a mentality foreign to the instincts of journalists and politicians. One national reporter told me of the Texas oilman who, at dinner, turned to the reporter and demanded to know why the damn press had any right to go sticking its nose into the oil business anyway. The reporter mumbled something about the First Amendment, but the message doubtless didn't sink in. It's hard to sympathize with businessmen who think they possess no social obligations, and the oil industry bears a large share of the responsibility for the treatment it receives at the hands of an angry, puzzled, distrusting public.

7

The Worker's Stake

THE RISE of the machine has meant the decline of the artisan, the craftsman who did his work painstakingly by hand and took pride in its quality. Machines have removed working men and women from the end product of their efforts. Standing at an assembly line, tightening screws on a succession of identical engine carburetors that will go into any one of a dozen automobile models, few people can muster more than a perfunctory personal pride in their contribution. Thus we have libraries full of the literature of labor discontent, relieved only by the occasional assembly-line interviewees who say they rather enjoy the mindlessness and lack of responsibility of their jobs.

But there's a more pervasive discontent in the present age. It is reported that American workers, whether on the assembly line or in the office, don't much want to work at all. Scholars and polltakers discover that the American people just do not believe any longer in the work ethic. Whereas the early postwar years saw generations of nose-to-the-grindstone people, ambitious men and women who pulled themselves up by their clichéd bootstraps, in the latter decades of the twentieth century such attitudes of industrious rectitude seem quaint. Little kids all say they want to be movie directors or sex therapists when they grow up. Adults expend their mental powers trying to figure out how to do as little as possible; yet they go deep into debt for huge motorboats and campers. Robert Schrank, a sociologist, has looked into the problem. In his book *Ten Thousand*

Working Days, he speaks of blue-collar workers who no longer wish even to think about their jobs. "Some," he explains, "prefer to make bowling the center of their lives. That may be a greater demonstration of autonomy and creativity than building a better high-speed gear box." Schrank found that people naturally still want the steady income a job provides, but want to do as little as feasible to earn it. He presents America as a giant civil service bureaucracy in the making, full of workers who draw weekly paychecks and in between spend their hours dawdling at their desks or guzzling beer on the assembly line. Schrank goes on to suggest that if we continue offering incentives for laziness such as welfare and unemployment doles, and if we remove the remaining punishments for not working—not having money, for instance—then few people in America will continue to do anything productive.

American management must take part of the blame. One can recount the history of such rogue corporations as J. P. Stevens & Company, the southern textile company that takes great pride in its resistance to unionization and its contempt for the well-being of its employees; or the notorious Hooker Chemical Corp. of upstate New York, the company alleged to have allowed its workers to be poisoned for years with chemicals that have caused grotesque, even fatal, job-related illnesses. On a more subtle plane, the technique of American management has never been to devote itself to worker satisfaction. The clever Japanese have taught us as much in recent years, for their management style has been successfully transplanted to a few American factories. This style reverses the American; rule is from the bottom up, rather than from the top down. In other words, Japanese managers consult seriously with their employees, replacing master-slave relationships with equal-to-equal relationships. They consciously try to build worker confidence and to engage the assembly-line employee in a sort of decision by consensus. Along with this effort goes an unusual commitment to worker job security. At a Sony plant in San Diego, when slack times come about, workers are not laid off or fired, as in American plants. Instead they are given house-cleaning chores in the factory—repainting, renovating, and so on. The plant manager says the long-range happiness of his factory "family" is more important than short-range profits. Another practice of the Japanese is to emphasize factory cleanliness and orderliness, for they believe that workers take pride in a clean, neat work environment.

American skeptics demur that the paternalistic, con-sensus-oriented management style works well in Japan, where the society is homogeneous, but wouldn't here. How-ever, it does work here, and its success can be seen in the growing number of American manufacturing plants owned and operated by Japanese. At that Sony plant in San Diego, the worker productivity is higher than at any other Ameri-can television manufacturing plant. The management style of the Japanese is in part responsible for that nation's 9 to 10 percent productivity growth rate, compared to a laggard American rate barely reaching 1 percent a year.

We cannot realistically expect, however, that the more considerate Japanese management methods will overtake American management traditions. The latter are too well en-trenched after so many decades. Instead, we will continue to hear laments over the demise of the American work ethic. But when a Richard Nixon or any number of professors decry the unwillingness of American workers to sweat for their pay, we are left unconvinced that slack morality and the absence of Victorian habits is the reason. If American workers don't any longer have much taste for tedious, unprestigious employment in factories presided over by snarling supervisors, perhaps we can find the reasons in the changed institutions of the modern economy and the changed values that they have fostered. For a beginning, the United States is well past the stage of industrial as-cendency born of World War II—and past memories of the

Great Depression before it. For after the war, America was full of youthful naïveté in assuming that hard work and economic growth would lead to personal fulfillment and untold wealth. Growth became a secular religion. The man with grease on his hands was a patriot, contributing to the Gross National Product. If you wanted to get ahead, you studied bookkeeping at night, in the hope that one day you could join the ranks of the white-collar class of men who kept a shine on their shoes and a smile of conformity on their faces. Selling vacuum cleaners door to door was honorable if only because it was one kind of work. Every wife was exhorted to conceive and raise more babies, because American industry needed the new customers that the babies would one day become.

Now, however, the ethic of depression-fed struggle is the province of today's retirees. Workers of the present generation often find themselves employed by corporate bureaucracies so large that the individual's contribution becomes almost imperceptible. His tie to the corporation is as impersonal as the computer-printed paycheck he receives. Then, too, whether a worker is employed by a billion-dollar corporation or a small shop, his concept of work is shaped by many years of television viewing; in television programs, and even more in TV commercials, the glamorous attainment of money and the subsequent pursuit of expensive pleasures suggest that the birthright of every American is easy affluence. In the world of television, who does not possess a beautiful lover, a Mercedes, and a sprawling home in Beverly Hills? Oh yes, one can recall Archie Bunker, the warehouseman from Queens, and a few compatriots of lowly station. But Archie was a buffoon, an anachronism from a past generation, the last residue of the dull 1950s. And the working-class characters of commercial television today mostly inhabit situation comedies hardly meant to glorify their lives. No, the heroes of television are dashing detectives, flush with money, and executives who have already made it to the top. Money comes easy in television land. Work is either exhilarating or, at worst, a minor inconvenience.

Are we not after all living in a "postindustrial" society? If the Japanese and the Koreans outproduce us now, is it not because they are only now entering their own industrial ages? If so, then it is probable that attitudes in those hardworking nations will also change when their living standards have matched our own. This line of reasoning implies that poverty is the breeding ground of the work ethic, and that the hope of alleviating it is what spurs workers to their most strenuous efforts. A few strange types, mostly in the arts, are goaded onward by the yearning for fame, but it seems that for most, dread of poverty is the obvious inducement. When affluence reaches a certain comfortable level for the majority of citizens, the work ethic dissolves. In the present secular age a species of pleasure ethic is all that's left. The basic needs all sated, one begins to pursue the more elusive riches of human pleasure, of hedonism. We are at the doorstep of Lasch's "Culture of Narcissism."

But there's a giant trick being played. What the television ads and Hollywood bedroom novels don't tell us is that every job, finally, is boring. Every job involves some kind of repetition. Details must be attended to. One comes to see the rough skin behind the pretty makeup. If you've ever worked on the production of a Hollywood movie you'll appreciate this. Actual movie production work is often dull, grueling, tedious. Writing for a living is even worse. Psychologists say that, contrary to every appearance, musicians are among those who suffer the most stress in our society. This news contradicts the image we have of carefree band musicians, getting paid to "play" with a gaggle of lithe, blond groupies waiting backstage. And of course we know that comedians are among the most miserable people on earth.

The view of the American worker as musician is becoming closer to reality than the image of him as a rough-hewn factory worker. For years, laborers have moved from factory work to jobs in the service economy. The flight attendant, the newspaper editor, the manager of the car rental agency, and the rock star are all service workers: i.e., providing services rather than physical goods. The significance of the shift is that these industries are less dominated by unions, though organized labor has made some inroads in recent times. The shift accelerates as manufacturers replace workers with cheap, compliant machines and is greatly encouraged by the government's policy of heavily taxing human labor through employer payments for unemployment insurance, Social Security, and the rest. Even labor unions have added their encouragement by forcing employers to contribute to expensive pension funds.

The character of work has thus changed. Walk through a typical chemical plant and you will understand why its workers are heavily unionized. The place reeks with the stench of acrid fumes. It is dusty with chemical wastes. The labyrinthine pipes and valves add to a vision of hell on earth. But then tour a newspaper office. You are in clean, more or less quiet, surroundings. The need for union representation is not so compelling. Reporters who earn a minimum of $500 a week don't seem to be unduly exploited, despite their claims of hardship. Editors are considerably more restrained in their criticisms than are foul-mouthed shop foremen.

In fact, the change in employment to the service sector, along with government standards such as the minimum wage and worker safety rules, have stripped away the traditional raison d'être of labor unions. No longer do they find much opportunity to protest horrible working conditions or fight industrial tyrants who enslave workers in a Dickensian nightmare. Those unions which are still active have become political powers used to force the redistribution of income to their members. Unions in the traditional mold—such as the United Auto Workers and the Steelworkers—along with the new breed of service-worker unions such as the American Federation of Teachers, all throw their weight around in the political arena to extract as much money as possible, without regard to how much actual work their members contribute to society.

Living in New York City, I am reminded of this nearly every day. New York, as they say, is a labor town. On this day, I walk past my apartment building and there in front of it garbage is piled in large mounds. The reason is that the building personnel are on strike and the sanitation men refuse to cross the picket lines. Eventually the building workers' union will settle for a higher wage. Their higher pay will come out of the tenants' pockets. For as surely as the building workers demand and get a contract that raises their wages faster than the higher cost of living, that raise will be translated into higher rents. A part of my income, and the income of all other tenants, is removed from our wallets and put into those of the building workers. Is it because the building workers have done better work of late, or because they suffered unduly in the past? No, it is merely because their union has the power to severely inconvenience tenants.

Even in the large industrial centers, however, unionism seems to be on a long-term slide; membership in the old-line unions has slowly fallen off over the decades. Yet the wealth of these unions has increased. Between 1966 and 1975 the assets of American labor unions rose some 78 percent, from $2 billion to nearly $4 billion. This is wealth locked into union pension funds, and some claim labor unions may well wake up and realize the power that this wealth confers. It is predicted that labor unions will begin to manipulate their pension fund investments to play big political games with corporations; the unions could compensate for waning membership by pulling investments out of corporations that refuse to do the unions' bidding, and, conversely, putting their pension fund money into the stocks and bonds of companies that toe the proper union line. One has doubts about this. After all, federal law would make the labor unions liable for any losses caused by poor investment of their workers' future pension money. Good investment strategy rarely equals good politics, no matter what your prejudices may be.

It has long been recognized that some labor unions do positive harm to their members, milking them for large dues payments and at the same time ignoring workers' real concerns. After all, unions have become fat bureaucratic institutions no less immovable than the largest corporations. The largest labor unions are fully as monopolistic as any corporation ever was. Some have wondered why the antitrust laws have never been used to break up monopoly unions. (I asked the question of Senator Edward Kennedy, who as chairman of the Senate Judiciary Committee has power over such matters. As I expected, Kennedy offered me a nonanswer, a mumbled reply that the unions have been of great benefit to the American worker.)

The degree to which organized labor has evolved from an institution concerned with the basic security and welfare of its members to a monolithic, power-hungry institution was demonstrated in 1978. President Carter set forth his voluntary wage-price guidelines in a failed attempt to fight mounting inflation. As the program progressed, it became evident that organized labor was the uncooperative party. Carter had succeeded by early 1979 in getting the *Fortune* 500 corporations, and most smaller companies, to comply with the guidelines, even though compliance cost them millions of dollars in paper work alone. Privately, White House officials admitted that having these corporations keep their price increases within the standards would not really end inflation, because inflation was worst in the prices of food and fuel and housing—products controlled not by the large corporations but by farmers, OPEC sheikhs, and small building contractors. Still, the officials argued, big-business compliance was essential because otherwise the labor unions would refuse to comply, claiming that it wasn't fair for labor to limit its demands while business didn't. Ironically, while the corporations dutifully complied with the wage-price guidelines, the labor unions ignored them. Labor leaders were quoted in the newspapers making fun of the guidelines and, in the same breath, accusing big business of causing all inflation.

The squabble over fairness has nothing to do with economics. It is purely a political question. Labor unions point to corporate profits as if their very presence were proof that business is greedy. Labor leaders engage in a power struggle over how the nation's wealth is distributed, and their criterion is not who is producing the most but what seems fair. What seems fair to most labor leaders is that their members should earn higher incomes than anyone else in the economy. This rhetoric is what gets labor union bosses elected, after all, and it comes to be what they believe.

Economists attempt to gauge the degree of equality in the economy by what they call the "distribution of income"—what groups in society get what portion of the riches. According to various theories of income distribution (none of which is any more than an intellectual plaything) laborers are rewarded with wages, the owners of land get a special theoretical rent, the owners of wealth-producing plants and equipment get profits, and investors get interest as income. This suggests that society is neatly divided into these factions, so if we wish to know what group is getting rich—the dirty bastards—then we just compare the share of national income accounted for by wages or rent or profits or interest; the Commerce Department compiles a "national income" account that tells us just this. Thus, for example, we can find in the tables that the percentage of wages in total national income has risen from 60 percent in 1929 to 75 percent by 1980, while the percent of profits has fallen from 28 percent to 17 percent. Judging from those numbers, we'd have to say that workers are doing better than their employers as a group.

But before we get tangled up in statistics and arcane theories, let's pull back a moment and bring this discussion closer to reality. People aren't divided into rigid groups; today's worker can be tomorrow's boss or even tycoon. We don't want to pretend that there's some solidified "mass" of workers out there, borrowed from a Marxist's stale dream. Our society is somewhat fluid, for people do move from class to class. Often the amount of income received by some workers or employers is determined more by politics than economics; for example, when a militant labor union bullies an outlandish contract settlement, or when the owners of large corporate farms get the government to subsidize their crops. The most we can realistically say about the distribution of income is that we live in a society where opportunities abound to earn wealth, and where the basic living standards have vastly improved for everyone over the last century. Visit many a country, developed or not, and you'll generally see a small coterie of the very rich and a large lump of the uncomfortably poor. Or if you visit a socialist nation, you'll see that everyone is pretty poor.

But our fabled land of opportunity does not satisfy the requirements of crypto-totalitarians who demand that everyone earn exactly the same income. So we are led to talk about economic justice. Let us begin by quoting the late Frank Knight, an economist who said: "The ownership of personal or material productive capacity is based upon a complex mixture of inheritance, luck and effort, probably in that order. . . ." No justice in that formulation, is there? Isn't it just awful that David Rockefeller lives in the cradle of luxury from the day he's born, while you and I don't? But it is still worse. What about the old Mafia kingpin who left his daughter $10 million, with which she built up a $100 million estate through clever investment? Said estate was then used by her son to found an eminently respectable international real estate empire. Up in Westchester County, New York, everyone knows about the handful of millionaire distillery magnates who got their start in the rum-running days of Prohibition and who were at that time closely connected with organized crime. What of the highly fashionable women's store in a certain southern city that is reputed to have been set up with funds made in the prostitution racket? We could go on with accounts of marijuana millionaires, Texas wildcatters who struck oil by chance, and young mistresses made into wealthy starlets by their paramours. There is no justice at all—certainly no meritocracy by which each person is paid on the basis of his or her productiveness. Such a meritocracy, in strict terms, has never been uncovered anywhere. Even when employers give tests to prospective workers, much more than the test scores will enter into the calculation of whether the worker is "suitable" for the company. Is he from the right background, did he go to the right school, is his wife vulgar, will he make trouble? These questions weigh more heavily than raw skill or ability for most jobs. It happens even in socialist countries like the Soviet Union, where an elite has evolved within the bureaucracy: an elite which, like all others, has little to do with the merits of its members and much to do with their power. Often such power derives merely from longevity. If an astute bureaucrat can survive purges and unfriendly bosses, if he or she (women are particularly good at this) can outlast the contretemps of the moment, that person will emerge after ten years or twenty as a powerful figure regardless of ability.

Let's talk a little about the distribution of wealth rather than the distribution of income—in other words, how much people own, as opposed to how much they pull in each year. John Brittain, a Brookings Institution economist of good repute, has taken the trouble to investigate inherited wealth, though the subject is missing from theories of income distribution. The available statistics show that the most affluent 1 percent of Americans possess one quarter of all the wealth, and that their share has remained stable despite recessions and the government's most obstinate efforts to tax away inheritances. And, Brittain says, the figure of one quarter is probably understated because it doesn't include trust funds, which, escaping estate tax, are not included in the data used by researchers. Other figures reveal that the top 6 percent of families in the United States own 57 percent of the wealth and the top 16 percent own three quarters of it.

Can we doubt that every true parlor socialist must seethe with envy and hate when he peruses statistics like these? If he can't line those rich sons of bitches up in front of firing squads, he'll line them up in front of the Internal Revenue Service to make sure they have their pockets cleaned. Scratch an egalitarian of the Left and you find an incipient regulator underneath—and nothing so angers a compulsive regulator as someone or something that refuses to be regulated out of existence. And in the eyes of laborites, when wealth is possessed by non–"working people," then it must be ill-got fortune. But let us see what the studies show about how wealth is obtained. Brittain draws on previous work tending to confirm that large old fortunes are passed on from generation to generation: cf. Rockefeller, Ford, Du Pont, et al. Huge new fortunes are the extraordinary result of the private-enterprise system. However, since old fortunes were new fortunes a few generations ago, they, too, had mostly been accumulated quickly, in some especially lucrative endeavor. This happens simply because the economy, growing and forever changing as it does, presents opportunities for fat rewards, if an entrepreneur is smart enough and bold enough to exploit them.

From time to time, *Fortune* magazine looks into the mores of American wealth; the last time was in 1979, when the magazine listed some of the richest Americans. One on the list had amassed his fortune by starting Wendy's hamburger chain to compete with McDonald's and Burger King. Another was a middle-aged woman who owned a chain of gas

stations. Several were Texas oilmen. Not one was a glamorous movie star, and only one was a doyen of Manhattan society life. Opportunities lie in wait; one need only spot them
and exploit them. I'd like to tell you that I have done this
with success, but it's not so. Oh, I could make a handsome
sum from sales of this book, but the rewards are not as-
tronomical because neither is the risk. For this act of writing
a book doesn't qualify as a venture in the same league with
starting a new chain of hamburger joints in the face of
strong competition; there may be room for only a few such
gambles at any given time in the American economy. But
many thousands of books hit the stands every year. If very
high risk carries with it the chance of very high reward, and
if only a few are willing to take on the risk, this helps to
explain why only a small handful of people in our society
are extremely wealthy. These few gambled and it paid off,
whether it was buying IBM stock cheaply when it was
brand-new, or spending a life's savings building the prototype of an airplane, or daring to become the numbers king
of Harlem.

After much study and analysis, Brittain concludes that
inherited wealth is responsible for the inequality in the distribution of wealth; his conclusion suggests that the government has utterly failed in its efforts at redistribution. For it
is a principal purpose of both estate and income taxes to
shift wealth from those who have it to those who don't. If
your parents leave you $1 million, the government will grab
60 percent of it in taxes. If you come to earn $500,000 a
year, the government will seize $250,000. Then it will hand
this money out to bureaucrats and to con artists who use
poverty programs to get rich and to senators who feel the
urge to order a new government limousine. This is egali-
tarianism at work. But despite all the efforts of the government, Brittain shows that the wealthy stay wealthy.

And I say, good for them; because if I make a killing, by
damn I want to keep it and enjoy it. The prospect of wealth

is a powerful incentive to contribute to the economy by investing in risky projects, by working hard, by starting up new businesses. We are speaking of the profit motive, and it's not to be denigrated. When governments tax the profit motive into oblivion, they are taxing the entrepreneurial spirit and thereby deliberately inhibiting economic growth. And of course it is economic growth that raises everyone's standard of living. Yet to some people the sight of extreme wealth is an offense. They have merely elevated their primal envy into a form of political self-righteousness.

8

Corporate Power on Trial

IN THE very early days of the Republic, government regulators were as zealous as any in America today. But in post-Revolutionary America, there was a slight difference; the government officials were adamantly pro-business. They fought each other tooth and nail to give merchants the most amenities. In the early 1800s state legislators offered tradesmen state-chartered corporations as a new way to raise cash, and the legislators would often vote to invest some of the state's money in a company. Broad business powers were freely granted to newly chartered banks, shipping firms, manufacturers, and insurance companies, which were especially important to the development of seagoing commerce. The port of New York battled Philadelphia and Boston for preeminence in commerce. New York won by issuing the most favorable regulations for merchant auction sales, building a handsome mercantile exchange building in 1825, and facilitating credit for businesses. This is in stark contrast to the New York of recent decades, which saddled businessmen with so many taxes and regulations that until 1978 companies fled the state in droves. (In 1978 even the most anti-business state officials began to have second thoughts.)

The pulsing growth of business in the early 1800s set the stage for an upward leap of national commerce in the 1850s. The pressures of America's huge market, now stretched over a geographical expanse, called for stepped-up manufacturing, often in several different parts of the nation at the same time. Between 1820 and 1850 the population more than doubled, growing from 9.6 million to 23 million people.

The steam-powered technology of the day was improving. By the late 1850s the railroad and the telegraph had extended from New York to the Mississippi River. In Washington, the U. S. Patent Office was beginning to be deluged with inventions. Whereas in the early days of the nineteenth century the Patent Office recorded an average of less than 100 patents a year, by the 1850s it was recording more than 2,500 a year. In fact, by 1850 the Patent Office pleaded with Congress for more funds, saying it had an inventory of 17,000 model prototypes for new inventions stacked up in its offices.

American managers had no experience with nationwide enterprise. Ready or not, however, economies of large scale demanded large organizations. Thus, as business historian Thomas Cochran has pointed out, they first tried imitating the organization of the familiar merchant ship, with its omnipotent captain, his officers, and the enlisted seamen below. This model didn't work, and neither did the military method of organizing. The problem was that managers hadn't come to grips with the fact of offices and plants spread out over hundreds of miles. This was in the days before telephones or automobiles, so there was little direct communication by which the managers could see to it that the junior supervisors and workers out in the provinces were doing their jobs. Often workers took advantage of the situation by turning out poor work or defrauding the company.

Thomas Cochran, in *200 Years of American Business*, cites American railroads as exemplars of inexperience in the management of big technology. He says the railroads started out as American factories did, with merchants hiring technical people to operate the machinery. The merchant, under this system, could get away with only occasional inspection of his spread-out operations. Not so, however, with the railroads. The great expansion of long-line railroads through the West in the 1850s required new planning skills, to obtain the necessary property rights for the laying of a railroad track, to finance construction of the road, and to keep it in good order. The outcome of poor management was widespread scandal in railroad finance and low productivity of railroad workers.

The scandal is epitomized in the dealings of Jim Fisk and Jay Gould, who made fortunes through the manipulation of railroad stock. Cornelius Vanderbilt owned the New York Central Railroad in the 1860s. The competing Erie railroad refused to raise its freight rates along with the New York Central. Vanderbilt, outraged, endeavored to buy the Erie. In doing so, however, he crossed paths with the corrupt Dan Drew, owner of the Erie, who worked in league with the even more dishonest Fisk and Gould. As Vanderbilt bought Erie stock, Drew "watered" the value of the stock by issuing more and more. Then he loaned his company several million dollars, taking Erie stock and bonds in exchange, and selling the securities short (i.e., selling the stock for delivery later, when presumably the price would have fallen and he could profitably buy the shares he was committed to deliver). Then he sold out his Erie assets, causing the stock to drop in price, which made his short-selling pay off handsomely. Next, Fisk and Gould printed Erie stock certificates and sold this stock to Vanderbilt, until Vanderbilt got one of his hired judges to stop the sales. The battle went on and on, with each side using the powers of corrupted government officials and legislators to harass each other and get each other arrested. But they were never impeded throughout years of unscrupulous wheeling and dealing. It was an era of laissez-faire.

As the nineteenth century came to a close, the railroads were learning how to manage large operations and had discovered the advantages of splitting a company into divisions, with a headquarters staffed by lawyers and accountants and chief executives. The system of divisions in turn gave rise to modern double-entry accounting, first pioneered in Britain. By 1900, what with the quick dissemination of

the technologies of electricity, the telegraph, and the gasoline engine, large companies were sprouting to take advantage of economies of large scale, economies so great that for
decades they would camouflage bad management. The
efficiency of large-scale technology was the greatest boon to
American industry. Entrepreneurs still existed by 1900: they
were the Carnegies of the steel industry and the Rocke-
fellers of oil, but now they were empire builders. When they
died and their families were no longer able or willing to take
their places, they left faceless corporate managements at the
helm, and these managements still run their companies
today. The faces change but the anonymous style does not.
Meanwhile, the recurrent waves of mergers, beginning in
1887, combined hundreds of small businesses into a relative
handful of big ones dominated by these magnates and their
heirs.

If the big company was the *sine qua non* of large-scale
technology, it also constituted a legal innovation. More important, it was a political organization. The corporate laws
established in the American mid-nineteenth century gave
the corporation the same kind of property rights as those
allotted to the individual. These laws permitted a corporation to subsume under the reign of its management the
property rights of individuals, i.e., the stockholders. This
was in full accord with Locke's theory of the social contract,
as was the limitation of a stockholder's liability for the actions of the corporation, based on the idea that no person
should be held accountable for any more than he has actually contributed in the form of cash.

In law, the corporation has no intrinsic power. It has only
the legitimacy necessary to acquire power. Still, a few
scholars, such as Henry Steele Commager, have argued that
the law establishing corporations is unfaithful to the United
States Constitution. They argue that the men who designed
the Constitution in the agricultural society of the middle of
the eighteenth century had in mind an equal distribution of

power, which the constitutional system of checks and balances was meant to ensure. But, these scholars insist, the law of corporations allows high concentrations of business power that remain unaccountable to anyone. Ergo, they say, the Constitution has been thwarted and the people have been cheated of their power to rule over corporations. This argument seems ingenuous, for the laws governing corporations do not endow them with any powers except for the ability to own property as any private person can. Power derives from what a corporation does with its property rights, just as the power of an individual derives from what he does with his property rights—subject, of course, to his abilities, in the same way that the corporate acquisition of power depends on the skills of its managers.

Another curious argument is that corporations have subverted the intent of American law by wresting from stockholders their right to help direct the company, if only by electing the board of directors. This is extremely naïve because, although in theory the stockholders are the actual owners of the business operated by corporate managers, in practice stockholders have demonstrated over many years that they have not the slightest interest in participating in a corporation's affairs. Stockholders exercise their influence only in the most general way, by refusing to bid up the prices of corporations with poor growth records or glum future prospects. And most of this influence is wielded by the sophisticated institutional investors—bank trust funds, colleges, and so on—and their well-trained stock market analysts. Stockholders do not want to be otherwise bothered with company affairs and regularly sign over their voting rights to the corporate executives. Investing in corporate stocks is a gamble to make money, pure and simple.

When American Express tried to take over McGraw-Hill in 1979, the managers of the latter firm howled that such a conglomeration would compromise the reputation of *Business Week* and the Standard and Poor's bond rating service, both owned by McGraw-Hill. Did McGraw-Hill's stockholders valiantly come to the rescue of their company by refusing to sell their shares, at an inflated price, to American Express? Did they question the propriety of having a financial company at the helm of a business magazine and a bond-rating service? Not at all. The McGraw-Hill stockholders turned angrily against the company's management and several filed lawsuits. The stockholders said, in effect, be damned with the integrity of the corporation, we insist on selling out to reap the profit offered us by American Express. The suits demanded that the McGraw-Hill stockholders be given the right to reconsider the stock tender offer which the company's management had already refused. The stockholders cared about one thing: money. Whether this is good or bad is an academic question. This is the way it is.

Dating from even before the great merger waves in the late nineteenth century and the one after World War I, and continuing through those of the 1968 stock market boom and of the late 1970s, the economic concentration of American industry has steadily increased. By 1978 the top fifty corporations in the *Fortune* 500 list held half the business assets of all 500. More striking is the fact that the top ten companies owned one quarter of the assets in the 500. This bigness spells economic power, and it implies political power. It is the potential to exercise political power that so worries regulatory Washington.

The corporation presents an ominous façade. It is faceless, formless, beyond or perhaps beneath morality. One discovers no human side to the business corporation, except for the unctuous, public relations spokesperson who babbles in bland clichés, making all too clear the universal intent of the corporation to conceal its motives and its actions. The corporation president is less accessible than a Mafia kingpin; at least the Mafia chief can be seen on the television news as he walks to the courtroom. When corporations present the public with their financial results, they customarily scramble most of the pertinent information so that no stockholder or journalist can tell from the annual report, much less from the flatulent news release accompanying it, what is really going on inside the company.

Feelings of suspicion and hostility toward big companies are all but ingrained in us, for sound reasons that derive from our natural yearning for maximum individual freedom. This kind of freedom is hardly enhanced by the specter of large, rich private organizations wielding economic and political power, shielded from public view by tradition and the big businessman's long-standing antipathy toward openness. This understandable distaste has bred the facile notion that all big corporations got to be big by evil means and perpetuate their bigness by preying on smaller businesses and consumers, often with the complicity of the government.

When we hear stories of how old Henry Ford used to go into the rest rooms of his auto plant to check the toilets and make sure workers who claimed they needed to defecate actually did so, our suspicions are confirmed. When Walter Cronkite reports on the evening news that Lockheed paid some $22 million in bribes to foreign interests since 1970 and that from 1963 to 1972 Exxon routinely paid out a total of $27 million in secret to Italian politicians, thus to better the prospects of its affiliate in that nation—when we hear this our suspicions are compounded. Public opinion polls consistently show that Americans distrust corporations. Whenever a pollster asks citizens whether they think the energy crisis is real or has been invented by profiteering oil companies, they always choose the latter explanation.

The fact is that most corporations are more or less innocent of the kind of conspiratorial wrong-doing of which rhetoricians and the public accuse them. The people who manage companies are hardly able to do that job, much less run power plays behind the curtains. They're just not clever enough, not sophisticated enough. If they were, you'd think

that at least they could figure out some scheme to create a
more appealing image. Yet any number of academic radicals
perched in their ivory towers, drawing nice salaries and protected by tenure, are ready to divulge elaborate and silly
scenarios of corporate conspiracy. Perhaps the most rabid
and extreme of these paranoid academics is Jeremy Rifkin,
who presides over the "People's Business Commission" and
who of late plies his trade in various radical think tanks.
With hottest venom and suspect accuracy, Rifkin proclaimed in his 1976 rewrite of the Constitution that the
"giant corporations" have "pursued a policy of industrial
negligence which kills 14,000 workers and permanently disa-
bles 900,000 more each year; manufactured unsafe products
that kill 30,000 and permanently disable 110,000 Americans
each year; turned our nation into a weapons factory, wasting valuable resources and labor that could be utilized for
basic human needs; used the energy crisis to double the
price of fuel and make record gains in profit; fostered ten-
sions and conflicts between races, sexes and ethnic groups in
their arbitrary and discriminatory employment practices;
pillaged the resources, exploited the people and systematically intervened in the domestic affairs of other nations in
order to profit their corporate treasuries; subverted the Constitution of the United States and the principle of government of, by and for the people. . . ." The list drones on in
the harsh tones of the militant extreme Left, until corporations are blamed for every ill that afflicts the human race.
This, to be charitable, is drivel, the sort of puerile propa-
ganda that many times makes the far Left resemble the far
Right in its overdone absurdity. Over on the Right, one
could find a John Birch Society pamphlet leveling the same
charges against the dirty Commies.

If the corporation is entirely a creation of the state, then it
has no rights but those granted at the pleasure of the government. In reality, it is the state governments that hand out
corporate charters, and state governments are rarely known

for their sophistication. To the contrary, the states compete with each other in laxity of corporation regulations, so they may attract comfortable revenues from the licensing operation. Delaware is the champion of the corporate chartering game. It has few rules to bother the mind of any corporation counsel, scrupulous or not. So you'll find a lopsided proportion of American corporations chartered in the state of Delaware. Regulation aficionados call for the federal chartering of corporations, thus to put the matter in the hands of a hard-nosed Washington bureaucracy. Crypto-totalitarians see corporations in general as agents of greed, hypocrisy, decay, and sometimes Satanic evil. One fears that the federal chartering idea, sensible perhaps in moderate and judicious hands, would open a Pandora's box of new regulations that might smother corporations entirely. History shows repeated precedence for the stifling of entrepreneurial spirit by excessive regulation and taxation. It began back in the Roman Empire of the fourth century B.C., when bureaucrats so oppressed the merchants and farmers of the age that foreign trade literally ceased and the Roman middle class slid backward into poverty.

In the long run the surest antidote to monopoly is change —technological change, organizational change, and change in consumers' tastes. But we live in the short run, and the hope of eventual industrial evolution demands more patience than we have any right to expect of ourselves. The faint future reward almost reminds one of the promise that religion has held for centuries to the downtrodden, that if they just wait till death retrieves them from this miserable earth, they will at last be delivered. Our nation long ago decided to hasten economic deliverance by instituting the antitrust laws. For good or ill, these laws have only served as the window dressing of jurisprudence. They have manifestly not been effective.

These laws arose first in response to the industrial upheavals brought on by radical new technologies in the post–Civil War epoch. The spread of electricity, railroads, and more efficient ways of manufacturing chemicals and metals led directly to the large-scale economies that provided the impetus for small firms to be merged into a few giant companies. The first great merger wave occurred from 1887 to 1904, during which more than three thousand small companies were swallowed up in mergers. Among the most notorious merging companies was U. S. Steel, which combined nearly eight hundred independent steel plants into a single multibillion-dollar corporation. General Electric was created from a merger of Edison General Electric and Thomson-Houston, already an electrical conglomerate. And we must mention Standard Oil, which began by merging some twenty Ohio refineries and then proceeded to undercut competitors or buy them, until Standard Oil comprised more than one hundred refineries and dominated the petroleum market in the country. John D. Rockefeller, who engineered the oil conglomerate, was infamous for his alleged use of goon squads and industrial terrorism to intimidate competitors.

Out of this rush to concentrate came the Sherman Act of 1890. It prohibits the formation of any trust or other conspiracy meant to stifle competition, and it subjects those who act to create a monopoly to criminal sanctions. It was followed in 1914 by the Federal Trade Commission and the Clayton Act, which bans anticompetitive corporate mergers and outlaws such uncompetitive practices as unfair price discrimination and exclusive agreements to divide up markets. In the early 1900s President Theodore Roosevelt had given the Justice Department the power to enforce these antitrust statutes. In its first antitrust cases, the Supreme Court upheld a "rule of reason" which stated that only "unreasonable" business behavior would be prosecuted. Thus if a monopoly had evolved because no other company wanted to stay in its business, then obviously the monopoly was guilty of no sin. Price undercutting was allowed if a company could prove that its lower prices were justified by lower costs of production, rather than by the evil intentions of predators out to bankrupt the opposition. Of course, Congress has exempted some industries, such as baseball teams and failing newspapers, from the antitrust laws, in the supposed interest of society—so these enterprises will not be forced to shut down just because they are big.

Antitrust actions never had great impact, and recently some new, harsher interpretations of antitrust theory have surfaced to toughen the laws. One is the *dominant firm theory*, which says any corporation that gets a large share of its market should be broken up. So, for example, when Du Pont came out with a cheaper titanium pigment as a result of a new, more efficient pigment production technique, the company quickly beat out the higher-priced competition and took nearly half the market. Flushed with its success, Du Pont increased its production facilities for the pigment. It was then that the Federal Trade Commission, under the hot-blooded social engineer Michael Pertschuk, decided to interfere. The FTC charged Du Pont with monopoly. The ultimate lesson of this theory is that companies are to be punished for their success. Only small, poorly managed firms will escape Pertschuk's legal storm troopers. A variation of the dominant firm theory is the FTC's argument that if four or fewer corporations share half their market or more, they should be broken up. Thus the auto industry would have to be split into several dozen highly inefficient small companies. The FTC has tried to break up General Foods, General Mills, and Kellogg since they sell three quarters of all breakfast cereals bought in the United States.

But let's see what the practical effect of antitrust enforcement has been. Professor Frank Kottke, a Washington State University economist, has delved into the subject and finds many a false premise embedded in so-called pro-competitive theories. First, Kottke says prosecution under the Sherman Act has never added more than two rivals in any market. A rather piddling result. He explains that when companies are broken up, the newly formed competitors tend to act like their older brothers, politely competing in advertising and the quality of service offered, but never in price. Another misconception pointed out by Kottke is the notion that breaking up an oligopoly will thereby restore the status quo existing before the companies became "partners" in a shared monopoly. When one company merges with another larger one, the formerly independent firm will be dismantled to some degree. Its brand names will be absorbed into the larger conglomerate, or, if a brand has a poor reputation, it will be quietly retired. Some of the company's plants may be closed. Its warehouse may be sold so that the conglomerate can save money by using already existing warehouses for the new division. People who were the backbone of the former business will have left or been fired after the take-over. So, if the government decides to break up a conglomerate, the division, restored to its independence, would be hard put to survive on its own. Kottke adds that the status quo ante can't be restored after a divestiture, simply because businessmen, once hooked on the comforts of non–price competition, are loath to return to costly price battles.

What effect does the antitrust law have in practice? The best answer is offered by the spectacle of the government's case against International Business Machines for monopolizing the computer industry. The case began in the 1960s and no end is in sight. Meanwhile, literally millions of documents have piled up in government files. Millions of dollars have been spent by IBM and the government. What gain is there for the American public?

The antitrust laws have, ironically, fostered the very kind of large corporation they mean to curb. For since the antitrust laws prevent cartelization—formal agreements between a few companies to sell the same amounts at the same prices and to pay the same wages—they have fomented mergers, the only alternative in industries where profits are so hard to earn that any heavy competition saps them and thus destroys the smaller, weaker companies. That is, if two or three American corporations see that the only way for all to survive is to restrict costly competition, they cannot, like their European brothers, create a legal, formal cartel. The only alternatives are to merge into a megacorporation or accept eventual bankruptcy.

Of course, the effect of a cartel on prices is identical to that of a merger: no price competition. Still, the merger effect of the antitrust laws may be more damaging than cartelization. Cartels almost always break up sooner or later, since there is powerful incentive, especially in times of slack sales, for one or more of the cartel members to discount its prices secretly and thus steal the market from its rivals. The incentive becomes overpowering if a company's plants must be working at a certain capacity before they operate efficiently. The cartel itself is the victim, and out of its demise may come corporations now ready to stand on their own feet. In contrast, the merger is forever, even though conglomerates do sometimes sell off money-losing operations if they can. Usually they're sold to other conglomerates.

As mergers inexorably continue to concentrate economic power in fewer and fewer hands, the natural political impulse has been to go beyond the antitrust laws, to come up with new legislation that would halt or even reverse concentration. Senator Edward Kennedy's 1979 bill to ban all mergers among companies above the $2 billion size is a major effort. (In 1979 and 1980 a number of mergers were attempted by large companies because the acquiring corporations feared that if they didn't hurry up and consummate their mergers, the Kennedy bill might eventually pass and outlaw them.) The Industrial Reorganization Act of 1975, which failed in Congress, would automatically have broken up any companies that dominated their markets. The proposal differed radically from traditional antitrust, because the antitrust laws are aimed at bad business practices. The

Reorganization Act was meant to undermine the structure
of corporate power, regardless of the presence or absence of
unscrupulous behavior. Ironically, the approach taken by
the Reorganization bill was more in keeping with the traditional economist's views of industrial power than the antitrust laws are. Economists contend that economic and even
political power flows from the way an industry is structured.
The usual American structure is oligopoly, with a handful of
corporations ruling a market and a "fringe" of small competitive companies scavenging at the sidelines.

The Kennedy bill and the failed Reorganization Act proposal are major initiatives that suggest the degree to which
burgeoning corporate power disturbs our most basic instincts for individualism and decentralized power. We can
expect more such initiatives. Of course, the business community, arguing for the merits of large-scale efficiencies, rejects
such plans out of hand. Yet we cannot dismiss the issue so
easily.

Beyond the plans to break up big corporations, the Securities and Exchange Commission has pushed hard for reform
of the way most corporations are run. The agency, hoping to
purify the air in corporate boardrooms, has proposed that
the board of directors be made up of people who have no
connection with the company. It also wants to make sure
that no bankers or lawyers who do any work for a corporation may serve on its board of directors. Moreover, the
agency would set up a passel of committees composed of
outside board members. One, already a requirement in New
York State, would audit the corporation's accounting practices. Another would check on the corporation's compliance
with environmental rules. Still another would watch over
the company's social responsibilities.

The idea behind all this is to make the corporation more
of a public organization, less a private, self-interested institution. But corporate executives aren't thrilled about the

proposals. Some claim requiring outside directors would frustrate corporate ladder climbers who hope one day to make the boardroom. Others say having the company president as the only insider on the board would place too heavy a burden on him to know everything that's going on in the company. More claim that lawyers and bankers make great board members and shouldn't be barred even if they do work for the corporation. The general feeling is that corporations don't want do-gooding amateurs on the board of directors; they want hard-nosed businessmen.

But people like Robert Townsend, author of *Up the Organization,* claim the board of directors has little more function than a rubber stamp. The corporate managers and not the directors are in the driver's seat, after all.

The emergence in the 1970s of the "unfriendly" corporate take-over has left some officers of companies dubious about corporate bigness, too. After all, any corporation with publicly traded stock is a candidate for take-over by a magnate or corporate organization that can afford to buy up its shares. This possibility becomes especially troublesome when a corporation's executives find its common stock to be worth less per share than the per-share value of the actual property it owns. This is when the stock is said to be priced at less than the company's *book value;* in the late 1970s many stocks were thus "undervalued."

The commonplace method of the unfriendly take-over is the stock tender offer, by which the corporate bridegroom offers the stockholders of its chosen mate a higher-than-market price. For instance, in 1978 R. J. Reynolds Industries, the metals conglomerate, sought a forced marriage with Del Monte, the maker of canned foods, and in the process bid up Del Monte's stock from $26.50 to $48.25 a share. If you had owned 100 shares of Del Monte stock and you sold out to R. J. Reynolds, you would have made a profit of $2,175, almost doubling your money. That kind of temptation is hard for most stockholders to resist. In fact, some savvy stock market investors try to predict which companies are about to be taken over in a tender offer. They then buy that company's stock and wait for the acquiring corporation to bid it up. If their guess is right, they walk away with a fat profit.

Obviously, in the unfriendly take-over, the executives of the corporation fear for the fate of their company and themselves when and if the suitor wins. In the American Express effort to take over McGraw-Hill, for example, the worry was that a huge financial corporation such as American Express would exert undue, unethical influence over McGraw-Hill's business magazines. In other take-overs, the executives of the courted company may fear they will be fired or may simply dislike the idea of becoming somebody else's employees. So, to try and hinder the unfriendly merger, a sought-after corporation will attempt to file all sorts of lawsuits against the acquirer. Failing that, the reluctant corporate maiden will call in a "white knight"—a friendly large corporation that will start competing with the unfriendly bridegroom for the lady's hand, in the hope that this will bid up the price of its stock high enough to ward off the unfriendly suitor. If the ploy doesn't work, at least the courted corporation feels it will be better off under the wing of the "white knight."

The modern corporation, as wealthy and powerful as it may be, still faces a multitude of challenges from government and the business community itself. If take-overs are on the increase, attempts to break up the resultant large corporations haven't slowed either. It can be predicted that efforts to curb corporate power will continue and perhaps succeed in the future as they have never succeeded in the past. This is because the power of big business—or at least the power it is perceived to have—has been recognized by the populace as a political threat. In the turmoil of the 1980s, with energy shortages, pervasive inflation, and political discomfort, it is doubtful that corporations, no matter how sophisticated in the arts of public relations, will be able to uphold the image of benign benevolence.

9

The Regulatory Nemesis

IF ONE SPENDS any time in official Washington, one gets used to seeing on office bookshelves a long row of large, thick black loose-leaf binders, each crammed with hundreds of pages of small type. These are the regulations of the United States Government. They grow every day, for every day scores of new regulations are published in the government's *Federal Register.* Every single one of them is costing the American people money, for every regulation adds to the cost burden of business, and business in turn must pass that added cost along to consumers.

Doubtless some amount of regulation is necessary. But government regulation has become profoundly overbearing, excessive, even irresponsible. Regulators wield unrestrained power; they aren't voted into office and are in no way bound to respect the desires of the populace. Under the feudal protection of the civil service system, they can't even be fired. Rather, these bureaucrats have the unearned license to impose their values on society, forming regulations that punish the American people, not through the court system, but through the pocketbook.

Horror stories abound. For example, the Occupational Safety and Health Administration tells meat-packers that the concrete floors in their processing plants are required to have a rough texture so the workers won't slip and fall. But then the Department of Agriculture tells them that the concrete floors must be perfectly smooth, so they are easy to clean. What are the meat-packers to do? Or take the case of brown lung, the disease caused by inhaling cotton mill dust. OSHA decided that the textile industry must buy nearly $3 billion worth of dust-filtering equipment, which would cost the industry more than a quarter of a billion dollars a year to operate. For all that, the expenditure would cut down brown lung disease by only 1,700 cases a year among the 130,000 textile workers exposed to cotton dust. This is quite a high cost. But OSHA rejected out of hand a much cheaper and more practical method of curbing brown lung when it declined to consider having workers wear simple face masks. The masks already protect textile workers in countries like Japan, but OSHA didn't like the plan. It found it more expedient to add a huge cost burden to the textile industry, just at the time when the industry is already suffering badly from cheaper textile imports and the growing use of synthetic fibers. Chances are that unless it can be subsidized by the government, the domestic textile industry is all but finished. OSHA can take a portion of the credit for that.

Kaiser Aluminum announces that every year it is required to send more than 10,000 reports to government agencies, at a cost of $5 million a year. Dow Chemical says it had to spend $147 million in 1975 because of government regulations, and half of that money was just thrown away. An independent would-be oil refiner spent $7 million and nine years just trying to get his refinery project approved. The litany of complaints goes on and on.

You know regulations must be getting out of hand when a person like Stewart Brand, father of the back-to-the-farm movement of the counterculture and now publisher of the *Co-Evolution Quarterly*, joins hands with upstanding businessmen to protest inane government rules, and when Clarence M. Ditlow, spokesman for the National Clean Air Coalition, joins with the hated oil industry in calling for the government to end its price regulations. Something is amiss. Even inside the White House, there is protest against regulatory irresponsibility. In 1978 Barry Bosworth, then President Carter's director of the White House anti-inflation council, bitterly denounced the refusal of the Environmental Protection Agency to take account of the cost of its regulations. Robert Strauss, then President Carter's special adviser on inflation, proposed that some of the more stringent and inflationary regulations be relaxed.

But alas, the regulators of Washington became fed up with this carping. A chief lobbyist of the Environmental Defense Fund, in a secret memo, vowed to "crush" Strauss. Soon enough Strauss was issuing apologetic "clarifications" to the press. All was once again right with the regulatory bureaucracy. One wonders, if the President's adviser is cowed into submission by the regulators, what power can check their excesses? None, apparently.

To what audience are agencies like the EPA and OSHA playing? It's surely not the business community, nor is it humble consumers. In fact, one learns from spending some time within the walls of regulatory castles that their high officials have a constituency of environmental lobbying groups and labor unions. Dozens of groups claiming to represent environmentalists and consumers have their offices in Washington, where their lawyers can keep a sharp eye on the regulators. If some tiny regulation seems too lax, too generous to business, these watchdogs howl and make threats until the regulators tighten up the rule to their liking.

Why do these lobbies, clearly out of step with the feeling in the rest of the nation, hold such sway in bureaucratic Washington? Apparently it is because they are at the leading edge of the kind of philosophy espoused by the regulators themselves. They act as a Greek chorus to the bureaucrats. If by chance a regulator becomes convinced of the hardships he is imposing on some industry, the chorus is there to lead him out of the wilderness and back toward the straight regulatory line.

This incestuous and elitist totalitarianism can go on because Washington is isolated from the rest of the nation, out of touch with the realities in southwest Missouri, northern Oregon, or even upper New York State. Regulatory Washington is a separate ideological country, operating entirely within its own cloistered version of reality. If this sounds exaggerated, I beg you to spend some time among the regulators. The agencies have made themselves into legislative and even judicial bureaucracies, and this without consulting anyone. Their power is reinforced by what political scientists call the "iron triangle" of mutual backscratching: members of Congress, in exchange for constituent rulebending, approve fat regulatory budgets, and special-interest groups support both the regulators and their pet representative or senator in exchange for special favors.

Ironically, the typical Washington regulatory bureaucracy acts like a corporate monopoly at its worst. Since there is no need to make a profit, and since there are no antitrust laws against big bureaucracies, the regulators are free to aggrandize their agencies without limits. As the bureaucracies become ever larger, they become ever more hierarchical and authoritarian. There are plenty of incentives to foster non-stop growth. For one thing, the regulator who has more people on his staff gets paid more. For another, as the agency becomes a giant, the chances for promotion within it multiply. Then regulatory bigness feeds on itself, for the bigger the agency, the more layers of bureaucrats there are and the greater is the need for internal paper work. Bureaucrats come to spend so much time writing and reading and shuffling memos that they literally forget what the agency's purpose is.

Naturally, the bureaucrat's incentive is not to cut costs but to increase them, since the less an agency spends this year, the smaller its budget will be next year. Even when a member of Congress finally complains that the budget is too fat he rarely wins, because only the bureaucrats can fathom the labyrinthine complexities of a regulatory agency and thus estimate how much the agency "needs."

We expect corporate executives to complain about government interference, but what are we to think when such a solidly liberal think tank as the Brookings Institution joins in with biting criticisms of government regulators? The New York *Times* has even issued its criticisms. Brookings first entered the fray with Edward Denison's 1978 study, which found that environmental and worker safety regulations have significantly lowered industrial productivity since 1967. A year later, Robert Crandall, a senior fellow of the institution, complained that there is no way to force regulators to look at the economic alternatives when trying to achieve some regulatory goal. They seek, he said, to issue their regulations at the minimum political cost to themselves, and not necessarily at the lowest cost to society. In fact, the regulators care little about the impact of their rules on society at large.

Crandall asserted that since the populace can't know how much alternative regulations might cost in higher prices, the regulator takes advantage of this ignorance to institute politically safe but needlessly expensive regulations. "Only by changing the incentives facing an administrator, or by informing the electorate of his profligacy," said Crandall, "can more sensible regulation be achieved." He offered the example of the Occupational Safety and Health Administration's poorly designed coke-oven standard, which was effected at the behest of the steelworkers. The rule protects fewer than 30,000 workers out of 9 million in the labor force, but everyone has to pay the resultant higher cost of producing steel. As Crandall added, "Most social regulation involves a transfer of economic resources from a large number of people to a small number of beneficiaries." We all pay for it whenever we buy the products made in a process saddled with such regulations.

Years ago, Joseph Schumpeter saw that business corporations would become vulnerable to attack and that the attack would constitute an intellectual war on capitalism itself. The argument (stated in *Can Capitalism Survive?*, in 1947), refreshed in recent times by Irving Kristol, says that in fact the corporate milieu breeds its own enemies. Schumpeter noted that first the glamorous old-fashioned entrepreneur would give way to the large anonymous corporate bureaucracy; and, as he said, "The stock exchange is a poor substitute for the Holy Grail." Accounting books and cost calculations only exacerbate the businessman's petty, unheroic nature. Even worse, said Schumpeter, "A genius at the business office may be, and often is, utterly unable outside of it to say boo to a goose—both in the drawing room and on the platform. Knowing this, he wants to be left alone and to leave politics alone."

Unfortunately, the businessman tends to become a political target. For the tendency of the corporation is to grow bigger over the years, to absorb smaller companies into the larger hemisphere of the conglomerate, or to drive them out of business altogether. However economically efficient this process may be, it is politically unpalatable. In proportion as corporate business divorces itself from the ideals and purposes of private enterprise, we lose any feeling for it. Schumpeter said it well: "Dematerialized, defunctionalized and absentee ownership does not impress and call forth moral allegiance as the vital form of property did. Eventually there will be nobody left who really cares to stand for [the corporation]—nobody within and nobody without the precincts of the big concerns."

Schumpeter places the origin of what Kristol calls the "new class" in the last decades of the eighteenth century when the "free-lance intellectual" became part of the scenery of the English mindscape. The "new class" is that group of college-educated professionals who have embraced all the anticapitalist dogma of the traditional Left, not on economic grounds—they are profoundly ignorant of economics—but on political and metaphysical foundations. They envisage an eventual burgeoning of communal cooperation under the mandate of a socialist bureaucracy.

Irving Kristol says the "new class" advocates freedom in all spheres but the economic. Yet this is too generous. Freedom is really rather low on the agenda in any sphere. When the "new class" shows its true nature, its symbols become the chains of oppression and the bullhorn of political harangues. Where to find the "new class" at work? In the more prestigious universities; in Washington, running the multitudinous government agencies that have sprung up to do their will—the Environmental Protection Agency is the classic example—and often in journalism, though many "new class" journalists are merely camp followers of the current chic dogma. You can find the "new class" wherever there are parties serving Perrier water.

What mischief has the "new class" wrought on the modern corporation? While considering itself to be the very vanguard of progressive politics, the "new class" is in fact extremely reactionary. Its members would like to push us far back into medieval times, when there were no corporations; neither, however, was there much freedom of any kind. In the Middle Ages, regulation was thick and heavy. It was meant to enforce the values of the Church. The Church believed that charging interest on loans was sinful (as the Saudis still believe) and that every price should be a "just price"—not a market price, but a fair one, whatever that means. So, as Barbara Tuchman writes in *A Distant Mirror: The Calamitous Fourteenth Century,* "to insure that no one gained an advantage over anyone else, commercial law prohibited innovation in tools or techniques, underselling below a fixed price, working late by artificial light, employing extra apprentices . . . and the advertising of wares or praising them to the detriment of others." Obviously the church scholastics of the Middle Ages, like their intellectual heirs in Washington today, had no sympathy for the workings of the market system and its incentives to earn a profit.

Scholars such as Paul Weaver have proposed that the "new" social regulation is almost entirely the bailiwick of the "new class" that Kristol has identified—their bureaucratic weapon against the corporation. Weaver, in fact, has written that, under the banner of the public interest, members of the "new class" brandish their "new" regulation to instigate a second managerial revolution. The first managerial revolution accomplished the displacement of the old middle-class entrepreneur-managers by the corporate managerial class, running quasi-public corporations. And now the "new" regulation would, in the hands of the "new class," shift the power to fully public institutions: i.e., the government.

Thus we have, among others, the Environmental Protection Agency, the Occupational Safety and Health Administration, the Federal Trade Commission, and the Securities and Exchange Commission as the feudal lords of American business. These agencies form regulations that undoubtedly curb the excesses of business. But in fact the tremendous added cost burden hurts small firms the most. The expense of governmental regulations is getting so oppressive and the regulations themselves so pervasive that more than a few businessmen, large and small, say their decisions are affected more by what the government does than by what the marketplace does. That's quite a radical departure, with unhappy consequences for our economy. It opens the way to a regimen of perverse incentives.

Of course, business has dealt with government regulation for many decades. But before the mid-1960s it was economic rather than political or social regulation. In other words, agencies like the Federal Trade Commission and the Federal Communications Commission ostensibly stood watch over industry, while state commissions granted utility companies monopoly rights in exchange for the right to check their books. This sort of regulation continues today alongside the new regulation. But the economic regulators are not possessed by zeal so much as by the lust for money. Executives of regulated companies—television stations or electric power companies, for instance—bribe regulatory commissioners and staffs with vacations in Mexico and the use of yachts in San Francisco Bay and even plain cash under the table. In the late 1950s this kind of corruption became so profligate that it spilled onto newspaper headlines. Sherman Adams, President Eisenhower's assistant, was forced to resign when it was revealed that he had taken lavish gifts from Bernard Goldfine, a New England textile executive whose company had been accused of shoddy practices until Adams intervened on Goldfine's behalf.

But what truly endangers the corporate structure is the regulation that blossomed after 1967, overseen by the Consumer Product Safety Commission, EPA, OSHA, SEC, and the rest. These aren't regulators of monopolies. Their mission is to cleanse the nation of environmental dangers, remove harm from the workplace and the home, squash fraud in the stock market: in general, to eliminate all risk from life in modern America. The impossible nature of their goal is viewed by the more militant regulators as only a temporary challenge. As time goes on, they design to fill the already crammed rule books with enough regulations to cover every moment of every person's life.

Richard Wilson, writing in *Technology Review*, wonders if it isn't true that since in the modern world the major risks of the past have been eliminated, the small risks now loom large. Wilson takes his readers through a day in the life of a Harvard professor. "The moment I climb out of bed I start taking risks. As I drowsily turn on the light I feel a slight tingle; my house is old with old wiring and there is a small risk of electrocution. Every year 500 people are electrocuted in the United States. I take a shower, and as I reach for the soap, I wonder about the many chemicals it contains. Are they all good for the skin, as the advertisements claim? My clothes have been cleaned with the best bleaching deter-

gent. Most bleaching agents contain a chemical that
fluoresces slightly in the sunlight to enhance the whiteness.
Does this make bleaches carcinogenic?

"I ponder this risk as I walk down to breakfast, taking
care not to fall upon the stairs. Falls kill 16,000 people per
year—mostly in domestic accidents. Shall I drink coffee or
tea with my breakfast? Both contain caffeine, a well-known
stimulant which may be carcinogenic. I have a sweet tooth;
do I use sugar which makes me fat and gives me heart disease, or saccharin which we now know causes cancer? It is
better to abstain."

Wilson continues through his day, past the dangers of bi-
cycling to Boston, breathing the polluted air, drinking chlo-
rinated water at the hall fountain, sitting in an office whose
brick walls contain small amounts of radioactivity, and later
settling down in bed with a glass of beer. Alcohol, notes
Wilson, causes cirrhosis of the liver and is associated with
various cancers. The green glass of his beer bottle contains
chromium that seeps into the beer. Chromium is a known
carcinogen, though small quantities of it are necessary to
life. Then, upon reclining in his bed, Wilson wonders about
the flammability of his pajamas. He remarks to himself, "I
remember the truism 'more people die in bed than anywhere else,' so at least I'm in the right place."

Wilson's account captures the panic of the American intellectual, the fear that someday he might actually die. Perhaps this panic is a consequence of the fading of traditional
religion. For it is the agnostic who has nothing to look forward to in death; no vision of heaven consoles him, and thus
he clings anxiously to life. The agnostic's cowardice reigns in
the regulatory bureaucracy.

It is the excessive aggressiveness of Washington's regulators that upsets businessmen the most and suggests that regulators have motivations that go beyond their assigned regulatory duties. This becomes clear in a study conducted by
the Wharton School's Industrial Research Unit. Part of the

study looked at how OSHA regulations have affected the
U.S. aerospace industry, which happens to be one of the
environmentally cleanest industries in the world. And since
aerospace firms do much of their business with the government, the industry is accustomed to what bureaucrats are
fond of calling "oversight"—the government looking over
the industry's shoulder. The aerospace industry is dominated by a few large corporations, among them General
Electric, Rockwell International, and United Technologies.
The requirement for heavy investment in research and the
dependence of the industry on government contracts make
the business somewhat rough for small companies. Even the
big ones—like Lockheed—can run into trouble; they face
feast or famine according to what the government decides
to spend on space and weapons systems.

Each of the large aerospace companies had its own safety
department long before OSHA set up shop in 1971. For
years they had one of the best safety records in all of American industry. The average work injury rate for all manufacturing firms ranged from 12 to 15 injuries per 100 man-years
of work, but for the aerospace industry the range was from
3.5 to 4.5 injuries per 100 man-years. The industry's excel-
lent record has been due in part to the clean, precision
processes used and the high level of automation. Continuing
military inspections of plants under defense contracts also
played a part, as did existing laws concerning plant safety.

None of this deterred OSHA, however. The agency wasn't
inclined to leave the aerospace industry alone just because it
already had an exemplary safety and health record. To the
contrary, OSHA was and is intent on interfering, imposing
expensive new regulations even if they actually cause existing safety and health conditions to deteriorate. This is the
message of the Wharton report. Aerospace plant safety professionals found out quickly that the kinds of rules OSHA
officials were concerned with had little to do with worker
health and safety. The OSHA regulators, according to

the Wharton report, were obsessed with Standard 1910.141(c)(2), "Construction of Toilet Rooms," which went into great detail about the rearrangement of toilet stalls to suit the government. Another major OSHA regulation explained exactly where to mount fire extinguishers. But aerospace safety officials say the most costly OSHA standard that had little to do with actual safety was the one requiring the grounding of office coffee pots and electric typewriters. A lot of companies have been forced by OSHA to rewire their entire offices and plants, largely because it's easy for OSHA inspectors to spot two-wire electric plugs in place of the three-wire plugs called for by the agency.

One gets the picture of OSHA officials as a cadre of Captain Queegs, neurotically obsessed with insignificant details while leaving important matters to percolate unattended. The safety and health professionals surveyed by the Wharton School all said that even the strictest compliance with OSHA standards would have virtually no effect on the health or safety of the aerospace workers, but these professionals were nonetheless required to rearrange their priorities to suit the regulators. A Southern California aerospace corporation determined that it would cost $3.5 million to comply with OSHA rules, but only $400,000 of that money would be spent on measures that would actually enhance worker health and safety. And that $400,000 would have been spent without OSHA. The company's safety professionals are much better trained than OSHA inspectors, and their program functioned efficiently before OSHA was anything more than a bureaucrat's wet dream.

Like Captain Queeg, OSHA tends to be ruthless in its madness. The high cost of compliance threatens to break many an aerospace company division, especially in view of the huge investments that must be funneled into future research if these companies are to stay competitive. The Wharton report states that strict compliance with the rules may be economically unfeasible for many aerospace companies. Yet while employment in the aerospace industry has fallen by one third in the past five years, OSHA has in the same period dramatically increased its requirements. In particular OSHA has stepped up its monitoring of toxic materials, which leads to problems in aerospace because some workers are exposed to a variety of chemicals for brief periods, in well-ventilated places. In other words, the exposure, though frequent, is safe. But OSHA doesn't care about that. It wants each exposure monitored, at the company's expense. Things are likely to get worse when OSHA approves its proposed four hundred "mini-standards." These will call for even more monitoring, record keeping, and health examinations. It will call for the hiring of more doctors and industrial hygienists and the use of expensive computer systems. All this is nonproductive investment, especially since it's made in what is already a quite safe, healthy industry. The cost of OSHA's unnecessary regulations will prove to be high, and consumers will ultimately pay it, either in the price of airline tickets or in the taxes paid to a government that buys planes and missiles.

Some groups have tried to estimate just how much regulations are costing American companies. Of course, they can't make an accurate appraisal of the indirect costs: construction delays, reduction in corporate international competitiveness, loss of factory productivity, discouragement of investments, shortages of supplies, and sundry other consequences of the government's heavy hand. They can, however, measure the direct costs of complying with federal regulations.

One study done by Arthur Andersen and Co., the accounting firm, for the Business Roundtable took forty-eight medium-sized and large corporations and looked at how much they had to spend in 1977 for regulations. The study results are not reassuring. Overall, these companies had to spend $2.6 billion to meet regulations, and much of that amount was judged to be wasteful. That $2.6 billion was equal to one eighth of those companies' profits for the year. And most of the costs—$2.3 billion—were incurred by manufacturing companies. These costs were passed along to consumers and added substantially to the inflation rate.

Three fourths of all the costs were due to EPA rules, according to the study. Two EPA rules accounted for $900 million in costs. One was the rule controlling air pollution from new cars. The other was a national air quality standard for particulate matter. These regulations are expensive, but on the other hand who cares to breathe polluted air? How does one distinguish between necessary regulations and superfluous, Captain Queeg regulations? Unfortunately, only a specialist who has plowed through mountains of detail and talked to a wide variety of people—regulators, businessmen, economists, medical researchers—can glean a clear idea of the extent of overregulation. The Wharton School study of OSHA is one example of diligence in uncovering unnecessary regulation. But the very difficulty of separating the good regulation from the excessive, ineffective regulation gives all regulators a mantle of protection from criticism. Many are wont to meet any attack by countering with the charge that the complainant is a selfish pawn of big business, ready to have the citizenry die from air and water pollution. Unless one is an expert, one is hard put to defend oneself.

The difficulty of being able to tell the valid regulations from the rest is what arms the worst of regulatory bureaucrats with a sense of supreme, unchecked power. Too often, they demand to have full jurisdiction and a free hand. Since lay people, whether members of Congress, journalists, or voters, are in no position to argue with them, regulators exercise powers befitting a Roman emperor. President Carter, for example, set up both a White House Regulatory Review Group and a Regulatory Council to monitor the value and efficiency of the government's multitudinous regulations. Neither was able to make the slightest dent. Carter then proposed to Congress a set of reforms that would force regulators to gauge the costs and benefits of their regulations and to review past regulations to see if they are effective in practice. But even if Congress were to pass such a proposal, no one expects it to make much difference.

The real problem is simply that the regulatory bureaucracy, trading on the good intentions that instigated its creation, has become an uncontrolled, ever-growing governmental tumor. It formulates rules that may or may not protect the people but definitely render our technology inefficient or obsolete. A solution has yet to be found.

10

War of the Bureaucracies

WHERE SHOULD we turn for truth but to a novelist? Norman Mailer, though a practicing writer for all his adult life, graduated from Harvard with an engineering degree. Thus his fascination with the metaphysics and philosophy of technology. In fact, many of his cleverest literary metaphors come from a happy marriage of the technical and the sensual, as when he describes electricity as "an avatar of hate" in *Of a Fire on the Moon*. Now let us indulge Mailer's feeling for the roots of what he sees as the totalitarian sensibility in America: ". . . America was altered from a nation of venture, exploitation, bigotry, initiative, strife, social justice and social injustice into a vast central swamp of tasteless toneless authority whose dependable heroes were drawn from FBI men, doctors, television entertainers, corporation executives and athletes who could cooperate with public-relations men." He finds a sense of technological totalitarianism in "corporate techniques . . . in the image of the commercials on television which use phallic and vaginal symbols to sell products which are otherwise useless for sex . . . in the jargon of educators, in the synthetic continuums of prose with which public-relations men learn to enclose the sense and smell of an event . . . in the taste of frozen food, the pharmaceutical odor of tranquilizers, the planned obsolescence of automobiles. . . ." Mailer sees this totalitarianism as resembling a plague rather than a formal ideology. It emanates from the abortionist's needle and the corporate executive's computerese more surely than from a politician's podium. It is, then, the Zeitgeist of modern technology, administered from the large corporation's antiseptic corridors. (In a burst of prescience, Mailer, writing in 1969, suggested that the 1970s would be a decade of technological narcissism, as reflected in the nature of the computer, which, he said, is the essence of narcissism because the computer cannot conceive of its inability to correct its own mistakes.)

You may complain that, after all, this is Mailer's literary license in the service of paranoia, that in real life technology has wrought wonders at the hands of the giant corporation. I disagree with the dismissal of Mailer's ethics, however. To ignore his charges is to ignore reality, and not the other way around. Most of us do sense a vague contempt for the TV dinner we unwrap and for the plush authoritarian austerity of corporate headquarters lobbies. Something deep in the psyche reminds us of other possibilities, of another more pastoral life glimpsed only in dreams. Is it the imperative of nature that rebels from the concept of the human being as a packaged adjunct to the electronic machine? I like to think that it is. And friends appear to be startled when I speak of the philosophical conservatism of Norman Mailer.

Let us venture for a spell into the corporate utopia of tomorrow as envisioned in Florida's Walt Disney World. Our unlikely tour guide is Michael Harrington, writing in *Harper's Magazine*. Here, Harrington points out, is the amazing technology of a corporate heaven: where trash is quietly sucked through underground tubes at sixty miles per hour, an air-conditioned electric monorail unobtrusively whisks visitors to their destinations, and unseen computers exercise complete control over the physical environment and at the same time calculate the profit-maximizing proportion of guests to be shunted through this amusement or that. The designers of Disney World, says Harrington, feel their village embodies one of the most powerful desires of the decade: to attain an apolitical, anti-intellectual, corporate technocratic solution to the problems of society. Planning and control are complete here. It is a perfect state monopoly, attended to by blond, blue-eyed, short-haired boys and girls who are prohibited from chewing gum and drinking alcohol.

But listen to Walt Disney himself and you'll hear the dream of an unadulterated technological socialist. His village will be "a planned community, controlled community, a showcase for American industry and research, schools, cultural and educational opportunities. . . . There will be no slum areas because we won't let them develop. There will be no landowners and therefore no voting control. People will rent houses instead of buying them, at modest rentals. There will be no retirees. Everyone must be employed. . . ." Could Mao Tse-tung or Fidel Castro have said it any better? This is corporate socialism of the most unambiguous character. It embraces whole the ideology of technology. It is the direct intellectual ancestor to the rationalist philosophers of the eighteenth century who, like Disney, craved a society ordered by the authority of strict rationalist mandates, distributional justice, and unqualified regimentation (provided this time not by ranting dictators but by silent electronic machines). Thus the Experimental Prototype Community of Tomorrow, so named by Disney planners who hope to spend half a billion dollars, financed by corporations and the government, to bring their ultimate socialist fantasy to realization. Is this sheer madness or is it the shape of the American corporate future?

Extending the limit of large-scale economies, we confront at last the hazy zone where the economic bends and twists the social. Television came to prominence, not to say dominance, because it offered mass efficiencies in the transmission of information. It permitted the whole nation to be wired with nerve strands, so to speak, with the brain in New York and the spinal cord lying across Middle America. The automobile, too, represented a revolutionary innovation. Our society has gained untold benefits from these inven-

tions, but have we not lost an incalculable amount? Both of
them work to destroy any traditional sense of community.
We watch television alone, or sitting silently in a rapt group.
We drive alone, or with one or two passengers. We are thus
separated from the necessity of social intercourse with people around us.

Driving in their little boxes, they become things, not people. This suggests why otherwise decent folk become mur-
derous maniacs behind the wheel. And rather than cultivate
the art of conversation, we let the television set provide it
for us. We can listen to a starlet complain of her bunions
and a famous writer pontificate on the mysteries of the ether
and his next million-dollar contract. Savor the contrast with
peasant societies. I had the privilege of living for a spell in
Colombia, as a Peace Corps volunteer, in a town of 15,000
called Miranda. There were only a half-dozen cars, maybe
as many television sets, and no refrigerators. People never
shut themselves in their homes to stare at a television
screen, because there wasn't that option. I'm not so much of
a romantic as to claim that if television were available
they'd ignore it, but still its absence led people to sit on ve-
randas on warm afternoons, talking. When they felt like
going somewhere, they didn't hop into the Buick. They
walked, and greeted fellow townspeople they passed, often
stopping to talk. Not having refrigerators, they went to no
supermarkets for frozen foods. Instead the citizens bought
at the marketplace on Sunday morning, and it was a carni-
val, a social event of major proportions. There in a clearing,
where burlap bags were spread on the ground and covered
with every species of produce, where makeshift stalls held
tools and old magazines and unimaginable junk for sale—
there was a place for a community to thrive. This small-town
warmth and openness is not peculiar to Colombia. It is common in every place where old ways still suffice. It is essentially the way Americans of a much earlier age lived, in the
eighteenth century out in the rural heartlands.

Have we not lost by our surrender of tribal society to technological isolation? The posing of the question assumes that we could have stopped the march of technology. And we could not, for it crept up on society by inches, powered by the iron logic that man succumbed to when he traded theocracy for democracy. Technology becomes, in our scheme, the nexus between economies of large scale and the corporate form of organization with its totalitarian sensibility. A species of technological socialism follows logically from this sensibility. Allied against it are the natural impulses of the free spirit, the artist, and the entrepreneur. Democracy, loosely defined, can accommodate the free spirit, but can it also accommodate the authoritarian bureaucrat?

Witness how contorted the line of reasoning has come to be in modern discussions. Conservatives typically champion the entrepreneurial spirit as a means of defending the great corporations from the encroachments of state control. Liberals condemn laissez-faire by calling for more regulation of big business and the breakup of monopolies into small companies that would compete fairly. The confusion clears when we set aside their rhetoric and look at the actual practice of these factions. Conservatives invoke nature to wash the aims of corporate technology in the glow of natural righteousness. Liberals invoke nature to shroud state control with the mantle of opposition to the corporate oppressors. Both appeal to the spirit of political and economic freedom, thus to wrap their goals in all the glory of visions and impulses that we know instinctively are right. Any politico who can attest that he is on the side of natural freedom will win the confidence of his constituency. Any who shows himself too closely in league with cultural totalitarianism will lose the election.

This is part of our dilemma. We may understand that large-scale technology is necessary to the progress of the human race, but still we dislike it at the deepest levels. Sus-

picions are confirmed when it's revealed that the nitrite in
our packaged meats causes cancer, that the smoke from the
fertilizer factory rots our lungs, and that Nixon's corrupt
presidency was supported by laundered $100,000 contri-
butions from some of the most prominent major corporations. I have even heard corporate executives, in the quie-
tude of their executive dining rooms, express faint
misgivings about the meaning of what they do. At the most
personal level, the natural instincts are at war with the technological imperative.

At the social level, the conflict lives in the tension between
bureaucrat and citizen; between the inexorably increasing
authority of corporate and government bureaucracies and
the yearning to break out; between the imperatives of natural freedom and imposed order, security, equality, and perceived justice. Yet even the strongest impulses to freedom
have been subverted by the false doctrine that individual
freedom is granted at the behest of the state. As Bertrand de
Jouvenal has said in his *Essays on Power*, when viewed his-
torically the right to liberty wasn't an act of generosity on
the part of any government. Rather, liberty was in ancient
societies an achievement of the individual, and one that won
the name of subjective right by force of self-assertion. Jouvenal accuses modern man of becoming so inured to state
authority that he has lost the collective memory of the free
man, who was a reality and not merely a philosopher's
dream. Freedom, he contends, is a subjective right that be-
longs to those who will seize it and defend it. Are we knock-
ing at the door of anarchy here? No, because Jouvenal's
view of freedom was one constrained by fundamental intui-
tive decency.

So to the paradox of totalitarian democracy. It was Mon-
tesquieu who warned of the confusion, common to democracies, of the power of the populace with the liberty of the
populace. We must emphatically add that even the power of
the populace in present-day democracies is largely illusory.

Voting is a rather impotent exercise when the candidates are chosen by the dictates of acceptability as delineated in newspaper columns and network news commentaries. The scholars of public choice at Virginia Polytechnic Institute have demonstrated algebraically that voting for candidates itself is an irrational act, because a single person's vote has an extremely narrow chance of affecting an election's outcome. Mankind has never devised any mechanism, after all, by which every citizen can share in the exercise of power. Hence the notion of the people's sovereignty is a sham, trumpeted most loudly by those who hunger to grab the levers of power for themselves—to be manipulated in the name of the people, of course. (Is it not ironic that technology may offer the potentiality to allow everyone at last to have a hand in policymaking, when advanced cable television makes it feasible for every household to vote electronically on any issue?)

With a centralized power, then, a democracy is no more amenable to personal liberty than a monarchy, for the democracy also acts with absolute authority even if criticism is permitted. Thus democracy's true claim to legitimacy has been that it would free people from the tyranny of more openly oppressive powers: in the American case, from King George III.

Every philosophy student knows that, by Kenneth Arrow's Impossibility Theorem, in a democracy the majority can and does oppress the minority. De Tocqueville foresaw this. It is thought to be the major defect of the democratic form.

Yet some say that the American democracy overcomes the opportunity for tyranny by operating a system in which special interests have their influence on legislators, and instant public opinion polls tell Congress when it is fulfilling the popular will. Herein lies a paradox. Jouvenal notes: "We are told, that the general interest is exactly represented by the government. From this postulate flows a corollary; that no interest is legitimate which opposes this general interest." And democratic governments differ chiefly in the permissiveness with which they tolerate the selfish interests of the minority. Jimmy Carter let farmers demonstrate in front of the White House and rip up the turf of the Washington Mall with their tractors, but he condemned their request for higher price parity as inflationary and opposed to the general interest. Carter doubtless was correct, for regardless of his permissiveness in allowing the special interests their fit of anger, his task was to juggle the manifold special interests inherent in a highly advanced society, each of which is necessary to the functioning of the society and none of which is endowed with any special claim on the decisions of government. The result is that economic and political muscle always wins out in the battle of the special interests, and the fiction of popular sovereignty loses what credibility it possessed in those ancient times when fewer special interests came trooping to Washington to redress their grievances.

Among the most visible and powerful of special interests are those of the large corporations. It has been amply chronicled that thousands of business lobbyists inhabit Washington, financed by millions of corporate dollars, seeking hundreds of special favors from the government. It is in the political power that flows from this corporate economic power that the danger of corporate clout most dramatically shows itself; this influence peddling would be called extortion and bribery in other contexts. Still, in a regime of battling interests, corporate America cannot reasonably be denied its opportunity to enter the fray. Why is it that when Ralph Nader claims to be speaking for the people, his voice possesses more credibility than that of, say, Grumman when it speaks of jobs on Long Island that it wishes to save for the benefit of the community? Nader, of course, has dressed himself in the ascetic's hair shirt to prove his bona fide identity as a true champion of the people.

It would seem apparent that a balancing of selfish interests is the only recourse of modern society, but what of Reinhold Niebuhr's assertion that the fundamental error in the philosophy of democracy is precisely its confidence in arriving at an easy resolution of the tension between self-interest and the general interest? Modern society, says Niebuhr, did at least seek to give the individual a greater freedom than that obtained in the old feudal orders of society; it sought to free people of the restraints placed on them by religious authority. But it never, claims Niebuhr, defied the general interest in the name of self-interest, individual or collective. Such moral cynicism was manifest only in the darkest hours of Nazism, according to Niebuhr. Thus he names selfish partisans as evil when they know no law beyond themselves. And this is consistent with the constrained sort of freedom we visualize as the ideal. But Niebuhr calls the "children of light"—those who uphold the common good —foolish for not recognizing the dark power of self-interest to push toward selfish ends. If democracy began as an enlightened revolt against aristocracy and feudal restraints, has it evolved into a darker reality? What is the reality that seeps through the cracks of the democratic myth? It is that social organization will inevitably be "corrupted" by the instinctive selfishness of nature's imperative. But people have refused to recognize the truth about democracy. Seeking solace, they contend that people would act rightly if the government and political parties didn't corrupt them; or if the economic system didn't exploit them; or if their education were only more complete. But one wonders why no apologist ever asked how it could be that the essentially good human race could have founded these tyrannical political institutions and oppressive economic systems and faulty educational institutions.

The logic of democracy springs from the soil of the French Revolution and ultimately from the reasoning of Descartes. Yet technology, too, springs from the Cartesian manifesto. The correlation is close enough to reveal democracy as consistent with technology, until technology becomes so powerful that it is the fomenter first of democracy, and then of technological socialism. Democracy is the application of the scientific method to society, just as technology is the application of the scientific method to production. And socialism is but the ultimate refinement of the democratic notion that human beings are basically good and thus perfectible, if only the slide rules of social engineers could calculate rational answers to all human problems.

Then it is technology that could finally lead us from democracy into bureaucratic socialism, not by the violent and perhaps premature revolutions of the Bolsheviks and the Chinese and the Cubans, but by quiet evolution, quiet as the Orwellian hum of an ice-blue computer mainframe recessed into the wall of a global corporate headquarters.

But there is something missing from this picture of the future. State governments may have been easy pickings for corporations, but the government in Washington costs a few more million dollars. It's true that Congress is a veritable snakepit of influence selling and buying. It is the private marketplace of government influence, as surely as the New York Stock Exchange is the private marketplace of shares in American industry. But opposing corporate power is the huge army of bureaucrats, the "new class," that is now struggling with corporate America to see which side will yield and which will at last possess the upper hand. This is no struggle between liberty and tyranny. It is a ferocious family argument among giants who wield great power and wish to have it all. The bureaucrats would bind and encumber corporations until they are impoverished and therefore lose effective power over the government apparatus. On the other side, the corporations would strip the bureaucrats of their license to make crippling rules and regulations. Of course, the power exercised by government bureaucrats was granted by Congress. But it is now an independent power, with a political base strong enough to frighten any President who dares to challenge a rule or regulation, to intimidate any member of Congress who would weaken the bureaucratic charter. The bureaucracy is the permanent government of Washington, and its power is such that it aims to defeat the power of large corporations and to control government. One totalitarian force battles another.

Scholars such as Jay Forrester of MIT believe this clash between government and corporations stems from misunderstanding between the two. He has said there is every reason for the two institutions to move in the same direction. And of course, Forrester is right. Government bureaucracies and corporate bureaucracies are identical in their organization and their intent. Both are authoritarian organizations directed by planners for the supposed greater good of the organization. The misunderstanding between corporations and government arises from the businessman's illusion that corporate, technological capitalism is equivalent to ancient laissez-faire capitalism. If the alternative to governmental bureaucratic power is corporate bureaucratic power, what is to be gained from this war? If the government triumphs, our society could quite possibly evolve into a governmental socialism. If the corporate structure should win, we would logically move toward technocratic corporate socialism. Neither choice is appetizing.

Who *will* win? Bureaucrats have license to make outlandish laws, but corporations have technology. Technology has shown itself to be an effective vehicle by which to usurp individual liberty and the very notion of individualism. Corporations, which are the masters of new technology, have at their disposal, therefore, a potent weapon in the war to dominate the populace. The bureaucracy can fight this advantage by passing regulations that outlaw or usurp technology, and it will retain its powers and multiply them as long as it can curry favors from Congress. One wonders how long the bureaucracy will be able to keep up the pretense that it is the defender of freedom from corporate oppression, risk, and the unlimited power of big institutions.

11

The Last
of the Entrepreneurs?

WASHINGTON AIMS its biggest regulatory guns at the major corporations, but small business is being slaughtered by the shrapnel. This matters, because nine of every ten businesses in the country are small businesses, with sales of $1 million or less a year. Ranging from mom-and-pop food stores to bubble gum manufacturers, they account for nearly half the Gross National Product, 80 percent of all new jobs, and more than half of all new inventions.

In fact, the small businessman (or woman) is the mainstay of the private marketplace. He fits most readily into the Adam Smith dream of freely competing independent entrepreneurs. Operating on the fringes of the turf lorded over by big business, the small businessman faces hefty odds; some 55 percent of all small businesses fail in the first five years of operation. Even when the business runs smoothly, he must have the sensibilities of a consummate gambler. Richard Cantillon, the Irish intellectual, summed it up in 1755. He said the task of the businessman is to buy goods for a known price with a view to selling them at a price which, at the moment of buying them, is unknown. To the extent the big businessman can set his own price, he cuts out the gamble. But the small businessman most often must just assume that he'll be able to sell at a profit. And the small manufacturer takes an even larger chance. He first guesses, or hopes, that enough people will buy his unknown brand. Then he has to back up his guess by spending thousands or even millions of dollars to build his factory and equip it and hire workers. If his gamble turns out badly, the loss will be enormous. He

can, of course, file for bankruptcy, but that is small consolation.

The demands and proclivities of consumers, flighty and
unpredictable as they are, is what any businessman must divine, whether he's starting a new enterprise, launching a
new product, or just joining the existing competition. A realtor, for instance, borrows $30 million and contracts to erect
a new hotel on Forty-second Street in Manhattan for the
year 1985. But he makes the decision in 1980, after some
years of tourist boom and an influx of rich foreigners who
open chic stores on Madison Avenue. It is also just after
the city has announced new plans to clean up Forty-second
Street and turn it into a showplace. At the time the realtor
decides to put up a new hotel, the prospects look good. All
the hotels in town are booked solid for months on end.
Other new hotels have just opened. Is the realtor therefore
swimming in safe waters? One doubts it. How can he know
that the need for hotel space will not have been satisfied by
the time his hotel opens its doors five years hence? How can
he know New York City won't have been blown off the face
of the earth? The short answer is that he just can't, so he
places his bet and takes his chance. But it's more than common to see this kind of project end in disgrace. Businessmen
rush in on clouds of optimism. Then, when they have satu-
rated the market with hotel rooms, they all lose money as
the rooms go begging for occupants. Only eventually will
the demand for rooms catch up with the new supply. When
it finally does, and good rooms become hard to reserve in
the city, the wave of building will resume. (When this happens en masse, we begin to see the outlines of what's known
as the *business cycle*. Optimism spurs investment in pursuit
of future profits. Overoptimism, however, brings losses to a
critical mass of businessmen, so that the psychology turns
black. Businessmen all retrench and withdraw their investments or withhold them. Instead they put their money in
safe government bonds and wait for economic euphoria

once more. In the meantime, their reticence creates, in large part, a recession.)

No artist ever takes such high risks as a dull businessman. Most artists take no risks at all, and for those who do, it is at little cost: a little time spent, a little bad publicity if the project goes wrong. If an artist is sufficiently clever, he can easily wheedle his way out of his bad experiment by averring that he was only putting the public on. Businessmen can't get away with lame excuses. After all, there's the solid, heavy machinery of industrial production sitting in factories and mills to attest to the folly of the businessman who has missed the mark. There is the bank account bleeding from a million-dollar hemorrhage.

Why should anyone care to gamble his money, time, and reputation catering to the public whim? The prospect of profit, of course, must rank at the top of any listing. Then, too, who doesn't want to be his own boss, to be independent and sovereign in his own sphere, theoretically at liberty to go as high as his sweat and his wit will take him? Not only that, but many a small businessman yearns, in his daydreams, to become a magnate, the founder of an empire that can be passed on to his heirs.

Consider this question: Should you invest your $100,000 in a bookstore, or put it into a nice, safe Treasury bond? If twelve-month T-bills are yielding an interest rate of 8 percent, and you figure that a bookstore would earn you a 12 percent return, then you can go for the bookstore. For this means that the bookstore will earn a profit of 12 percent of $100,000, or $12,000, each year. Mind you, we're talking about what the store will earn you after all pretax expenses, including your salary.

How do you calculate what a bookstore will yield? There are two simple ways. You could look at the profits earned in existing bookstores. That is, you can figure the average return on investment, known in the money trade as *ROI*. This figure equals the net income for the year divided by the value of all the assets—the property—used in the business. The resulting percentage number is analogous to an interest rate and can be validly compared with whatever the going interest rates are. The difficulty with using an average return on investment for all bookstores is that each is different. The famed Scribner's on Fifth Avenue in New York is housed in a fine old building that was bought dirt cheap many years ago. A bookstore on New York's Upper East Side may be frequented by a famous author and his coterie. Another's return may be held down by the rudeness of the proprietor, who spits on the floor. The average is therefore only useful as a comparative tool, so you may contrast the return on investment for bookstores with the return on china shops and delicatessens, not to mention the return on bonds. To get the information needed to figure simple return on investment you'd need to look at a bookstore's income statement to find the *net income* (literally, the bottom line), and you'd have to look at its balance sheet to find the total assets. But businessmen don't wish people to obtain this information; and besides, the fact that one or a hundred bookstores make 10 percent a year doesn't assure you that yours will.

A more sophisticated way to estimate how much a bookstore will yield in a year is through *discounted cash flow* analysis. This is based on the idea that a dollar now is worth more than a dollar a year hence, simply because you have to wait for next year's dollar. The idea that the present value of a dollar is higher in the present has nothing to do in this context with inflation. It has to do with the forgone spending opportunity. If you can dig up an estimate of the market value of the bookstore if you sold it after a year, and an estimate of the net income it will pull in for the year, you can simply divide net income by the market price and get a percentage, which is the yield on your investment. For example, if you can calculate that the bookstore will take in at least $100,000 a year after all expenses, including taxes, and if you know from reading classified ads and checking the inflation rate for real estate that you can sell the bookstore next year for $1 million, the answer is 10 percent minimum return—minimum because you said the $100,000 net income is the least amount it would earn in a year.

One thing is clear: there is no hard and fast way of figuring out whether you'll get rich or starve, because in trying to calculate a rate of return on the bookstore you have either to extrapolate into the future what has happened in the past with other people's bookstores, or to use estimates, which are likely to be more in the realm of guesses. This truth, that even with the fanciest formulas you can only hazard an educated guess as to the profitability of an enterprise—unless that business is protected from competition by the government—this explains just why a businessman must be a gambler.

What is it, therefore, but optimism that motivates people to embark on uncharted waters? Men of business are incurably optimistic; even in the depths of gloom, they still look upward. I cannot explain this persistent hopefulness. It may grow out of necessity. Businessmen need to see profits coming—eventually—because any other sight would repudiate their being. But sometimes business optimism runs riot. Some economists see this foolhardiness as the precipitator of the business booms that always end in dismal crashes. It happened most notably in the weeks before the stock market crash of the Great Depression, when speculative fever, nourished on pure avarice, pushed asset prices skyward until the bubble burst and Wall Street financiers started bailing out of eighth-story windows with no parachutes. It happened again in the late 1960s when the stock market burst forth on growth stocks and young men made and lost fortunes in a day. Shady dealers built paper empires that collapsed, leaving ordinary stockholders to pick up the pieces in the early 1970s.

The small businessman may cherish his competitiveness

and he may speak proudly of his freedom, but he knows he isn't so free anymore. For the government comes down hardest of all on these businessmen who don't have platoons of accountants and lawyers to take care of government paper work. President Carter's Commission on Federal Paperwork estimated that small businesses in the United States are required to file a total of 10 billion sheets of paper each year. All that paper work costs $20 billion a year and eats up the equivalent of the working hours of 68,000 employees each year. Agency regulations increase the costs of small businessmen proportionately much more than those of big corporations, because the small businessman can't spread his regulatory overhead among several different divisions. A lot of small businessmen just ignore as many of the regulations as they can, because if they complied with every one they'd have to shut down completely. Among small-time entrepreneurs, OSHA is the most hated of all agencies. The sight of an OSHA inspector at the door of a small factory means official citations, fines, and threats for picayune violations of rules that are excessive when they aren't inane.

A few small businessmen have always been talented at exploiting government regulations, often unscrupulously. For instance, consider the "teakettle" refiner. He found out that lurking within the bureaucratic maze that administered federal crude oil price controls was a special favor. It was for tiny refineries, so they wouldn't be at a disadvantage to larger refineries. In fact, it gave the small ones the advantage of cheaper crude oil. So the teakettle refiner bought some old, used refinery equipment, just enough to make heavy, bottom-of-the-barrel heating oil. Given the advantage provided by the regulations, he could pay back his investment in six months and skim off the cream afterward—to the tune of millions of dollars.

Or consider the teakettle refiner's brother, the crude-oil trader who made fast bucks by tinkering with the government's classifications of crude oil. Now, what the government deemed "old" oil—that in production before the 1973 OPEC price hike and the imposition of controls—sold for half the price of what the government decided was "new" oil. But oil is oil; it's only "old" or "new" on paper. So if you could buy "old" oil at the low "old" oil price and sell it as "new" oil at the much higher "new" oil price, you'd make some easy money. Indeed, a few Texas good ole boys did just that—and laughed all the way to the bank.

And what about the small construction firms that name the janitor president so the company can qualify for government contracts meant for minority-owned small businesses? When in 1976 the Economic Development Administration offered construction contracts that called for the contractor to do 10 percent of his business with minority companies, it turned out that more than 30 percent of such companies were hastily formed minority fronts. So much for anti-recession aid designed to help minorities.

More examples can be delineated, but the lesson is that somebody's always going to be smart enough to turn regulations around to their advantage, and this is almost a natural impulse. The marketplace, broadly defined, keeps popping up no matter how hard the government tries to suppress it. And market forces are no respecters of laws (if they were, we wouldn't have a Mafia). Small businessmen, ironically, are invisible enough, insignificant enough sometimes, to pull off regulatory tricks and get away with it.

But mostly small business gets the blunt end of the regulatory stick because independent businessmen are too busy running their businesses to roam through the halls of Congress twisting arms. Even if they had the time, they don't have the financial clout of the *Fortune* 500 companies or the friends in high places. Like consumers, small businessmen are left mostly unrepresented in the Washington catfights over power. You'd think that the bureaucrats would naturally favor small businesses. But in fact the philosophy in vogue along the Potomac seems to be that all business is bad, and to hell with small businesses. If they can't float in the same regulatory waters navigated by billion-dollar corporations, let them sink.

Now, small business has always been the prime source for new technology, for innovations, for creative breakthroughs, for new products and new ways to sell products. But the tax laws and securities laws and the ways of Wall Street make it tough for small businesses, especially new ones, to raise money. What small businesses need most of all is venture capital, money with which to gamble. Ideally, this should come from the sale of stock, as it often does for the large corporations. But Wall Street investors, many of whom represent bank trusts and big union pension funds, are leery of new stocks offered by unknown companies; they prefer to stick with the traditional blue-chip names of the *Fortune* 500. Stockbrokers, understandably, don't often recommend that their individual clients buy into risky, little-known stock issues.

Government regulations, compounding the problem, inflate the cost of issuing less than a million dollars' worth of stock. Capital gains taxes discourage investments in small firms. And the corporate income tax discriminates against small business, as do a number of Internal Revenue Service regulations. On top of that, government franchise and gross receipt taxes remove money from small business coffers whether they are making a profit or not, though it's true that most new businesses lose money for at least the first three years of existence. What can deal the death blow is the drain from required employer contributions to Social Security, Workers' Compensation, and unemployment insurance. There are always proposals to reform these and other impediments to small businesses, but the proposals somehow never get off the ground.

The Small Business Administration is supposed to be Washington's friend of small business. Yet it's acknowledged to be the most corrupt, sluggish agency in Washington—a happy hunting ground for tired bureaucrats who want the comforts of a civil service job but none of the hassles. So the SBA gets the worst and the dullest of the regulators. They while away their hours making loans to the wrong kinds of small businesses, and taking kickbacks on the side. The results are sadly amusing. According to several accounts, of some 3,400 small companies that have received loans with SBA help, only 30 are still in existence. Many of the 30 are front operations to skim money from the agency's minority business loan program.

None of this is surprising, if one considers the lopsided policy of the SBA. It won't give out any loans to new businesses because in theory it's not able to take the risk. In practice, however, the agency squanders its loan money on even riskier lost causes; by law it is the lender of last resort and can hand out money to an established firm only if the banks have turned the loan application down. Naturally, the loan proposals rejected by commercial banks are likely to be poor risks. But the SBA doesn't care; it seeks only to fill its quota of loans. The agency ought to be helping out promising new ventures. Instead, it throws money away on faltering companies.

Small business has no national voice, no powerful advocate, and few friends in Washington. Despite all the political oratory praising small business in the same breath with motherhood and the flag, the institution is a sitting target for every pipsqueak politico with a notion to find an easy victim for government abuse.

12

The Natural Marketplace

THE WORLD of the small businessman and the neighborhood entrepreneur is a far cry from the corporate planner's large-scale economies. But the small businessmen and the giant corporations bump together in the private marketplace. There natural instincts take precedence over the scientific logic of technology. In the ideal private marketplace, natural selfish impulses are channeled in mutually beneficial ways—into the businessman's urge to earn a profit and the consumer's urge to acquire possessions. Big companies and small ones alike must accept the discipline of the market, unless they can successfully contrive to wrest some monopoly power. They often get away with it. (A twenty-four-hour gas station in a one-horse town can be as much of a monopoly as AT&T.)

The natural marketplace is as old as human society itself. And though some ancient tribes got along without an organized market, it has evolved in every part of the world and thrives wherever it's permitted. Even when the market is quashed, it manages to reassert itself. In Moscow, an American tourist finds a ready black market for American cigarettes and blue jeans, even though the market system is outlawed. In the U.S.A., marijuana possession is still prohibited, but the market flourishes because people want to buy it and some are willing to sell it. Up on 123rd Street in New York's Harlem, there's even a marijuana dealers' bazaar. One walks along the street from stoop to stoop, checking out the day's wholesale offerings. There is something infinitely human about what Adam Smith in 1776 called the "propensity to truck, barter and exchange."

Where once humans fabricated most of what they used, now we buy it all, or rent it. Our spending is the most important engine of economic prosperity. Our buying habits determine which businesses will succeed and which file for bankruptcy. On any given day, hundreds of new products pour from factories to take their chances in the marketplace, often backed by millions of dollars' worth of advertising and promotion. An Edsel fails, and a Polaroid camera wins. No matter that the Edsel was born in the comfort of a billion-dollar corporation while the Polaroid had humble beginnings in an engineer's workshop. Either a product catches the consumer's fancy or it fails, contrary to the arcane doctrine that giant corporations make the products they want to make and then brainwash consumers into buying them. It's true that a big company can more easily afford market research polls to see if a new bar of soap is going to send every housewife speeding to the supermarket. It can also afford expensive ads in national magazines and television commercials. Still, it is consumers' tastes that prevail; many a six-figure sum has been blown to promote a dud. Rather than an economy in which big corporations force-feed us their baubles, the obverse description is more accurate; a particularly attractive bauble can create a big corporation. Think again of the Polaroid camera, invented by an out-of-work engineer. It sold so well that it made him rich and formed the basis for a large and successful corporation that now sells a variety of cameras and other products. There is a consumers' marketplace out there, and there are some simple rules by which it operates.

The market is an organized system of exchange, and the organizing factor is an information medium. It tells producers just how much or how little consumers value each good they've offered for sale and tells consumers how much of society's resources were required to produce the goods offered for sale. This information medium is called the price system. It doesn't always work, and it almost never works properly for some classes of goods. But where it does function, it is a quick, efficient medium, compressing pages of information into a few digits preceded by a dollar sign. Price alone, however, is not sufficient; we must also take account of the quantity of a good sold. Price multiplied by quantity equals expenditure for consumers as a group, and at the same time it equals revenues for producers. Now, there is a "law of demand" that says the higher the price of a good, other things being equal, the smaller the quantity that will sell, and the lower the price, the greater the amount that will be sold. Simple enough! But it's a law that's often unheeded. Still, we have to think about the rule before we can understand its limitations.

When speaking of demand, we usually mean everyone's demand for a good or service. (*Demand* really is a poor word; it suggests to non-economists that buyers are pounding on shop doors, growling and "demanding" to buy things; all it really means is that people desire a good and are willing to pay a price for it.) But before using the notion of a product's overall demand, we should take note of the fact that each person has his own demand schedule for every object he buys. He has a set of quantities he will demand at each given price for each good. Only by conceptually adding up all the individual demand schedules do we arrive at a general, average demand schedule for any particular item. This schedule then tells us, within the severe limits of the "law of demand," how people, on the average, feel about the item, whether they want it very much or not.

The "law" has an important corollary that is sometimes hard for even businessmen to understand. Think what would happen if you, as a producer of coffee, for example, wanted to lower the price of a pound. The law of demand would say you'll sell more cans of coffee, but since you've cheapened the price, won't you wind up just breaking even?

Say last week you sold 100,000 cans of coffee at your usual price of $2.00 each, which is the going price. But this week, at the Coffee Processors Association dinner, a disgruntled waiter has spiked the gin with essence of lysergic acid. So you and your colleagues, all stoned on LSD, decide to cut the price in half. This week your company sells coffee for $1.00 a can, and as a result you have orders for 200,000 cans, double the ordinary amount sold. But you haven't made any more money this week. Last week you sold 100,000 cans at $2.00 for a gross revenue of $200,000. This week you sell 190,000 cans at $1.00 and receive $190,000 in gross revenues. You lost money. You get on the conference phone to your friends in the coffee industry and trade sob stories. You guys can't figure out what made you crazy enough to chop prices like that. In revenge, you all decide to raise them even higher than before, to $2.50 a can. At this new higher price, you get orders for only 90,000 cans. Gross revenue—price multiplied by quantity sold—is $225,000. That's a little better than before all this price-changing started. Lesson: That coffee is a good possessing what's called low *demand elasticity*. In other words, the demand for coffee is inflexible, and pretty unresponsive to change in price. Why? For one thing, coffee is a habit-forming substance. It is more a necessity than a luxury to most people, and the bill for coffee isn't really a huge part of their personal budgets. So they'll buy about the same amount of coffee even if the price goes up a bit. They might buy slightly less, but they don't give it too much thought except when the price changes very dramatically. Coffee, cigarettes, gasoline for cars, toilet tissue, razor blades, and a thousand other little necessities of life possess little demand elasticity.

Inelastic products, can however, become more elastic as time goes by. Gasoline is a good example. After the 1973 Arab petroleum embargo, when oil-producing nations raised the price of crude oil by four times and the price of gasoline at the pumps shot up from 25 cents a gallon to 50 or 60 cents (and more recently to $1.00) per gallon, there was no immediate diminution in the amount of gas sold. Everybody needed gas then as much as they did a month before. Gasoline was endowed with almost perfect inelasticity of demand. Consumers would buy the fuel at almost any price. What choice did we have? We had to drive our cars. So in the very short run, a span of a few weeks anyhow, the new OPEC price couldn't hurt sales. But from then on, people had the time to rearrange their lives to use as little gasoline as possible. At the same time, entrepreneurs mused that with gas at $1.00 a gallon, it might be cheaper to make alcohol fuel from corn husks or to extract oil from shale and process it into gas, or try any number of substitutes, including mass transit (one of the many great advantages of living in New York City is that you don't need a car and would in fact be a fool to keep one). The excessively high price of gasoline stimulated the substitution of now-less-expensive equivalents. Most products are surprisingly substitutable, because people are ingenious. Scientists have calculated that most of the things we use are made from a few common elements—iron, copper, et al.—and we could fairly easily adjust to a life without hydrocarbon fuels. Instead we'd need a little more energy from other sources, especially nuclear fusion and solar power. The resources that have absolutely no physical substitute are quite rare. And by 1980, seven years after the quadrupling of oil prices, statistics showed that Americans did indeed respond by lowering their demand for petroleum products, especially gasoline. People who didn't know that inelasticity of demand fades with time were stunned by the news. They will be even more stunned when they see the decline in gasoline sales after true gas substitutes hit the market in large scale. Even by 1978, major oil companies had decided to close at least one fourth of all their gasoline stations, because there wouldn't be enough business to support them. As time goes on, the demand elasticity of a product always increases. It's a rule to remember.

And what of a product with elastic demand, as opposed to inelastic? It's the other side of the coin. "Elastic" products tend to be non-necessities, even luxury items that can be forgone, and they tend to be expensive. Or if they're neither, they can still be of elastic demand if there are a large number of substitutes for a given brand. For instance, it may be that any particular brand of toothpaste has high elasticity because there are fifty other nearly identical brands sitting on the grocery shelf. Still, most goods of elastic demand fit the stereotype of the luxury item. And since the desire for the luxury good is flexible, its sales are quite responsive to its price.

In this case, raising the price very much can have disastrous effects but lowering it can give the merchant a bonus. He can actually bring in more sales revenue at the lower price—that is, more than enough to make up for the decline in per-unit revenues.

Let us say we no longer sell coffee; instead we hawk Mercedes-Benz cars. Now our four-door 280SE goes for a modest $25,000, plus taxes and dealer prep., of course. But we blow a pile of money in the casino of the San Juan Hilton and need cash. We cut prices to $22,000. We had been selling 15 cars a month at the $25,000 price, which came to $375,000. But at $22,000 we sell 45 a month, and that gives us $990,000 in gross revenues. Not only did we cover the extra units needed to match the former revenue, but we added $615,000 to our revenues. We could pull it off because of the Mercedes' demand flexibility, its elasticity for the great majority of consumers. Sure, there are a few flamboyantly rich souls who think of a Mercedes as a strict necessity, not a luxury, and they'd doubtless throw away any sum for one, and the more the better (because more extravagant). But they don't count here because they're not a large enough group to change the total effect of consumer feeling. It is taste and opinion and, more important, techno-

logical necessity or lack of it that determine the elasticity or
inelasticity of any good.

But demand elasticity may be meaningless when the law
of demand is bent. There exist powerful forces that subvert
the proper workings of the price system. One is the simple
fact that the price system is an information medium, and information often costs money. If information costs gum up
the works, the quantity sold need not necessarily fall when
the price of a good rises. On the other hand, drastic price re-
ductions may not result in a single sale simply because people tend to use price as an indicator of quality. No woman of
means would touch a mink coat priced at $500. She'd be
positively insulted if anyone dared to suggest that she
should buy such an obvious "rag." Instead, milady prefers to
shell out $5,000 for a coat she knows is worthy. And logic is
on her side nine times out of ten. In fact, no one but a slave
or a charity worker with a large bank account could make a
good mink coat for $500; that wouldn't even pay for the
pelts.

And who will buy a $60 television receiver? As is the case
with a multitude of technical products, ordinary consumers,
unless they happen to be engineers, can't make informed decisions about how well a TV set is designed and assembled.
We therefore have to assume that as one goes up the scale of
price one goes up the scale of quality. This is not true by
any means all the time, but it's the only working assumption
we have to go on. Ratings such as those published by Consumers Union are helpful, though they quickly become
dated as new models arrive in the stores, with new features
and specifications. (One sometimes wonders if the frequent
model changes are in part to confound the product testers.)

When product quality and price information are hard to
come by, advertising can heavily direct demand in favor of
the advertised brand. Rental cars come to mind. For years
Hertz has advertised heavily as the major car rental company. Avis, its main competitor, created some attention with

its "number two" commercials, but Hertz is the big name in the industry. There are, however, half a dozen other car rental corporations. Now, it's not necessarily true that these other companies are inferior; in fact, they're cheaper and in some cases do a better job because they need the business. But we don't have the ways or the means to test the quality of each car rental service, so we go for the highly advertised, expensive one, hoping that its familiarity and success mean the company is really better. If we follow the logic we've adopted in these circumstances, we reverse the law of demand. As something gets more expensive, we buy more of it.

Suppose a new car rental company, the Hollywood Flash Car Rental Co. (as written up in *Newsweek* and *People*), moves in next door to Hertz in the airports of America, charging double Hertz's rate and offering cars of the same quality. The only difference is that its cars are a touch more gaudy. The Hollywood Flash Car Rental Co. will be flooded with reservations from people wanting to flaunt their chic affluence. They assume the steep price must mean prestige, even star treatment. Hollywood Flash will make a gold mine from such premises. Here we have two violations of the law of demand, one by the use of price as an index of quality, the other by what is known as the snob effect. It, too, must be given due weight. Many a bright, trendy entrepreneur has earned a fortune by making his product chic.

A few years back, the Perrier Bottling Company, a French concern that sells bottled spring water, wasn't growing very quickly. Its sales were off in Europe and it decided to try its luck in America. Perrier water seeped slowly into the consciousness of the chic through ads in the New York *Times Magazine*, *New York*, and *The New Yorker*. Soon it became fashionable to order a Perrier with a twist of lime. Now shapely girls in running clothes drink Perrier water through a straw as they jog around Central Park. Monsieur Perrier makes a killing selling water—plain water—in a city where the tap water is unpolluted and good-tasting. This is not logical, but it's still economics, and the effect is measurable as profit on the bottom line of the Perrier income statement. The buyers of Perrier water know full well that they are spending their money for plain water, albeit enhanced by carbonated water and the cachet of fashion. These customers are voluntarily offering Perrier some quantum of monopoly power in the market for water, since to some degree —mostly determined in the minds of consumers—its water is different, a different product from New York City tap water, really.

But the other side of this coin is the amount of monopoly power granted to businesses out of plain ignorance. When it's hard to compare prices of alternative goods and their quality, then the seller of the "blind" product gets to be a monopolist of sorts. The most obvious case is where mere distance turns a mom-and-pop grocery store into a fierce local monopoly. Dear old mom and pop, operating what may be the only store for miles around, can gouge the hell out of their customers with prices double those charged by the half-dozen grocery stores in town. Sometimes little family stores will take advantage of calamities to jack up the prices further. When a hurricane hit New Orleans a few years ago, one small grocery store charged five dollars for each candle it sold, simply because no other store in a highly damaged part of town was open. "Convenience stores," the 7 Elevens for instance, get themselves a bit of monopoly power in their neighborhoods simply by being available and open twenty-four hours a day.

A less satisfactory example of the small—but powerful—monopoly is the single local bank in a country village. Until recently, townsfolk weren't apt to travel around the countryside seeking the best interest rate for their loan. It would have cost too much time and money, and besides they assumed the price of credit would be the same everywhere. Of course, lately, with time and space compressed so much by electronic technology, bank customers are likely to be more sophisticated.

Unchallenged local monopolies exist also in the largest cities, regardless of the most modern communications. I'm speaking of car repair shops. You turn your car in, tell the repairman what you think is wrong, then wait and hope. Eventually he'll give you a call to tell you the bad news, and you pay *whatever* he says you must. You can sue; but how many thousands will it cost, and how many years will it be before your case is even called before the bench? The repairman isn't unaware of these factors. He has all the information about your car's difficulties because (a) he is your mechanic, the technician who knows more than you do, and (b) your car is locked away in his garage. If he says the car has a busted cylinder, how can you dispute it? If you want to come by and inspect, he can make sure it has a broken cylinder by the time you get there. Once in South Carolina I put my former MG with New York plates into a repair shop. When I got it back, the car had beer can tops and cigarette butts on the floor, not to mention mud. Had the good ole boys taken the MG out for a night on the town? Indeed they had. Was there anything I could do? Yes, I could meekly pay the sixty-dollar repair bill and drive away.

It's the hypothesis of Richard Holton, a business administration professor at the University of California, that the consumer information problem is only getting worse. Holton says that because of our economy's success over the long haul, many more people have much more cash to spend. They also have many more artifacts to spend it on, and these products grow more complex as they incorporate the latest technological twists. And, he says, the rate of technological innovation is increasing, so that new products have a shorter life-span before becoming obsolete. The result is that it is getting harder to find and absorb accurate information on many of the goods and services we buy. And as soon as we learn the ins and outs of the newest video tape recorder, for example, it is outmoded, replaced by new digital tape equipment with a radical technology.

The information gap grows especially large for big-ticket items—refrigerators, cars, and stereo loudspeakers. We don't know how long the things will stay "modern," how long they'll last, how much servicing they'll require, or even whether the price we paid was fair.

The rise of official consumerism is intended to cut our product information costs and to punish the purveyors of false information. We have federally mandated package labeling calling for the listing of all ingredients in food products. We have cars that must list their gas mileage as determined in the laboratories of Washington. We have warning labels on packs of cigarettes. All this is still a drip in a very large bucket. Do we proceed to say that government regulation, as odious and costly as it is, can be the only solution for our growing insufficiency of information about the things we buy?

We are running up against a basic drawback of the market economy. Those who don't keep their wits about them will part with their money at the hands of swindlers, whether in the guise of streetcorner hustlers or faceless corporations. This has always been true, even if the problem is worse today. Look in an old Sears catalog, at the lurid advertisements for magic contraptions that promised to cure cancer by passing a weak current through the waist. I remember the story of a farmer who saw a newspaper ad for a "surefire" potato bug killer, for the then considerable sum of five dollars. Enthusiastic, he sent off for the new breakthrough in insect control. What he got in the mail was two wooden blocks. One had a small hole in its center. Printed instructions told the farmer to place a potato bug in the center of the block and slam the other block down on it. The instructions "guaranteed" that this method would work. Who could dispute the fact?

Consumer information or the lack of it can often thwart

the workings of the law of demand, as can people's feelings about the future course of prices. If people expect a recession within the very near future, they might expect prices to fall or, more likely, for prices not to rise so steeply as they had before the onset of slack times. Thus they would defer all major purchases not required for daily living. House hunting would be put off until a few homes started going begging from the lack of people with credit (though in these days homes sometimes become a drug on the market simply because they are too far out in the suburbs or threaten monstrous heating bills).

Yet in real life, few people can know just when a recession has arrived. Even when Tom Brokaw says so on "The Today Show," with the full backing of every government statistic, still prices may not obey the rules and neatly fall. Indeed, throughout the 1970s, prices tended to rise during the larger parts of most recessions. Schooled in the inflationary recessions of the last decade, Americans have come more and more to adopt the European habit of "investing" in durable goods, assets that will yield years of valuable service, whether one speaks of a mink coat or a Picasso oil painting. And they go ahead and buy now merely because experience has shown them that, if they don't, prices will simply be higher next year and outrageous the year after. When they do this kind of buying, they often do much of it on credit, which is also clever, because then they get to pay back their debts in dollars that are less valuable than the ones the banks gave them. All this is clearly wise behavior for the individual, even if the effect of all these individual actions is to help fulfill the inflation prophecy by driving prices up further, including the price of credit. When everyone with access to credit is clamoring to buy town houses, vintage sports cars, Gucci shoes, and "investment" furniture, prices can't help but be bid upward.

The extra inflation created by this strategy of putting one's depreciating dollars into hard assets, whatever the price, can distort markets in unpleasant ways. For instance, in the summer of 1978 I bought a couple of cases of 1976 Morgon Beaujolais wine, an exceptional vintage at a relative bargain price of $5.45 a bottle. During the months that I was casually uncorking my "investment" to taste its pleasures, 1976 *grand cru* Beaujolais was quietly disappearing from the shelves of the wine shops. By Christmas of 1978 there was no premier 1976 Beaujolais to be had anywhere in Manhattan, at any price. One frosty Saturday I went the rounds of every major wine emporium in the city and found only some second-rate bottles of '76 Beaujolais, none of which was worth the inflated price. I discovered that over a matter of months fevered wine demand had turned my modest Beaujolais into a rare wine. But alas, the investment was far too liquid. I had drunk all but two bottles by then. The hope of capital gain had been squandered in my ignorance of the unusual demand for fine French wines. However, the Beaujolais, while it lasted, did provide me with delightful service.

The law of demand is subject to more qualifications. For example, people's habits are often slow to change, so that a change in price will not immediately result in the expected change in quantity demanded. Some would-be buyers may be waiting for the price to fall further before they buy. If a potential buyer of a hand calculator had much patience in the 1970s, he could have waited until sixty-dollar calculators became eight-dollar calculators by the end of the decade. Of course, for him to wait so idly, his demand for calculators had to be extremely elastic.

Then, too, a change in the quality of a product can confound the rule of demand, because the relation between quality and price and therefore quantity demanded is left out of the equation. Suppose a television manufacturer adds a new circuit to his nineteen-inch color TV model, a circuit that "locks in" color transmissions. If the price of the set remains the same at retail, then what we have in effect is a lower true price. Assuming that the addition of the new circuit did represent an improvement in quality and not useless gimmickry, we are able to buy a better product at the price of the old one. And even if the television maker raises the price to cover the cost of the new circuit, he hasn't really raised the price of the old television set at all. We are now buying a new and different product at the new price. It may have the same look, the same name, the same model number, but the presence of the new circuit makes it distinguishable as a new product. So what looks like a price change on the demand schedule is not one at all and the demand analysis falls apart.

This law of demand, in fact, has so many quirks that it's only really valid as an impressionistic generalization, a sort of economic adage. This statement will shock many economists, who put great faith in the static decimal points of demand calculations. No doubt they are already aghast at my refusal to illustrate the hallowed law by the use of a graph showing the classical elementary downward-sloping demand curve on axes representing price and quantity sold. But the fact is that, even aside from the manifold exceptions to the law, demand for any good or service is constantly changing. To be accurate, the curve would have to be floating in the wind. Even if tastes stayed the same for a time, new products would be making old ones obsolescent; lower-priced models would steal the market from their high-priced prototypes; circumstances would alter the demand for a good, as when the oil price quadrupled and suddenly there was booming demand for home insulation, heat exchangers, solar heaters, and the like. Meanwhile, in the depths of the oil crisis, you couldn't give away long Cadillacs. (They were subsequently shortened and made gas-efficient, and since time eased the fear of Ultimate Doom that followed the oil price hike, their sales picked up over the years, at least until the gas shortages of 1979.)

In a Cambridge Union debate between William Buckley

and John Kenneth Galbraith on the energy question, Mr. Galbraith quoted some demand elasticity numbers for petroleum products. "Where did you get those figures?" demanded Buckley. "I made them up," retorted Galbraith. And he might well have meant it. It is safest to regard statistics purporting to indicate the exact demand elasticity of a product or service as extremely suspect. At every price there's a different elasticity. The idea of elasticity is fine and useful, however, as an impressionistic description of the degree of caution with which consumers approach the purchase of a good.

Before the first airline deregulation back in 1978, the executives of corporations such as Eastern, United, and TWA all assumed—nay, were convinced—that airline travel was a service that had quite inelastic demand, because they knew that the great bulk of their profits came from business people who had to travel. With such low elasticity, lowering fares would merely mean the same passengers didn't have to pay as much. The airline business would feel no perceptible change except for a smaller profit.

The companies were safe from low fares until Alfred Kahn, then chief of the Civil Aeronautics Board, and Senator Edward Kennedy forced deregulation on them. They kicked and screamed all the way, until one morning they woke up and found the airline business booming as it had never boomed before. After the record profits of post-deregulation 1978, airline executives had been proven dead wrong about the elasticity of their product. When tested in the marketplace, airline service turned out to be highly elastic. Ordinary citizens, discretionary travelers, responded quickly and forcefully to the decline in the price of airline tickets. In doing so, they provided the airlines with far more than enough to make up for the smaller per-unit revenue from each ticket. This is the lesson of demand elasticity. Many businessmen have never learned it. And not understanding how a simple analysis of demand elasticity can indicate the way consumers will respond to a price change, they miss the opportunities to reap rewards by lowering prices, or, if their products have low elasticity, of raising them.

What we have in the airline example is a case of beneficial *price discrimination*. That is, the airlines, unwittingly and involuntarily, by government deregulation, are more fully exploiting the different demand elasticities of different customers who fly. Business travelers have a rather inelastic demand. They fly because they are required to: so they can visit a plant, meet a customer, or write a story. Raising or lowering the price of an airline ticket won't affect them much. The company's probably paying for the ticket, anyhow. But at the other end of the scale are occasional airline passengers, whose demand for airline travel is very responsive to ticket prices. So the airlines, forced by the CAB, offered them up to 50 percent discount fares in the tourist class, if they were willing to wait on standby or be bumped from a full flight.

Price discrimination is also used by electric utilities when they lower electricity rates for those who use power during off-peak hours, say between midnight and dawn. Obviously, those who need electricity at a certain time, usually during peak hours of use, are the customers with inelastic demand, so there's little use in lowering their rates. For the most part they'll pay the going rate. But the lower off-peak rates can induce nonurgent electricity uses, thus spreading more evenly the distribution of electric power, and possibly reducing the chance of a blackout. There is, however, one kind of price discrimination that is justly outlawed by the 1936 Robinson-Patman Price Discrimination Act. Suppose a corporation is the sole regional supplier of bauxite to two firms that process it into aluminum, used in cars and home appliances. Suppose further that one of the aluminum firms is a subdivision of the supplying company. The supplier charges a rock-bottom rate to its own subdivision and charges an outrageously high one to the other processor. The supplier is trying to drive the independent processor out of business, by making him pay prices he can't possibly afford. This has been done many times, and successfully, to break the back of competitors. That's why it is prohibited.

Supply, as even the most naïve non-economist knows, is no more than the other side of the coin. Whereas the law of demand shows the quantity demanded dropping as the price increases, the law of supply shows that producers will supply more of their goods as the price rises. Again, this is a common-sense proposition. As the price of something is bid up by shouting consumers who demand more than is available, that new price offers juicy rewards for the producer who can make enough of whatever it is to supply it to them. Without the price increase, he might be unable to supply more. For that would require a new assembly line at least, with new packing and warehouse facilities, plus more trucks and more workers to run the expanded operation.

The old price was not high enough to yield the producer the extra money needed to invest in the expensive new machines and people he would need for increased output. But the new price offers him enough of a premium over the old one for him to know he'll soon have enough coming in to support a larger operation, pay back any debt he might have incurred, and perhaps make a fatter profit. Since the law of supply claims to describe the behavior of producers rather than consumers, our "exceptions" to the law of demand don't necessarily apply here. Producers' "tastes" don't really enter into their decisions of what and how much to manufacture. If a manufacturer is a dedicated businessman, his aim is to make a profit. Perhaps he's in, say, the dressmaking industry in the first place because of his tastes, but that's as far as it should go. He'll make decisions based on what will sell to consumers, whether the going price will support the operation he has in mind, and what will satisfy the stockholders, not to mention the banks that have lent him cash. If he doesn't make decisions that boost the profitability of his company, he'll be in trouble, sooner or later.

The law of supply is much less flexible than the law of demand. One can easily find products for which the demand increases, via the snob effect, as the price goes up. But I am unable to point out a good whose quantity supplied increases because the price falls. This can only happen in unnatural circumstances, as when the government distorts the marketplace with price controls or nationalization of industry.

Supply elasticity, like demand elasticity, is a nice little concept to remember in analyzing economic events, but it doesn't do to put it in exact denominations, for the same reasons true of demand elasticity. There simply is no such thing as a single supply elasticity number for any good. At every price the supply elasticity is different. Yet supply elasticity indicates how quickly and readily a good's supply can be augmented, and analysts have ignored this at their peril. Recall the early 1970s "housing crisis." It was a time when housing prices were climbing skyward, as they are wont to do. Television network correspondents clutched their microphones and sobbed that, with the price of housing up so high, average people couldn't afford homes anymore. Therefore, they concluded, we were in for a long, grave national housing shortage. By 1980 the populace of America would be huddled in apartments, except for those lucky few who had already bought houses. But by 1980 more people than ever were living in houses. To tell the truth, more adult singles had joined traditional families in home living. The news correspondents had forgotten that a higher price calls forth more supply, and the apparent elasticity of housing is such that it takes a relatively few months for the effect to be felt. Clearly the supply elasticity of housing is finally dependent on the technology of home building, and how quickly it can be mobilized.

Differing supply elasticity is simply the result of differing technology. It takes at least twelve years to erect a chemical plant—even longer, with the tight environmental legislation of the late 1970s. But it takes only a year to get corn back in the silos.

Agriculture, however, presents a special case. Farmers are dependent upon the uncertain bounty of Mother Nature. The supply of wheat and cattle and avocados depends on the vagaries of the weather in Russia and the high price of (petroleum-based) fertilizer in Pakistan. A drought or a freeze in one continent might pull prices to levels that make farmers of another gleeful. So what do they do? Of course, they double or triple their acreage and enlarge their herds, to take advantage of the new demand created by the inflexible supply of food. And as surely as night follows day, the shortage this year is father to a surplus the next, when there is no drought or freeze. Grain is so plentiful that it has to be piled outside the crammed grain elevators in the countryside of Texas and Iowa, where birds and mice will take their gluttonous fill of it. This seesaw of boom or bust is what prompted Congress long ago to concoct a large and intricate system of price supports and bank credits for farmers. The annual growing cycle of most farm products has proved insufficiently elastic to accommodate the whims of the agricultural market. Once farmers have planted their fields, they have fixed the maximum quantity of crops they can harvest, regardless of consumers' wishes, acts of God, political coups, wars, or Washington bureaucrats.

If consumers' tastes and habits govern the demand for consumer goods in the short run, over the long haul it is demographic change that controls trends in demand. This is hardly recognized by most economists, though Lord Keynes himself knew it. In fact, he ascribed much power to demography. He wrote in his *General Theory* (1936): "The great events of history are often due to secular changes in the growth of population and other fundamental economic causes which, escaping by their gradual character the notice of contemporary observers, are attributed to the follies of statesmen or the fanaticism of atheists." And demographic changes fail to capture the imagination of mainstream analysts because they occur over long periods, decades at least, and are rarely immediately apparent even after their completion. Yet the government has been collecting reasonably complete census statistics for years, and more than a few shrewd businessmen have plowed through these tracts to divine whether their product has a future or not.

A wise textbook publisher could have known as early as 1970 that his business would be slowly crumbling, as college enrollments dropped off after the post–World War II baby boom spent itself. That baby boom gave us a swollen population of young people who have now finished college and are in adulthood. No peacetime baby boom has replenished the supply of students. During the years 1946 to 1964, 76.4 million babies were born in this nation. Some 70 million are still living, aged sixteen to thirty-four, and the youngest make up some of the largest classrooms educators will see for a good while—at least until these people have their own children, for the birth rate has dropped dramatically in America, and there's no guarantee that we'll ever see again the huge young population of the 1960s, which gave us the counterculture of that era, among other things, such as high crime rates and large welfare rolls (for teenaged mothers predominate on these lists). Changing postwar styles mean childbearing is no longer de rigueur.

The important things to look for in the population are the birth (and death) rates; the median age of the populace; the mobility of the population; the rate of marriage and divorce; the education level of different age groups, and their levels of income. If we know the trend of these factors, then we'll be able to anticipate what kinds of products people will want in coming years. (We'll also have an idea of how competitive the job market will be in the future.)

But we have to add another slice to the pie before our

analysis becomes elucidative. It is a fact that as we travel through life we spend money in different ways. This idea is usually illustrated by three curves on a graph. The first shows how wealth changes as we get older. What happens for the "average" person is that he doesn't start to accumulate much wealth until age forty or fifty, and he reaches a peak at age sixty to sixty-five. The figure might seem a little conservative. What of all the movie actors and rock singers? But if you've ever been to a watering hole of the very rich, such as Palm Beach, you'll soon notice that the very rich tend to be very old. (One evening at the Royal Poinciana Theater I saw more walking cadavers than I've ever seen elsewhere.)

The second curve shows that the average person's physical assets—possessions like a house, a car, a set of furniture—begin to accumulate at age twenty and continue in an upward trend steadily until about age fifty, when the number of these possessions begins to fall. And since this average person is busy accumulating physical assets for a good thirty years, then during that time he's also in debt, from around age twenty to age fifty, more or less. So much for the life cycle of wealth.

Look now to the year 2000. The baby boom generation will be between thirty-six and forty-six years old. By that time these citizens will have finished any childbearing they are likely to do. They'll be raising their kids and moving up the job ladder. What's significant is that we'll have this bulging age group moving into a period when they'll have already bought homes if they're going to, and when they'll be spending plenty of money on food and clothing for their children, and more on education. Can we then expect slack housing demand and heavy demand for the latter items? All other things being equal, we can. What if the divorce rate continues to climb and the number of single adults retains its upward course? To that extent, these expectations will be foiled. But even with the large number of single people, the baby boom represents a tremendous blip on the demographic charts, and that has importance for the sellers of goods and services. From the viewpoint of the consumer, it means as much. For if housing demand is to be slack in the year 2000, then home prices will be lower than they might otherwise be. If food and clothing are to be in high demand, their prices will go up. In the job market, we can expect heavy competition for the middle-management and upper-management positions for which people aged thirty-six to forty-six are eligible. That's in strong contrast to the generation born before World War II. These folks had an easy time getting a good job since executives were in demand and the economy was growing in the 1960s. It could be said that they were born with demographic silver spoons in their mouths, for even before they joined the corpus of working people, they had passed through uncrowded classrooms in the 1950s. The members of the baby boom have not fared so well, and they'll be forever cursed with their numbers. They crowded the schools and have crowded the low-level job market so that more than a few have become downwardly mobile. They have turned out to be less affluent, less secure, less comfortable than their parents. Some have slipped from the middle class to the working class, or from the upper middle class to the lower middle class, if we demarcate the middle class by the possession of a college diploma. They have faced competition at every turn, and when they reach the year 2000 they'll see that competition in the things they buy. Competition will follow them to the grave, perhaps literally; in the year 2030, when the denizens of the baby boom are past retirement age, cemeteries may be very crowded, too.

And what of migration trends? Americans are extremely mobile, if not rootless, people. About 20 percent of us move at least once a year. The thing to know is where we move to. Throughout the 1970s we flocked to the hallowed Sunbelt, stretching around the southern and western perimeter of the

United States. But already, by the twilight of the decade, the golden Sunbelt had visibly dimmed, as pollution, congestion, crime, and decay had invaded its supposedly nice pastoral precincts. We began to hear talk of an urban resurgence. New York City has again become quite fashionable. It bustles with activity, and the flight to the suburbs seems to have reversed gears, at least a bit. The migration pattern has also reversed. In the most recent times it has been the wealthy who have moved back to the city and the poor who have fled to the suburbs. Now those businessmen who can forecast whether these trends will continue, and how strongly, will be able to make a profit if they act on their forecasts.

13

The Imperfect Market

THE MECHANICS of demand and supply, mediated by prices, are what makes the private marketplace work. Of course, like most human institutions, the market doesn't often work perfectly. Anyone would prefer to be an absolute monopolist instead of a competitor who has to scramble to make money. But as long as we are competing, who is going to draw the line between fair and unfair competition? Indeed, how can any competition be fair as long as consumers lack accurate information about prices and quantities and qualities?

Well, we can enter the theoretical vacuum just long enough to watch how the laws of demand and of supply mesh with each other in the most perfect conditions. We have the provisioners and the provided, the suppliers and the demanders, out in the marketplace. The amount of a good that's supplied increases as the price increases. The degree to which the supply increases—the supply elasticity— depends on technology and the costs of production. Now the amount of a good that's demanded falls as the price goes up. How much it falls depends on demand elasticity, that is, on consumers' needs and priorities and tastes. Suppose the price of beef goes up. Slowly, to be sure, the amount of beef supplied will increase, and at the same time the amount demanded will decrease, until ideally supply should exactly match demand. Then the market is said to be *cleared*. There are no more steaks on the grocery shelf. In this state of the cleared market, every consumer is left satisfied. Every producer has his pockets full of cash, at least enough to go on producing. Here is the exalted justice of the free and open market.

Sad to say, however, the only markets that regularly clear are glaringly noticeable for the fact that they do. And if they do, it is only for an hour, or a day. Remember, demand is always changing. With a changed demand for watches, for instance, you get a different set of prices at which different quantities are demanded, so the point of intersection of supply and demand schedules changes too. The market will no longer clear.

Then what will it do? There are two possibilities. In the first case, the new price of watches is lower than the market-clearing price. Now, the lower the price, the more quantity demanded but the smaller the quantity supplied, so we have too much demand for watches. Then what? All the demanders, like a crowd around a bin of sale items in a bargain basement, start fighting and harassing the seller, we shall say. In the process, if everything is working as it should, the low price will be bid upward. This is because price is a means by which to ration. The highest bidders get the few remaining watches. Those who are willing to pay the most will win the prizes. If not by price, how can a merchant dispose of his goods? The new higher price of watches, the new price that was bid up by the shouts of people demanding to buy watches, sings its song to the makers of watches. It says, make more watches and you shall be rewarded. It supplies incentive, this higher price. Soon, depending of course on the supply elasticity of watches, more watches will be in the stores.

It all sounds very smooth, and in the sweet, ordered heaven of abstract economics it runs as smoothly as clockwork. But out in the grimy streets, gremlins gum the works. They are the gremlins of information costs, whom we've already met, and expectations, whom we've also met, and there is a third—government interference, whom we'll get to know only too well. Assume again that the price of watches

—or, to give it reality, we'll say the price of Meadows brand watches—is below the market-clearing price. More Meadows watches are demanded than supplied.

Our first problem is to figure out just how, in actuality, the excess demand for Meadows watches will cause the price to be bid up. After all, these watches aren't sold at auction. So who's doing the bidding to whom, and how are the proceedings transmitted to Meadows, the somewhat dotty watch magnate? We'll assume Meadows watches are sold in jewelry and department stores across America, after having been shipped from the Meadows Watch Works in Geneva, via New York. Since the price of these watches is below the market-clearing one, people all over the country are snapping them up, leaving store shelves empty and stockrooms bereft. Things get worse when *People* magazine prints a photograph revealing that Catherine Deneuve wears a Meadows watch on her creamy thigh. Women are calling up store owners, and immediately store buyers are on the phone to the Meadows U.S. offices in Manhattan. They demand triple last month's order of watches, and now. The harried order taker says it'll take five weeks at least, but he'll see what he can do. He types out a message on the Telex to Geneva. It arrives at 11 P.M., Geneva time.

The next morning, the watch works manager confronts Meadows with the Telex message. "I can't produce that many watches in five weeks," he says. "We've got more than we can handle, m'sieur. New York wants all the watches we can make. Los Angeles says forget the price, just send watches." Meadows listens offhandedly while drinking his morning coffee and smoking his morning pipeful. He tells the manager to go ahead and start twenty-four-hour production. Then, for the remainder of the morning, Meadows paces back and forth in front of his gold-inlaid Provençal desk. Should he consider expanding the plant, adding another watch assembly line? But he couldn't just add an assembly line. He'd also need a new machine shop to shape

the parts that go into the watch, and new space to store
extra raw materials, and new warehouse capacity. So he decides to wait a month or two and see if the demand surge is
more than a fluke, more a tribute to Catherine Deneuve's
thigh than Meadows' watch. The twenty-four-hour production will hold them for now, he tells himself.

Meadows thinks he's being prudent, and he's probably
right. In being prudent, he's also confounding any notion
that, somehow, in the case of excess demand, consumers literally bid up the price of the wanted item, and in so doing
cause a larger quantity to be immediately supplied. This is
absurd in the case of most goods. If a jeweler, seeing the un-
satisfied demand for Meadows watches, raises the price 30
percent because that's what he learned should happen (in
Economics 101), he won't call forth a new quantity at that
price. He'll only cheat his customers. More Meadows
watches will come on the market only when old Meadows
finally decides to expand production. Since this expansion
costs big money, Meadows will undoubtedly offer the
watches at a noticeably higher price. Will it be the "market-
clearing" price? Only by sheer chance. How does Meadows,
or anyone else, know what that price is? He could assume
that it would be the price of a watch of comparable or
higher quality but different brand. Maybe, maybe not. He'll
have to find out by learning, over a period of weeks, months,
or years, how consumers react to the new price. In any
event, he's not likely to change the new price once he has
set it. Changing prices costs extra money for new price
tags, labor to take off the old tags and put new ones on, and
so on.

You may object that Meadows, though he be in his dot-
age, still has long experience in the watchmaking trade. He
knows how consumers react to different watch prices. Perhaps he does, to a very limited degree, but his knowledge
will not suffice. Prices don't usually fluctuate up and down,
offering businessmen lessons in consumer responses. Rather,

they tend to go only up. The question is how much they can go up before they choke off the market and store owners are left with a pile of unsold Meadows watches. No one can know that. It's dependent on the state of demand, not at the time the decision was made to produce a certain amount of watches, but at the time of sale, which may well be long afterward. Demand, remember, changes constantly. And market research won't help. Meadows could commission a study in which innocent consumers were asked if they would buy a Meadows watch, Catherine Deneuve model, at $275 instead of the old $250 price. The answers would be unreliable. People's opinions are one thing; their behavior in the store is likely to be another, based on the impulses, needs, and cautions of the moment when they spy a gold Meadows watch glistening in the window.

The unknowable nature of the market-clearing price explains why retailers must keep inventories of merchandise as buffers against misjudgment. But it costs money to keep goods in storage, so the retailer wants the minimum inventory possible. While he doesn't want to run out of supplies, on the other hand he doesn't want to be stuck with a big inventory that, in a business downturn, sits on the shelf eating up working capital.

Now we can generalize the thought: the concept of the market in which demand meets supply and the market clears automatically works well for an old-fashioned auction market, and it actually happens in organized commodity markets like the Chicago Board of Trade, or in stock markets like the New York Stock Exchange, or at antique auctions held by Sotheby Parke Bernet. Outside of these situations, few markets clear. Many may come close to clearing over long stretches of time. But the market mechanism corresponds to very little we know in twentieth-century life. The idea, however, is a useful fiction. It's another of those intellectual devices that lets one think clearly about an economic problem—as long as one doesn't take the device too seriously.

Now suppose that Bloomingdale's, the perennially fashionable store on Lexington Avenue in Manhattan, sells Meadows watches for $285; but there's a little hole-in-the-wall store down on the Lower East Side where you can get one for $250 cash. The difference in the two prices is accounted for, in part, by information costs. The price at Bloomingdale's is $10 above list price; half of the premium, we can say, represents the value of the time it would take to search out the little store on the Lower East Side. Part of it represents the advantage a Bloomingdale's buyer has in knowing he'll be able to exchange the watch or get an immediate refund if it should malfunction. Down at the store on the Lower East Side, you pay cash and there are no returns. That's what the hand-lettered sign on the display case says. (The rest of the $10 premium pays for the extra expense of Bloomingdale's fancy digs and the cost of running its large credit card offices.) On the other hand, what if a jewelry store uptown in Harlem sells the watches for no less than $300? The higher price is probably accounted for by the extra expenses of an armed guard and television security cameras and all the apparatus of security the shopkeeper is obliged to use in a high-crime neighborhood.

The government gets into the act, too. It regularly injects political considerations into the economy of the marketplace. Basically the government can tax a product or subsidize it—either with cash or by tax credits, which have the same effect—or it can directly control a good and, in extreme cases, outlaw it. When the government taxes a product we buy, the outcome will be different depending on the demand elasticity of the good. If we're talking about a tax on a good of inelastic demand, such as cigarettes or whiskey, that will raise money for the government. We're talking about products which, by the definition of elasticity, accommodate the addition of the tax to the selling price because these goods are considered necessities and they're small items in the grocery bag.

But if the taxed product has demand elasticity—that is, if it's a big-ticket item, perhaps a luxury—then buyer reaction to the added tax will be large. That's what demand elasticity means. So consumers will slow down buying, and the government won't raise any cash, yet it will discourage purchase of that item. Suppose the item were a gas-guzzling roadhog. If the government taxes low-mileage cars and lets the fuel-efficient compacts go free of taxes, then the government can encourage the purchase and use of small cars. This kind of thing was proposed in Congress a few years ago but hasn't yet come to fruition. One of my favorite ideas is that, to discourage the noise, congestion, and pollution caused by cars in New York City, the city government could charge five-dollar tolls on all bridges and tunnels leading into Manhattan, and charge maybe a dime to leave. When I mentioned this idea to the chief of the Environmental Protection Agency, he immediately and rightly declared that no, it wouldn't go. The idea is politically unmentionable. Many people who drive cars in Manhattan have clout.

If the effect of a tax depends on elasticity, that of a subsidy doesn't. This is a supply notion, not a demand one. Subsidizing production by grants or by tax credits such as the business Investment Tax Credit (to promote the buying of new plant and equipment) will of course encourage production of the subsidized product. It's also possible for a government to subsidize the purchase of goods. Egypt has subsidized rice so its citizens could buy the food at low prices. It cost more than the Egyptian government could afford, but that didn't seem to matter as long as foreign aid was flowing in. Governments can, in general, use subsidies along with taxes to redirect consumers and producers.

But our national legislators are not all of rational disposition, so they often tax the wrong things and subsidize the wrong things and end up distorting the economy. For in-

stance, a few years ago the government set up cash subsidies
for small independent oil refineries, to encourage their
growth in the face of competition from oil giants such as
Mobil and Exxon. As it happened, this subsidy inspired a bizarre growth in small refineries, which happen to be so
small that they're much less efficient than the large-scale
models with their economies. Farming has long been subsidized to protect farmers from nature's vicissitudes. Non-
profit radio and television broadcasting is partly subsidized by the government, partly by corporations. The arts
are subsidized by grants distributed by the National Endow-
ment for the Arts. College students are subsidized by cheap,
liberal federal loans. In fact, a whole American middle class
was formed on government subsidies, though the patriarchs
of this generation have most bitterly complained of subsidies to the poor. This was the World War II generation,
the generation of men who came home from the war in the
1940s, married, bought homes subsidized by the Veterans
Administration, got college degrees paid for by the Veterans
Administration, and got job preference, too, because of their
veteran status.

It's interesting that a subsidy of another nature has
done much to create or perpetuate urban slums. The subsidy in question is the indirect one of rent control, whereby
a renter has to pay only a fraction of what the landlord
would charge if the apartment were on the open market. This is quite helpful to the tenant, except that if the
landlord's total rent isn't enough to pay for the increased
cost of the building's maintenance and repair, then he won't
be able to afford to keep the building in working order.
Then the boiler bursts and there's no heat for months and of
course the tenants decide to pay no rent at all. The landlord
gives up and abandons the building. The city thus loses the
landlord's real estate tax money, and soon the tenants leave
for warmer and safer buildings. If any tenants are too poor
or ill to move, they might be burned to death, for sooner or

later the abandoned building falls into the hands of vandals who torch buildings for fun. Hence the ugly, burned-out specter of a place like the South Bronx. In turn, the high rate of building fires means that no one will construct new buildings in the neighborhood because, among other things, the fire insurance rates are too high. The neighborhood thus further deteriorates, until finally, as is happening in the South Bronx, grass begins to grow where slums once stood. This may be the only hope. Some have predicted that in a decade or two the uptown New York slums will have been transformed into a neighborhood of new luxury apartments and town houses. It will thus rise Phoenix-like from the ashes of urban stupidity.

Direct government controls have a different character from taxes and subsidies, which can encourage or discourage but can't actually prevent anyone from buying or making what they want. Direct controls, such as wage and price controls, call for ceilings on all wages and prices, on pain of jail or fines for violators. What, then, is the result? If the government puts a ceiling on the price of bread, what happens when the cost of making bread becomes more expensive and eventually, as the population grows apace, there is an increased demand for it? Sooner or later more bread will be called for than is in the hands of grocers. With the passage of time, what once was an appropriate market-clearing price for bread has become too low to ensure a supply. And the grocer can't raise the price. We get a shortage of bread. But then some smart sidewalk entrepreneur might go to the bakery and buy some bread at a premium over wholesale prices, to sell on the sly at a black market price. He can supply bread, if people are willing to pay the higher price. If not, they'll get none, because, since the grocery store can't raise its price, the bakery has stopped shipping bread. On the other hand, the baker might deal with the price controls by simply cutting down on the quality of the bread he produces and supplying the lower-quality bread at the same

184

price he used to charge for his best brand. All these things regularly happen when the government seeks to control wages and prices.

And every exception or exemption from the controls will breed all manner of efforts to take advantage of it. Suppose controls' clamp a lid on wages for workers but leave an exemption for the wages of newly hired people; they can start off at whatever salary they can fetch. Then people will take full advantage of the exemption by job-hopping, going from an old job to a new one to get a raise. This happened all too frequently during the latter phases of President Nixon's wage and price controls.

More damaging than these peccadillos, however, is that wage and price controls bottle up demand pressures on a large spectrum of products. When the controls come off, therefore, the prices of a thousand goods soar, quickly adjusting to their correct levels. The result is inflation—and, sooner or later, recession. But even after decades of proof that wage and price controls don't work except in wartime, Presidents still use them because they seem to remain popular with the public. Maybe it's the idea of coming down on those dastardly big corporations that makes wage and price controls so appealing to an untutored populace. They are assuming that corporations and unions are greedy and keep pushing up wages and prices because of their unquenchable selfishness. In fact, the controls attack only the symptoms of inflation and not its causes, as we shall see.

One curious way to escape the ravages of inflation and the grasping tax collector is at once ancient and quite modern. It is simple barter. Before there were markets it was the method of trading, and it has returned again in the inflationary era. A dentist friend agrees to yank your teeth if you'll do his tax forms. No cash passes hands, no prices are paid. The parties decide what each other's services are worth as services, instead of in terms of inflated, taxable paper money. So the amount exchanged depends not on how much the government has inflated the currency but on the "real" value of the goods and services. And it is tax-free.

Even without serious inflation, barter is always present. I saw my most memorable instance of barter in Bogotá, Colombia, about 1967. I was sitting with friends in a dimly lit bar-cum-bordello downtown. A prostitute and a shoeshine boy walked in together and passed to the back and into a rest room. In a few minutes the shoeshine boy came out, his clothes all disheveled. The prostitute followed, with two knee-length white leather boots in her hand. The terms of the trade became immediately clear.

One difficulty, however: a return to the barter system would be tremendously complicated because every product must be valued in terms of every other product, instead of just in terms of a single good, i.e., money. If you're selling your ability to fill out tax forms, you have to figure what that's worth in terms of dental service, or a friend's beach house, or whatever is offered in exchange. More important, the person offering has to calculate what your tax service is worth. It can get sticky. Yet during periods of inflation that disadvantage is outweighed by the prospect of dealing in inflation-free "prices" that also happen to be tax-free.

14

Inflationary Fallout

THE RUNNING BATTLE between the corporate power structure and the bureaucratic power structure is not fought in a vacuum. The fallout from the war settles on groups with lesser bases of power. Consumers pay higher prices when energy costs and regulations raise production costs. Taxpayers see their after-tax incomes dwindle when the government bureaucracy demands a fatter budget with which to fight for its turf. In turn, people want higher wages to compensate for the higher prices and higher taxes. And we come to the realization that the fallout from this war, this long-range power struggle, is *inflation*. Only thus can we explain the persistent inflation of the 1970s, when the battle reached epic proportions. Only thus can we explain its indefinite continuance. Throughout recorded history, inflation has been a curse visited on populations by tyrannies. If inflation is more pervasive than it has been in many decades, perhaps it is only because the present tyranny is larger and more powerful than ever and engaged in a conflict that only exacerbates the normal excesses of central governments. When corporate power tangles mightily with bureaucratic power, it is citizens who suffer the wounds.

Inflation, the scourge of economics, shows an analogy to cancer. Cancer cells are normal except that they're multiplying out of control—mad cells on some dark, unholy crusade. Inflation, in like manner, sends the profit motive wildly out of control, transformed from worthy endeavor to hot greed. Loosed from any moderation, the invisible hand of competition becomes the heavy hand of uncompromising selfishness, in which each higher price ups the ante in the struggle to stay ahead. The price of bread and milk goes up, and soon the secretary and the auto worker get higher wages so they can still buy the amount of food they used to buy. But these higher wages represent higher costs to employers, so they raise their prices to cover the new expenses. Then, of course, workers will want still another raise so they can once again buy the same amount of bread and milk as before, and more (for they also desire to progress in their lives).

This is the famous wage-price spiral. We can, for a moment, restrict our thinking to this spiral and try to figure out who is to blame for starting it all. If you are of a liberal persuasion, you'll prefer to believe, no doubt, that big corporations started the whole mess by raising their prices to unconscionable levels, since they naturally have the monopoly power to do it. But if you're a conservative, you'll declare that greedy monopoly labor unions forced wages beyond reasonable levels, and the poor employers were thus forced to pass these outlandish costs along (conclusion: we must break the unions). And if you're a touch wishy-washy, you'll say it was the work of unions in full obscene collusion with management. That is, the unions would negotiate fat pay increases, and the companies, with their monopoly powers, would pass on the costs to consumers in higher prices. After all, it would be worth while for the company, to avoid long and expensive strikes. Whichever theory you might subscribe to, you'll extend this labor-management misbehavior to the whole economy by assuming that union wages set the standard, if not the floor, for nonunion wages.

What truly links wages and prices is productivity. This is defined as physical output per unit of input. We can speak of output per man-hour of labor, or output per machine-hour of equipment, or output per BTU of fuel. Output per all of these inputs is known as *total-factor productivity*. It is the conceptually right version to use, but the government compiles output only per man-hour because it's easy to measure. Very well, an increase in output per man-hour is an increase in productivity. For if this output per man-hour has risen, that must mean the worker is more efficient or is using more efficient equipment. Whatever the source of his new efficiency, he is obviously providing his bosses with something for nothing. The employer gets more output to sell with no increase in his costs. But his free lunch doesn't last for long. The worker's labor union will be quick to point out the productivity gain: if labor productivity at a plant has increased by 5 percent, then a 5 percent wage increase will not be inflationary. In recent times, however, productivity has fallen behind but wage demands have not. If a union demands and gets a 5 percent wage increase but productivity has increased by only 1 percent, then after the wage raise goes into effect the same amount of factory output will cost the boss 4 percent more than it used to. He's going to try to recoup that lost 4 percent by tacking it onto the selling price of his products. The result is inflation, because productivity lagged.

For the better part of the twentieth century, productivity grew at an annual rate of approximately 3 percent. One reason was that workers were moving off farms, where productivity growth was perpetually low, to urban industrial jobs where it was high. Another was the high rate of industrial automation. Machines do take the place of people, but the effect on productivity is helpful for those remaining on the job because each can produce more per man-hour. By the end of the 1970s, however, the move from farm to city had been completed and has even been reversed to a tiny extent. And much formerly productive automated machinery has been rendered inefficiently expensive by higher world petroleum prices and anti-pollution regulations.

In connection with productivity, one often hears the term *capital-intensive* bandied about with considerable inaccuracy. It merely means that a high proportion of machines is used in a production process. Oil refining is capital-intensive because it requires miles of pipes and huge distillation stacks and only a few maintenance workers. Dressmaking factories are *labor-intensive*, in contrast, because they employ legions of workers at sewing machines. Most American industries tend toward the capital-intensive, in part because in this nation labor has always been the relatively scarce input, whereas in poor nations it has always been capital (plants and equipment).

But let's look at the wage-price dilemma another way. Recall that the wage is also a price. It is the price of labor services. Therefore the wage-price spiral becomes the price-price spiral. We might as well simplify it to the "price spiral," and wonder how it got started, rather than chasing our tails over whether unions or corporations are guilty of excess greed. If we reformulate the problem as a simple case of prices going up, then we must look to a different cause. Economic theories of inflation abound, but they come to little on purely theoretical grounds. A glance at history might be more enlightening.

Start after the Peloponnesian War, in the Greece of the fourth century B.C. Inflation, fomented by a large increase in the number of Greek coins, created unemployment and class hatreds. But inflation was worse in the Egypt of a century later, where kings minted too many coins, imposed stiff taxes, and had the government sell foodstuffs at excessive prices. In the Roman Empire, corn went up in price five times from the time of Christ's death to the third century A.D., but by the fourth century the corn price had risen one hundred times. Thus in 301 the Emperor Diocletian issued wage and price controls. From whence did this inflation arise? From the excesses of tyranny, for the empire's bureaucracy was swollen with regulators and the citizens were crushed with taxes. The imperial army was simply too big and too expensive for the empire to support. Productivity slid, farmlands returned to weeds, and anarchy reigned. Trust in the Roman currency disappeared. Rome was in fatal decline. Not until the reign of Heraclius was a currency established that kept its value. But then Pepin the Short introduced into Europe the silver penny, which stayed fairly stable and became the internationally accepted currency of the 1100s.

As we go further, we can speak of the wage controls in the England of 1349 due to the wage demands of those who survived the Black Death, with the government's debasement of the coinage again a factor. We move to Spain of 1600. The heavy burden of a government bureaucracy, oppressive taxation, military spending, and the removal of silver from the Spanish coins eventually brought Spain down from the pinnacle of worldly power. All this culminated in the Great Crash of 1680, a terrible depression.

What of America? By the late eighteenth century the American currency was so inflated that a pair of shoes cost $5,000. Inflation recurred regularly up to the Civil War when it became virulent, fostered by war spending and the profligate printing of greenbacks. After the war and up to the end of the nineteenth century, gold production in Colorado, Alaska, and overseas kept inflation on an upward trend, though it had leveled off for a time after the fall of the South and the end of Civil War hostilities.

During World War I, consumer prices rose only moderately, but wholesale prices climbed twofold as the government spent its money on raw commodities needed for the war effort. By the end of the war in 1920, these prices fell. The drop was precipitous. It was a massive deflation that cut most prices in half, back to their prewar level or below. Inflation later resumed its upward course, but in 1933 the Great Depression sent prices plummeting as the nation's money supply abruptly began to shrink (on the bad advice of the nation's bankers, who nursed a rather silly theory that money didn't affect the economy. Bankers relied on the notion that their only task was to offer short-term loans to businesses at fair interest rates).

But because of the huge deflation of prices, nominal interest rates fell, though the "real" interest rates were quite high if deflation was taken into account. Bankers of the day, however, didn't take that into account. So they felt justified in keeping credit tight, thereby worsening the situation disastrously. Meanwhile the Federal Reserve system stood by passively as more than six hundred banks failed. Milton Friedman has suggested that the whole mess could have been avoided if Benjamin Strong, the wise and effective chief of the New York Federal Reserve Bank, had remained healthy and had steered the national banking system through its crisis.

Often when the American economy looks bleak, as it periodically does, citizens wonder about a repeat of the Great Depression and latter-day Cassandras predict another crash. But the possibility is no longer realistic, since President Franklin Roosevelt established the Federal Deposit Insurance Corporation to insure bank accounts and thus end bank panics. Then, too, national unemployment insurance, Social Security and welfare, and "countercyclical" federal budget provisions guarantee that we'll never have mass starvation except in the most unimaginable of catastrophes.

America didn't really come out of its depression until the Second World War, and though prices rose as the war was financed, the rise was not dramatic. Price controls administered by John Kenneth Galbraith and a bureaucracy of thousands kept prices bottled up until peacetime, so that when controls were lifted at the end of 1945 prices doubled within three years. A small recession followed, then the Korean War with its escalation of inflation due to war spending, and then a period of stable prices. The quiet years lasted only until 1958, however, when a recession came, which made way for another era of creeping inflation, fueled at first by a loose monetary policy and government deficit

spending and later by the war in Vietnam. There were the
ineffective Kennedy "guideposts" to get business and labor
voluntarily to slow down the wage-price spiral. President
Johnson's tax cut in 1964 sped it up.

Still this was only baby inflation compared to the inflation
of the 1970s. Prices were rising at rates of 3 to 4 percent. Yet President Johnson's politically motivated failure
to call for a tax increase to pay for the Vietnam War,
and Congress's failure to pass such a tax surcharge early
enough, caused the inflation to proceed heavenward at rates
of 5 percent, a level that was considered devastating at the
time. The 1968 tax hike came too late, and rapid growth of
the money supply had by 1971 presented the nation with
something of a crisis. When inflation hit 11 percent in the
summer of 1971, labor leaders, led by AFL-CIO president
George Meany, were calling for wage-price controls. Even
conservative Arthur Burns, the chief of the Federal Reserve
System, delivered a famous speech at Pepperdine College
calling for some sort of wage-price mechanism. But President Nixon righteously spent his hours playing the ardent
foe of mandatory wage and price controls. Now it so happened that the Democratic Congress of Nixon's reign had
passed legislation giving him the authority to impose wage-
price controls. Congress handed Nixon the legislation to em-
barrass him, back before inflation had gotten virulent. So on
August 15, 1971, Richard Nixon, that staunch opposer of
government interference in the marketplace, pulled his
wage-price authority off the shelf and shocked everybody by
declaring mandatory controls. (At the same time Nixon announced the end of the system of fixed money exchange
rates.)

Even by 1980 the nation had yet to be rid of the deleterious effects of those Nixonian controls. For the controls
had done no good. Prices did fall back to less than 5 percent
rises while controls were in effect, but this would have happened anyway because of slack demand. It is quite possible

that prices would have fallen even further if Nixon had not imposed his controls. But no matter, for when the controls were finally dismantled in April of 1973, what followed was the worst American recession since the depression of 1933. It happened this way. Quite simply, the Nixon controls had clamped a lid on pressures that burst forth when the controls were lifted. These pressures grew from suppressed demand. Shortages had developed during the control period, because suppliers weren't allowed to raise prices so they might expand their output and satisfy the desire for their goods. As controls came off, prices shot upward to finally adjust supply and demand. By the end of 1974 inflation was close to 14 percent.

Then came a giant straw that broke the economy's back, a dynamite blast whose effects spread beyond the economy to menace the national psyche with scenes of the Final Apocalypse. First, in October of 1973, the Arab oil-producing nations slapped an oil embargo on the United States and escalated the price of crude oil. These unprecedented, continuing increases in the oil price created an instant and massive transfer of wealth from the bank accounts of Americans to those of oil sheikhdoms. Suddenly the nation, and much of the rest of the non-Communist world (Russia and China have their own oil) were meek hostages before Bedouins of the desert. Americans saw it as an unpretty spectacle of ill-deserved wealth, of windfalls created by the sheer whimsy of nature: it just happened that the dry, poor deserts held most of the world's known reserves of petroleum. Our enforced homage to the Arabs put a permanent end to American self-images of insuperability. It put a huge dent in the economy, as people started adjusting to spending considerably more for gasoline—sixty cents a gallon where a few months before it had been twenty-five cents—and home heating oil and all the plastics, chemicals, fertilizers, and countless other things made from petroleum.

The coup de grace was brought off by the Federal Reserve System when it abruptly ended the growth of the money supply. Credit became unavailable. Businessmen's confidence was shattered. Investors ran from the stock market, and it duly plunged to record low levels for the postwar period. The stock market fell to the 500 range in December of 1974. The die was cast, and corporations all over America began mass layoffs. The news was grim. At the time I was living on Cape Canaveral, Florida. In a masterstroke of bad timing, I had only a few months earlier resigned a job as a newspaper editor and columnist. At the Cape Canaveral unemployment office I had more than enough company. The place was like a Manhattan subway at rush hour on a rainy day—packed to the rafters with the victims of OPEC's machinations. Layoffs hadn't been unusual at the Cape, what with the space program and regular cutbacks that put thousands at a clip out of work. But the recession that began around August of 1974 outdid any layoffs Congress created when it curbed space spending.

The gloom was all in the news then, and when Walter Cronkite intoned in a solemn voice that the American economy was going to hell faster as every hour passed, the gloom naturally deepened. Businessmen, their confidence lost, retrenched even further, canceling all plans to expand their operations, firing workers, closing plants. Investors nursed their wounds from all the cash they lost when they panicked and ran away from the stock market. Journalists and pop philosophers wove theories of Imminent Doom, the end of growth, the twilight of modern civilization. But if the days were black for most of us, they were glory days for every manner of amateur economist and political faith healer. Books poured forth explaining how Americans who wanted to save themselves from the Final End should buy gold bars, stock their cellars with canned fruit, and oil up their shotguns. The dollar was worthless, they declared. One author warned that people who really and truly wanted to be safe should move to a house isolated deep in the country, away from paved roads and sewer lines. All this was necessary, the author confided to the select few millions who shelled out two dollars for his paperback, because soon the economy would fall away into anarchy. Americans, not unlike rabid rats, would be roaming the streets in mean packs, foraging and stealing food, looting indiscriminately, killing for survival.

The irony of all this doomsaying was that the people who preached hell on Earth called themselves "realists" and even turned out a magazine with that title. Thank goodness their "reality" never descended from the pages of their literature into the life of the real world. No, these gentlemen had followed a path of logic that had taken the wrong turn at a crucial crossroad. True, the nation was in bad shape by 1975. But it didn't follow that things would get worse at an accelerating speed. Too much would be at stake for that. Panic on Wall Street is one thing, but panic on Main Street will bring out troops. Men of reason won't let our affairs get so out of hand. Did the "realists" think the President would lounge in the White House as madness took over the nation? Even Gerald Ford would do better than that. And we experienced no nightmare scenario, perhaps proving—for all who needed proof—that civilization is cemented by the decent instincts of most people and their willingness to preserve that civilization.

At the other end of the political spectrum from the "realist" seers of anarchy were the remnants of the counterculture, who saw the energy crisis and the stock market dive and the lowered living standards of high unemployment as a further beckoning call to Mother Earth's rustic life-style. The recession became the rallying point for Stewart Brand and his *Whole Earth Catalog* band. It was time, they claimed, to get back to nature, to go to the countryside and build a log cabin and spend one's days churning butter and learning to play Appalachian hillbilly music on the violin. The Whole Earth types, who loved to piddle with contrap-

tions for making natural gas from chicken droppings, really
shared a vision of doom not too different from that of the
"realists" of the far Right. The message of the counterculture, Whole Earth division, was that the modern industrial
society was running out of fuel forever and civilization must
revert to something approaching the Middle Ages by today's
reckoning—crude hand technology, mule-drawn plows, all
the homely arts of frontier life, arts that somehow seemed
imbued with goodness compared to the giant automatic machinery of factories owned by the fathers of upper-middle-
class Whole Earthers. That machinery of course, was in-
herently sinful in their myopic view. Economies of scale
meant nothing to them, nor did the reality of raised living
standards for millions of the unprivileged. But after all, this
kind of back-to-nature romanticism has existed for many
centuries; European ladies and gentlemen of nobility retired
to farms to elegantly entertain themselves by playing rustics
for a week or two.

Obviously, these Whole Earth people are a partial rein-
carnation of the Puritan tradition that reaches back to the
founding of our nation. Deeply hidden in their collective
psyche is the notion that pleasure is wrong, that the hair
shirt is the only proper vestment. I didn't fully realize this
until I found out in the early 1970s that the back-to-nature
movement, though it counted itself as in the forefront of the
counterculture, detested the marijuana and hard rock of the
generation. These were sinful was the unstated message.
These types—the men with nineteenth-century beards down
to the chest, women in long drab floor-length dresses, no
makeup—spent their leisure hours playing old Appalachian
bluegrass tunes of many generations ago.

I found this puzzling. It occurred to me that in their
world of solar energy and horse-drawn wagons there would
be no electric guitars to tear the filaments of the ether with
fine energy. And with the sound of the electric guitar the
very essence of rock music, I decided that these people of

the Whole Earth communal camp were not my kind of people, which is a judgment I'm sure they'd be the first to confirm. Then, too, I have lived in rural Colombia where life is little changed from what it was in the seventeenth century. Charming, yes, but only for an affluent American who has his modern conveniences and can fly home again whenever he takes a notion. For the Colombian campesinos, walking barefoot on dirt floors and using strips of old newspaper for toilet paper are not so charming. Back in New York, I met some Colombian immigrants—illegal ones, doubtless—who cleaned the toilets in the newspaper office where I worked. I often spoke to them, in Spanish, and finally asked how they could prefer cleaning toilets and living in New York slums to the lush, beautiful countryside of Colombia. Their answer was devastatingly simple: money. Yes, Colombia was lovely, but there was no work and life was too crude. If it seemed pleasant to middle-class American youths, that was because they didn't have to live as many of the Colombian people lived.

Much to the amazement of recession-bred doomsters, the American economy slowly revived. Soon people who spent heavily on gold bars were taking a bath, and people who had sold out of the stock market at a loss when it hit 500 were weeping as they watched the market climb back up past 800 again. In retrospect, December 1974 was the optimum time to buy into the stock market, not pull out. I wish I had realized that. I could have made a small killing. But I, like everyone else, was immersed in the psychology of economic holocaust.

The economy had revived by 1978, when employment reached record levels and 3.5 million people joined the work force. Inflation, which had dropped off to a "mere" 6 percent after the recession, climbed to 8 percent in 1978. By summer the Carter administration was getting worried enough to hire Robert Strauss, the smooth-talking Texas Democrat, as its anti-inflation jawboner. By the fall of 1978 the Administration saw deadly political handwriting on the wall and instituted a program of voluntary wage-price guidelines not unlike the guideposts tried earlier by Presidents Kennedy and Johnson. Also resembling Nixon's wage-price controls, these guidelines were based on the theory that inflation is caused by greedy businesses and labor unions. But unlike the Nixon crew, the Administration was wise enough not to make them mandatory, thus avoiding the tremendous boom of inflation when the controls were taken off.

In fact, Carter didn't have the legislative authority to impose controls, and he faced tremendous tactical problems if he ever tried to acquire it. First, the influential congressmen who controlled the banking committees that rule over such legislation said they were opposed to controls except in a national emergency. Even if they weren't opposed, however, the process of getting the authority would call for public hearings, during which businesses would be raising their prices like crazy, in anticipation of the new controls.

Still, the talk of wage and price controls persisted. Right-wing business analysts and corporate executives enjoy scaring luncheon audiences with their "inside" information on imminent controls. A few labor leaders whine for controls as a way to punish big business. But by 1979 even the liberal Joint Economic Committee of Congress came out with a report showing in precise numerical tables how wage and price controls fail to work.

Well, if we look back at the sketch of past inflation and the subsequent recessions and depressions, what is the conclusion? It is that in past decades and centuries, government fiscal and monetary policy has exacerbated inflation. It has debased the currency, bloated the nation with money, taxed its citizens into the poorhouse, and perverted the workings of the marketplace. When inflation grew to insupportable proportions, a deflation followed with attendant unemployment and general hardship.

In the present era, government's economic policies continue true to form, making worse what is an already deleterious situation caused by the conflict between big business and big government over the shape of the American democracy to come.

15

How Money Works

MONEY, said to have been invented by Croesus, is the lubricant and the medium of the market system, though it isn't strictly necessary to the marketplace and many tribal societies have existed, albeit at a rather primitive level, without its use. The convenience money offers is the elimination of the costs of barter, whereby each thing to be traded must have a "price" in terms of every other thing for which it is to be traded. If you manufacture and trade shoes, you'll have to figure out how many pairs of shoes you're willing to give for a pound of sugar and for a lamp and for socks and for anything else you want to own. At the same time, you'll have to reckon whether you could get more value by trading for other goods. Then the people offering sugar or lamps have to determine if your shoes are worth so many ounces of sugar, and so on. Very tedious.

Money becomes the common denominator and thus allows much greater efficiency. It also serves as a storehouse of wealth. Rather than have your wealth in cattle, which you may not be able to sell immediately if you want to, money is acceptable to everyone. It is liquid. In reality, its acceptability is what makes it money—whatever people accept as money *is* money.

The concept that money is whatever people accept as money comes as a great shock and blasphemy to those authors and self-appointed seers who claim the economy totters on the brink of disaster because our money is no longer "backed" by gold. This is a favorite theme of recessionist doomsters; it is their general theory of catastrophe, good for a best seller every few years (long enough for readers to forget that the disaster predicted in the previous volume never occurred).

When the major currencies really were "backed" by gold —that is, when they could be exchanged for gold bullion— then economic health depended on, of all things, the vagaries of gold mining. When a new vein was discovered, boom times followed, for the money supply could expand. But the more usual result was long recession. The system was arbitrary, as silly as determining monetary policy by consulting the stars or groundhogs.

In the present era, the gold market is ruled by fear just as the stock market is moved by greed. When the inflation indexes start to flutter skyward, "gold bugs" come out of the woodwork to invest in gold bars and coins and even gold mine stocks. They exhort their frightened compatriots to buy gold, too, and, of course, to oil up the shotgun. Then the price of gold, sure enough, rises. However, once it becomes clear that Armageddon isn't imminent, the gold fever slacks off. In any case, the people who made money in gold made it years ago, by purchasing the stuff at $40 an ounce and selling it at $200 an ounce. Since the mid-1970s the gold market has often been a suckers' market. The professional gold hustlers make their cash from books and newsletters offering black visions of the future, along with assurances that salvation lies in the purchase of gold.

With or without backing, money has a huge flaw as a trading mechanism. Stated simply, too much of it equals inflation. To see how this happens, consider that money, like any other good, is supplied and demanded. But it has its peculiarities, which we will note. For the moment, however, think what happens if consumers and businesses are supplied more money than they need for the day-to-day paying of bills and for the savings account. They will spend the rest, right? And when they go on a spending spree, they bid up the prices of the things they want to buy. These people have extra money and they are willing to pay an extra $500 for a Persian rug or Provençal antique desk. So the prices of these and countless other goods and services rise. After a period of time it takes more money to buy the same amount of things. Workers are quick to understand this, so they ask for higher wages to enable them to buy as much as, if not more than, they used to be able to buy. If their employers give them higher wages, they're better off only for a brief time. For those higher wages mean higher costs to the employers. What will they do? If they can, they will pass on these higher costs to consumers. Workers, with their increased paychecks, are back where they started. If they ask for still higher wages, as they are wont to do, then prices will rise by the same amount. Around and around we go.

Economists distinguish between anticipated inflation and unexpected inflation. The conventional rule is that if consumers expect more inflation they'll buy in advance before prices soar, while if they are hit with unexpected inflation they'll pull in their horns and stop spending money. The only problem with this is that nobody fails to expect inflation anymore. It has been such an integral part of our financial experience for so many years that few are inhibited enough to save their money. To the contrary, we read of inflation in the papers and hear its every turn announced on television news. When it promises to get worse, we merely think more intently about what we ought to buy, which nice big expensive thing we should "invest" our emaciated dollars in.

The peculiar thing about the inflation cycle is that money is supplied, not on the basis of any market supply and demand, but on the basis of what the government surmises to be the right amount of money circulating in the economy. Let's see just how money is created. It's a cascading process; money is fed from one institution to another until it's spread around the country at about six times the value of the original money the government released onto the financial market. This neat trick is possible because of what banks call *reserve requirements*. For example, if a bank's reserve requirement is 10 percent, then that means for every $100 put into the bank's checking accounts, $10 must stay at the bank to cover checks cashed and money withdrawn from savings accounts. So the other $90 can be loaned out.

It is by loaning money that a bank is supposed to make its money, via the interest rate it charges. The great majority of a bank's borrowing customers are businesses, but it obviously lends consumers such things as car loans and home mortgages, and even lends cash to the government. Of course, banks would rather not put up with the risk of loaning money to people in the community. It would be infinitely safer, and therefore more profitable, to take all that idle checking account money, minus the 10 percent reserve requirement, and invest it in Treasury securities and bonds issued by big companies. But the law prohibits banks from spending more than 10 percent to purchase securities; their job is to loan money and thus facilitate commerce in the community where they are established.

Now, keeping in mind that the reserve requirement percentage is all the bank has to keep locked away in its vaults (actually, most of it is on paper, in the account books), notice what happens as money multiplies throughout the economy. It begins in a smallish room on the fourth floor of the stately Federal Reserve Bank Building in lower Manhattan. In that room, with its sleek computer terminals and banks of telephones, Federal Reserve *open-market* operations are executed. Suppose the Fed's Open Market Committee, a group of hoary financial men, decides to loosen up the money supply of the nation. Then a specialist in open-market operations will immediately go on the market by telephoning some dealers whose sole task is to buy and sell Treasury securities from or to the open-market desk at the Fed. Well, the open-market operations man will say he wants to buy $1 billion worth of Treasury securities (T-bills they call them in the trade—"Treasury bills," "bonds," "securities" are all synonymous). He and a dealer work out the technicalities for a minute or two, and teletypes click, so that the government, in the guise of the open-market man, has bought the T-bills and in exchange has deposited a billion dollars in the bank account of the T-bill dealer. Now watch what happens. The bank that holds the T-bill dealer's account—we can name it the Last National Bank—is now able to loan out $900 million, as long as it keeps the other $100 million safe in the coffers. (What the Last National Bank does is deposit that $100 million in its own account at the Fed bank, which is its *reserve account*.)

Suppose the Last National Bank, after many weighty meetings and reference checks and discussions, decides to loan the $900 million to the Zilch Corp. so it can develop and market a new kind of electric toothpick. Well then, the Zilch Corp. naturally deposits the check for $900 million in its bank, the River Bank. Now the River Bank keeps the 10 percent reserve requirement—it comes to $90 million—and loans out the $810 million that's left over. Suppose the River Bank loans the money to Mervyn's Fashion & Fuel Corp., so it can build a shopping center outside of Dallas. Then Mervyn's deposits its check for $810 million in First Cowpoke National Bank of Greater Dallas. First Cowpoke sets aside 10 percent—$81 million—in its Fed reserve account, and then loans out the remaining $729 million to Formaldehyde Estates, a real estate development on the outskirts of Dallas. The builder of Formaldehyde Estates deposits the $729 million check in the Dallas Bank of Commerce and Rodeos. Do you see where we're leading? Isn't it fun? The process keeps on going, like a successful chain letter, until that $1 billion the federal government issued has multiplied to $6 billion, though in reality the system has leakages. The money supply is now fatter, which simply means that people have more money in their hands. Which means they spend it. Which means prices go up, as people escalate their demands for everything under the sun.

But if the government can spread cash around, it can also make it scarce. This fact, along with the government's ability to spend money directly to buy things allowed in the budget, offers the chief means by which the government directly influences the course of the economy. Of course, it affects the economy indirectly in other ways, by imposing costly regulations, for instance. But it is through monetary policy, combined with fiscal policy, that the government tries to steer a course toward healthy growth and full employment. That it has failed so miserably in doing this is another matter, and one that we will not ignore.

A curious thing happens every time the government adjusts the money supply. It is that interest rates change. This can hardly be surprising, since when the government increases the supply of money, it is making more money available to loan out, and thus the price of borrowing money gets cheaper: that is, interest rates fall. And if the government takes money out of the economy by selling T-bills to its dealers, there's less to be loaned out. The demand for credit is greater than the supply of it in this case, and the price of credit—the interest rate—goes up, to ration the available new money. So, according to whether the government tightens or loosens the money supply, interest rates will go up or fall—in the short run. The degree of the change varies, depending on how busy the credit market is. In other words, if a lot of companies are hot to borrow money—if there's the equivalent of a boom in loan demand, and a rush to bankers' offices —then the price of credit may rise regardless of what the Fed does to lower it. This actually happened in the late 1970s. The Fed bought T-bills like crazy, trying to expand the money supply and therefore lower the interest rates which then prevailed. But heavy loan demand in 1977 kept interest rates high despite its efforts.

Rising prices can also add their bit to the interest rate, independent of what the Fed does. If prices are going up at 6 percent a year, then a year from now a dollar will buy 6 percent less than it can buy today. A banker realizes this, and he wants all of his original amount when his one-year loans are due next year. So he will have to charge an interest rate above 6 percent, because if he charges just 6 percent, then when the year is up and the borrower pays him back he'll have only what he started with. There's no profit in that. Instead, the banker charges 6 percent plus a premium. He may charge 8 percent so he can make a 2 percent profit after subtracting the 6 percent inflation.

We have loan demand and inflation both influencing interest rates, independent of whatever the Fed does. In view of this, does it strike you as odd that the Federal Reserve has always judged the condition of the money market by looking at interest rates rather than at the actual dollar amount of the money supply? It ought to.

The government is losing its grip on the money supply because there have grown up new institutions that free credit from the bounds of the Federal Reserve's will. Let us point out first that not all banks are members of the Fed, nor are they required to be. In fact, more and more banks prefer not to be, since state charters often allow them to keep a smaller percentage of reserves than the Fed does. The result is that there exists a *competition in laxity* between the Federal Reserve System and the state bank-chartering agencies, so each may win the most charters. The Fed has naturally lost out because it penalizes members. It used to be that all the biggest banks were members of the Fed—they are distinguished by the word *national* in their names—but the situation has deteriorated to the extent that Congress looks ever more closely at schemes that periodically come before the banking committees to require all banks to be members of the Fed.

Some new wrinkles in credit have confounded the government's control over interest rates. While realizing that a bank no longer relies on deposits to get money it can loan out, for illustrative purposes let us consider a bank that offers 5 percent on its savings accounts and charges 8 percent on the loans it makes. Clearly, the bank makes 3 percent profit. But what if a government rule makes that 5 percent the highest interest rate a bank can pay to savings account depositors? Then when most interest rates rise to 10 percent, the saver is more clever if he pulls his money out of the savings account and into a bond that offers the 10 percent interest. In fact the government did, until 1974, keep a ceiling on what banks could pay out, but this wasn't so damaging because securities that paid off the best interest rates could be bought only in large denominations, of $100,000 or more. True, some bank certificates of deposit, which are issued to attract loanable money, can be bought in denominations as low as $10,000. But by and large, banks were left undamaged by ceilings they could pay out on the savings accounts. They simply used CD's, which are "savings accounts" in the form of bonds, to raise money for loans. As long as the rates of interest the bank paid on its certificates of deposit were lower than the rates of interest it charged on its loans, the bank made money and interest rates stayed at decent levels.

Yet there was a persistent difficulty. Savings and loan associations, unlike banks, had no recourse to CD's to generate funds. A savings and loan takes in savings accounts on which it pays out an interest rate limited by law, and it uses the money to grant home mortgages. Whenever interest rates rose to high levels, people would pull their money out of S&L's so they could reap the higher interest rates found elsewhere, even in commercial banks. Savings and loan associations were no longer able to make many home mortgage loans. This put a halt to home construction and more often than not precipitated a business downturn.

But in 1978 savings and loan associations and mutual savings banks were permitted to issue *money market cer-*

tificates paying interest rates slightly higher than what Treasury bills offer. So savings and loans, and thus the home construction industry, are no longer totally at the mercy of swings in interest rates. Now high interest rates don't automatically crimp the housing market because savings and loans can get the money they need by selling the money market certificates. As long as the interest rates they charge on home mortgages are higher than the interest rates they pay on the certificates, all is well and the institutions make money.

These new money market certificates have had another, perhaps more profound, effect. They have given borrowers a powerful incentive to borrow whether interest rates are high or not. Interest rates can now soar to untold heights, beyond the 1975 recession's 12 percent prime rate (the rate banks charge their best corporate customers). And the incentive is all the more pronounced precisely because interest payments to banks can be deducted from the income tax payments of borrowers. And too, during an inflation it's always wise to go into debt, because the debtor pays his money back in dollars that have depreciated since the time he was given his loan. That is, he pays the bank back in cheaper dollars.

Therefore, if high interest rates no longer faze consumers, or the economy for that matter, has not the Fed been rendered impotent? Or perhaps the Fed should attend first to the money supply, where the signals are clearer. If Congress did force all banks to become members of the Federal Reserve, and if the Fed set about restricting money growth to match the economy's growth, it's quite possible some progress could be made in releasing the American economy from the fetters of inflation. Some economists, known as monetarists, believe fervently that monetary stability is crucial to the economy's health and that government deficit spending —fiscal policy—is harmful. You'd think that by now we would have at hand a body of hard evidence to confirm or deny that proposition. Well, there is plenty of circumstantial evidence that monetary policy makes a difference. The coincidence of growth in the money supply and growth in the price level (inflation) repeats itself throughout our history. But the cause of rapid money supply growth and the effect of inflation occur with a lag ranging from six months to two or three years. It isn't possible to predict the length of the lag. Hence monetarists call for strict, fixed growth of the money supply. Most monetarists say the money supply should grow at a steady rate of 3 or 4 percent: no more, no less, just enough to match the after-inflation growth of the Gross National Product. For example, if it was seen that 4 percent real GNP growth was most typical and healthy, then the money supply would be held to a strict 4 percent growth year in and year out, and to hell with the course of interest rates. More extreme monetarists want zero money growth. But after all, the population does increase, and the economy grows larger over time, as measured by the GNP, which has moved from $103.4 million in 1929, when it was first compiled, to something approaching $3 trillion in 1980. Zero money growth could give us a vicious permanent recession.

Still, why not hold money supply growth at 3 or 4 percent if that would help to stabilize the economy? Why has it never been tried? The answer lies in the traditions of the Federal Reserve Board and Congress. The Fed is independent of congressional action, but nevertheless it was established by an act of Congress and therefore is a child of that body. Members of Congress, hungry for votes at any cost, perpetually attempt to pressure the chairman of the Fed to keep interest rates low, because the popular political wisdom is that this will be favorable to constituents and will keep the economy buoyant. Do members of Congress care about inflation? No, they'd rather see the spigots open full. So they miss no chance to influence the Fed, even though it's nominally independent. Think what would happen if the

Federal Reserve's board members were appointed, and
fired, by Congress. Then the economy would be wrecked by
the Keystone Kops on Capitol Hill. The notion of steady
money supply growth would require presidential approval
or at least a congressional resolution—more likely a complicated new law. None of this is likely. Bankers, who carry big
clubs in Congress, would oppose it. But their opposition
would be as nothing compared to the opposition of Congress
itself, to whom the very idea of strict money supply control
is antithetical to the free-spending nature of the congressional tradition. Is not the main distinction of Congress that
its members win their votes in direct proportion to the quantity of cash they promise to distribute to their constituents?
Isn't this ethic of the government subsidy the quintessence
of American politics?

The object of fine-tuning monetary and fiscal policy is to
smooth out what we call business cycles: i.e., those recur-
ring bouts of expansion and prosperity followed by reces-
sionary doom, followed by a recovery and finally another expansion, which eventually end in a crash. The cycle repeats
itself with depressing regularity. Most economists speak of a
single business cycle as being two expansions and two recessions. And they blame the cycles on everything from sun-
spots to new inventions or the excesses of capitalism.

But let us keep it simple by starting at the trough of a
recession, and following the pattern as it happened in 1975.
Now the federal budget swings into action with unemployment compensation, welfare money, and even new programs to pay for make-work jobs. Then the Fed eases up on
the money supply so that, slowly, more and more people get
some cash in their hands. They start to buy again, and business picks up, until businessmen are so ebullient that they
rehire laid-off workers and even decide to expand. When
they actually do begin borrowing money to build a new
plant, then more jobs are created, everybody is spending,
and the economy heats up. At this point the Fed ought to

tighten up on the money supply a bit, but it never does so in time. And Congress ought to cancel those recession-born job programs, but it never does. So the economy gets over-heated with demand. The citizenry has money to spend. By this time even factories that run twenty-four hours a day can't produce enough to satisfy the lust to buy, so prices fly upward. This eventually inspires the Fed to slam the brakes on the money supply, to keep interest rates from going through the roof in the expansionary inflation. Then we are likely to see the nation plunge once again into the depths of a downturn. This is the pattern, more or less, but every cycle is different. If the recession of 1975 was worsened by the OPEC oil price shock, the recession that began in 1979, too, will have its own special treats in store.

In 1979 the economists in the White House offered a poignant illustration of the folly inherent in notions of doc-toring the economy by fine-tuning. White House advisers went around scratching their heads. Was the money supply growing too quickly or too slowly? they asked each other. What would those 1980 Social Security tax increases do? Must the Administration cut the budget, or would that bring on a recession in the election year? Should the White House engineer a quick recession and get it over with before the presidential sweepstakes? You see, it is possible to stimu-late the economy or brake it by budgetary and monetary policies, but no one knows the proper amount of stimulus or drag to apply in any given situation. Worse than that, it's not possible to predict when the fiscal or monetary pressure will begin to be felt. Fine-tuning the economy from the White House is like landing an Airbus at night without the aid of a compass or an altimeter. Frankly, I don't care to be aboard.

It seems that ever since the Vietnam inflation, when re-cessions come about the inflation rate doesn't fall, regardless of how much demand has decreased. This is a great embar-rassment to the nation's economists. They are forced to throw up their hands in dismay; none of the old panaceas have worked. Conservatives say the Fed just doesn't have the guts to tighten the money supply enough to wring out inflation once and for all. Of course, they don't mention that this would cost us a hard, long recession. Liberals, for their part, complain that if only the Administration would impose permanent wage and price controls, accompanied by a big trust-busting campaign to break up big business, then we'd at last solve inflation. But in such a large, diverse economy as ours, with literally millions of different prices and thousands of different wages, permanent wage and price controls would be a bureaucratic horror costing many millions to administer. No matter how efficiently it worked, the inevitable black markets and shortages would eventually break the controls down, unless the United States opted for a police state to monitor each transaction in the economy. And when controls come off, inflation dashes ahead to make up for lost time. The government reacts, creating a recession. Then, too, the breaking up of large corporations may seem attractive, but who will pay the costs of the breakup and what body will determine if a company is big because of the efficiencies it can exploit merely by being big? More than that, who will pay the price for the inefficiency resulting when such corporations are dismantled?

What both sides ignore is that government policies can no longer suffice to eliminate inflation. They may damp it down for a time, or worsen it. But getting to the heart of inflation involves getting at the root causes of our technology's present obsolescence. Only when the American infrastructure is again made cost-efficient, by repairing the old somehow, or by adopting new technology, can the basic inflation be reckoned with in a decisive way.

16

The Politics of Cash

Is it any surprise that the ever-increasing inflationary burdens imposed by government, not to mention those imposed by OPEC, had, by the late 1970s, incited taxpayer revolt? It was born in California, that wellspring of new and untried ideas. In the summer of 1978 one Harold Jarvis, a ruddy-faced Rotarian, mounted what in California passes for the altar of ideas. He called for a drastic cut in property taxes. Of course, the state's guardians of responsible government opposed the plan. Every major state newspaper cursed Proposition 13. Government officials hinted that schools would be closed and police departments would be shut down if the proposal passed. Governor Jerry Brown angrily denounced Proposition 13 from every podium in California.

In a brilliant masterstroke of political timing, the county of Los Angeles dramatically raised homeowners' property taxes just before the Prop. 13 vote. The die was cast. The tax cut passed 3 to 1. Well, who wouldn't vote himself a tax cut? Governor Brown, in what must have been the decade's most cynical game of see-where-the-people-are-going-and-run-out-in-front, named himself the co-author of Proposition 13 and proclaimed himself its guiding light. But Brown wasn't to stop there. Next he went around the nation calling for a constitutional amendment to balance the federal budget. Even the mainstream conservatives oppose such a radical measure, for it would hamstring the government in hard times, when it might need to spend in the red to bring the nation back to life.

Hard on the heels of Proposition 13 came the Laffer
Curve, also a product of California and, specifically, a creation of Arthur B. Laffer, a professor at the University of
Southern California. What Laffer did was to take an extremely simple thought and elaborate it into an economic
theory, a dubious one. Laffer began with the idea that if
people's income taxes were reduced, then they'd have more
incentive to work, since they'd keep a larger percentage of
their gross income than before. So they'd work harder and
spend harder. By spending their cash in unison, they would
create heavy demand for all sorts of goods and services.
Eventually, producers would respond to this outpouring of
new demand by expanding their production. In the process
they would hire more (tax-paying) workers. In the process
they would also make more (taxable) corporate income. The
net result, Laffer claimed, would be that the stimulus of
lower taxes would finally bring into the government's coffers
more taxes than it had lost in the first place by cutting them.
Does it seem a little perplexing? All Laffer was saying is that
the increased income and sales taxes from the new boom
created by a giant tax cut would more than make up for the
taxes lost due to the cut. Something for nothing, in effect.

You might have noticed, however, that there are a couple
of bad problems with this reasoning. First of all, when everybody starts spending all that extra money which used to
be taxed away, won't prices go up? Won't there be inflation?
Of course there will be. Even more fundamentally, how do
we know the tax cut would stimulate enough new business
to more than cover the government revenues lost? Let me
offer myself as an example. I'd be delighted if my taxes were
cut by, say, 30 percent, or any percent. But will it make me
work harder and, so to speak, "expand" my production? I already work hard enough. I hold down a full-time job at *Fortune;* at nights and on the weekends I spend my hours writing this book. What more can I do, unless I give up sleep for
good? No, I'll happily spend the extra money I would get

from a tax cut, but I don't see how it's going to make me
produce any additions to the Gross National Product. All I'll
be doing is pushing up the inflation rate. The lesson is that,
in the practical world, transitions aren't so smooth as in the
classical world of abstract perfection that Laffer sees when
he puts on his rose-colored glasses. Companies can't increase
their production overnight. Often they may not want to at
all, for reasons having nothing to do with taxes. Sure, they'll
take the extra profit from a tax cut, just as I will. But that
doesn't mean they'll use it as Laffer has theorized.

The Laffer Curve inspired the famed Kemp-Roth tax cut
bill that was proposed before Congress in 1978 by Con-
gressman Jack Kemp of New York and Senator William
Roth of Delaware, both Republicans. Their bill was designed to repeat the experience of 1962, when President
John Kennedy's tax cut seemed to push the economy toward
prosperity. But the Kemp-Roth bill had one fatal defect in
the eyes of most economists, including Walter Heller, who
had been Kennedy's economic adviser. The bill didn't limit
government spending along with government revenues.
Being a Fundamentalist concoction, the Kemp-Roth bill vio-
lated the doctrine that spending cuts must go with tax cuts.
Of course, since the federal government is loath to reduce
its beloved spending, we have gotten precious few tax cuts
in recent history.

The Laffer Curve, however, remains as a rallying symbol
for Republicans, who'd love to ride into the White House on
popular hopes of a massive tax cut that would lower all income taxes by no less than a third. For who except a few
spoilsport economists would attack such a plan to enrich everyone's bank account painlessly? In truth, the Laffer Curve
is a right-wing answer to the Phillips Curve inflation-
unemployment trade-off that led so many Keynesian economists to think they could indefinitely lower unemployment
by inflating the economy. The Laffer Curve is no less er-
roneous and no less seductive. Still, a few economists, while

fully recognizing the fallacy of the Laffer free lunch, have advocated passage of the Kemp-Roth bill because it might force Congress to turn down the spigots of federal spending or risk an enormous inflation. Milton Friedman, the dean of conservative economists, has taken this position. But in doing so, he placed his bet that Congress would come to grips with reason and voluntarily slice the very spending that is the lifeblood of congressional patronage and reelection. I doubt Friedman placed his bet wisely.

The Jarvis Amendment of California, the clamor for a convention to write the requirement for a balanced budget into the Constitution, the anger of ordinary citizens as expressed in news polls—all this has exerted its force on Congress and the executive branch, if only because the fellows fear they may not be reelected if they don't portray themselves now as the most devout promoters of fiscal conservatism. And if these protests against deficit spending do finally prevail by law or constitutional amendment, what will they have accomplished? Many old-line economists start coughing and harrumphing when they think of the consequences. For one thing, a statutory limit to budgetary spending would undo the cherished "stabilizing" role of the federal budget. It would destroy what economists think of as the all-important fiscal policy by which, when an economy falls into recession, the budget mechanism can automatically give some relief—in the form of unemployment insurance extensions, "countercyclical" money to create jobs, and more welfare for more people. Mainstream economists have always taught that this economic stimulus would soon reap rewards, for as money flowed into the economy anew, tax revenues to the Treasury would increase while the need to pay out unemployment and welfare money decreased; as the economy recovered, the federal budget would go into the happy state of balance, or it would run up a surplus. Yet the last time the federal government's budget was in balance was in 1969. Since then, through good times and bad, it has only gone into greater deficit. Why? Because over the years the munificent programs of the Rooseveltian New Deal and Kennedy's New Frontier and Johnson's Great Society and Nixon's New Federalism administration have expanded into monstrous bureaucracies that seem to be self-perpetuating. Congress has mandated government expenditures of millions and millions for everything from school lunches to academic studies of Peruvian prostitutes, and to finance government bureaus ranging from the gigantic Department of Health, Education, and Welfare to the National Pig Manure Commission. The federal budget no longer runs its cycle in phase with the economy's state. Rather, it remains permanently in the red.

Here we have to be careful. Much confusion reigns over just how the government's budget affects the rate of inflation. The truth is that it doesn't necessarily have to affect it, but under some conditions deficit expenditure can inflame demand, bidding prices up, and it can result in an expanding money supply. However, it's wrong simply to assume that budget deficits always increase inflation because of the so-called debt burden. A goodly number of pundits think that since the government's debt runs to more than $800 billion and the nation's debt totals more than $4 trillion, then this debt must be paid back in one gigantic lump sum, and that the government is cheating by paying it back with money printed by the Treasury and "backed" only by hot air. Yet, first of all, the national debt is what we owe each other. For every debtor there is a creditor, and thus for every liability there is an asset, and in this sense the debt represents wealth, too. Speaking more practically, a high level of debt means people are living higher off the hog, and who is to complain about that?

But take a look at how the government will finance deficit spending. Since it is a deficit, then by definition there are no taxes to finance the expenditures. Thus the Treasury must borrow the money, by selling Treasury bonds. When the government sells bonds to banks, it gets cash of course, and this cash goes into the government's bank accounts. This is known as "monetizing" the debt. When it creates new cash in government bank accounts (new in the sense that the bonds it sold to get the money were freshly printed for the purpose), the money supply is indeed increased, and this can heat up demand and thus inflation as the new money is spent by the government. But there's more: when the Treasury Department goes into the credit market to sell its bonds and thereby borrow money, the Federal Reserve System wants to make sure this offering doesn't squeeze out corporations that also need to sell bonds. So the Fed tries to keep interest rates at a reasonable level by expanding the money supply while the Treasury is in the market. This is known as *accommodating the Treasury*. And of course it can fuel inflation as the new dollars get spent.

It's curious how the money supply also changes with the tides of presidential incumbency. The patterns repeat themselves, President after President. Edward Tufte has described how it works in a book called *Political Control of the Economy* (1978). He says that between 1946 and 1976 Americans' income went up the most in the years when a President was running for reelection. In those years, by his calculations, income rose by an average of 3.4 percent. But when the President wasn't running for reelection, it went up by only 2 percent, and a measly 2.6 percent when Congress was out hunting for votes. He also found that unemployment rates fell lower in election years than they had been the year before or would be the year after. The only exception, says Tufte, was the Eisenhower administration. But another Republican, Richard Nixon, was a flagrant practitioner of the presidential scam.

How does it work? The President pushes for tax cuts or increases in health insurance benefits, veterans' benefits, old age benefits—the possibilities are manifold. And if a President raises Social Security benefits before an election, he surely doesn't make the mistake of also raising taxes to pay for the new benefits. If he does that at all, he'll do it after the election. The end result is what Tufte describes as a four-year "political cycle" whereby increasing unemployment follows a President's election, since he can relax his tricks then. Then, as complaints arise, he stimulates the economy until we get a healthy recovery and less joblessness near the end of the President's term, just in time for reelection. The cycle doesn't always work out so neatly, though. Some Presidents are overwhelmed by events—such as the monster recession of 1975—so that Gerald Ford, for example, didn't really have a lot to show when election year came around in 1976. He lost. Then, too, there are the occasional Jimmy Carters who find inflation a greater election liability than unemployment. Still, Tufte's "political cycle" is not to be forgotten when one thinks about the economy's so-called fine-tuning.

Pundits of a moralistic bent like to complain that we Americans, flabby with affluence and profane with material lusts, spend too much and save too little. A comparison is made with Victorian times when we are told that the populace exercised discipline enough to put some money away each week. These days, it is said, Americans save nothing. The government-compiled savings rate shows a marked drop over the recent past. Thus there is not as much money available in banks for bankers to loan out to businesses so they can build new plants and hire new workers. All this is blamed on modern American materialism, the lack of respect for the solemn duties and requirements of civilized life. We are now narcissistic creatures, so the argument goes, believing in no higher authority, accepting no sacrifices. Instead we are consumed by greed and the urge to buy now, to get our gratification immediately if not sooner.

Most of this is wrong. First, savings accounts are no longer the chief source of the funds that banks loan out to businesses. Second, what motivation is there to leave money idle in a savings account, even at the maximum interest rate, while inflation lowers its value? Better to spend it and buy something of value, something hard and durable and even useful. One might as well buy it now before the price goes up once again, as it inexorably does. The moralists fail to realize that inflation takes away the motivation to save cash. We consume more during years of inflation because that is the wisest thing most of us are able to do. Those who save are mostly investors who can afford to buy the high-yielding bonds that come only in huge denominations. For these wealthy people, saving pays off. For the rest of us, we're better off buying homes and trips to Paris.

So in a concrete sense, inflation does make gluttons of us. The incentives created by rising prices pervert the kinder "natural forces" of Adam Smith's "invisible hand." We end up with a species of selfish cynicism gleaned from the average person's repeated experience: being on the losing end of inflation, watching his paycheck erode, watching his living standard fall, in refutation of the old-fashioned idea that he should move up the ladder as he gets older. Many people find themselves, in an epoch of inflation, slipping down the financial ladder. This happens because salaries and wages never fully adjust to rising prices. A school principal who made $23,000 a year in 1960 was affluent in the manner that a school principal is supposed to be—not rich, but flush enough to afford a Buick and a new fall suit or two. In 1980 the school principal is paid $40,000. But that's not enough to make up for the increase in prices since 1960, so he probably drives a Volkswagen and buys his suits at Sears. His position has become devalued. Then can we not predict his reaction? If he can't make enough to pay for the living style of a school principal in 1960, at least he can buy as much as he can, going into debt to do it—to get while the getting's not any worse.

Businesses exhibit an analagous psychology; during a long

period of inflation, corporations prefer to take over smaller companies rather than invest in expensive new factories or go on the market with untried products. Building costs increase constantly, and inflation heightens the risk of building or venturing into unknown territory because inflation creates uncertainty about the future. Thus businessmen feel a mighty urge to merge their company with other companies, "buying" growth instead of building it. This explains the impetus behind the great 1960s boom in conglomerate mergers that accelerated in the late 1970s until thousands of firms had disappeared from the economy, all absorbed into larger conglomerates.

If the consumer's buy-now-before-the-price-goes-up-again inflation psychology increases inflationary pressure as prices get bid up still further, the businessman's buy-now-because-building-looks-too-risky inflation psychology is also a detriment to economic growth. For when a company buys another company, the result is a mere transfer of ownership. Nothing new is added to the economy. In contrast, if a company built a new plant instead of buying one, it would perforce be spending money, and that would boost the growth of the Gross National Product.

17

The Japanese Century

IN THE WARM spring of 1979 a Japanese industrialist donated a number of cherry trees to New York's Central Park. He also gave several hundred thousand dollars for the repair of the Bethesda Fountain in the park. The industrialist said he did it because in the past America has been generous to Asia, and he wanted to return the favor. There's something ironic about this. The tables seem to have turned on us. We no longer rule the international economy. We haven't yet slipped into the status of an underdeveloped nation, but who knows?

Well, of course, we could not have expected to sustain the world leadership that followed from our favorable postwar position. As the nations of Europe and Asia rebuilt, they began to catch up. Now nations like West Germany and Japan far outperform us in international trade. This used not to matter much, for our industry could sell all it wanted inside the nation. But in recent decades export business has multiplied, until it now accounts for close to 15 percent of our trade.

It would account for a good bit more if American businessmen were as adept in Paris and Jakarta as they are in Des Moines. American international competitiveness would be still better if the regulators of Washington didn't trip American businessmen up with onerous regulations. In Japan, by contrast, the government bends over backwards to aid Japanese industry with fat subsidies and favors. Not for nothing is it called "Japan, Inc." You may say Tokyo is full of air pollution as a result. Maybe so. I'm not claiming that the Japanese way is right for us. But we cannot deny that Japanese businessmen will better American businessmen every time, in part because they enjoy government advantages while our businessmen labor under disadvantages imposed on them by our government.

The result is that Japan's trade balance with the United States is so lopsided in Japan's favor—a massive $13 billion Japanese surplus in 1978—that the Japanese government volunteered to finance its own "buy American" program, complete with its floating American trade fair constructed on a ship, to help the poor, inept American businessmen even things out. Yet Japanese businessmen remain wary of U.S. products. They don't like the interruptions in supplying their orders when American workers go on strike, as they so often do. More troubling for us, the Japanese no longer consider American goods to be of high quality.

It may have seemed like Henry Luce's American Century in the years following World War II, but in the 1980s we must ask if it will become the Japanese Century. The Japanese people, sometimes described as a society of workaholics, have accomplished much with little, aided, of course, by our postwar contributions. Still, through ingenuity and hard work and a taste for business enterprise, the Japanese have outdone us, even using expensive energy. Japan must import almost all of her raw materials, including oil, but this has been only a small deterrent. For while we at home work out our problems with large-scale technology and our bureaucratic battles, countries like Japan, with no such difficulties, will be leaping ahead of us. Few foreign nations are much inclined to imitate our penchant for hobbling ourselves. The only countries that have taken up the sport are nearly weakened beyond repair. Britain is the classic example, the object lesson in the pitfalls of running a bureaucratic welfare state that systematically saps a nation's wealth for nonproductive uses. Britain has taken up to 98 percent of the income of its citizens who earn $35,000 a year or more, though Prime Minister Margaret Thatcher has endeavored to change all that. The taxes have gone to pay for things like a "free" health clinic system. But it's only free at the cost of removing the motivations for hard work. Mrs. Thatcher hopes to restore such motivations.

Since the United States is likely to face defeats on the international front despite presidential agreements to lower international tariffs and despite summit meetings in which the major Western trading partners pledge to help each other, then we ought to begin to address the problems America faces in international commerce. But first we must understand something of how international trade works. America can no longer afford its insular chauvinism and its ignorance of the way the wider world interacts.

Are imports inflationary? Economists and government policy makers often argue that they are, but some studies show that the imported merchandise sold in American stores is actually anti-inflationary. The traditional line of argument is that imports exacerbate inflation at home because the more we import, the higher our trade deficit usually goes. That in turn means the dollar depreciates in value due to the excess supply of dollars overseas. When the dollar depreciates, the home price of imported goods goes up, because it then takes more dollars to equal the same amount of yen or marks. And some analysts contend that when the price of Japanese cameras goes up, retailers mark up the prices of American-made cameras to match them. The grand conclusion is that the more we import, the more inflationary imports are.

Yet some experts say that if you go and check out the department stores, you'll find that imported merchandise is generally cheaper than its American equivalent. One study of 400 stores across the nation found that in 1979 imported goods were on average about 11 percent less expensive than American goods and thus saved American consumers something on the order of $2 billion annually. Even when Ameri-

can goods and foreign goods are priced identically, often the
consumer is better off buying the imported model, because
many times it is of higher quality and has more features
than the home product. So, in effect, the consumer is still
saving money when he buys imports.

Whether imports are inflationary, however, depends entirely on how much we import, how much we export, and
how retailers behave. If they sell imports at their lower
prices, Americans save. If they simply mark up the imports
to the same prices as those of domestic products, then the
retailers pocket the advantage. When import prices go up as
our trade deficit widens, whether this pushes up all U.S.
prices depends on whether sellers do in fact mark all prices
of a particular good the same. To understand the effects of
imports, one should first understand the balancing mechanism described in this chapter. Then, knowing that, one
should also know what retailers do when import prices go
up or down. And it is here where economics again approaches the status of applied psychology.

It is true, however, that to the extent we import, we
should also be exporting, so the exports can, in effect, pay
for the imports. It is only when imports badly exceed exports that the inflationary dangers of imported goods become apparent. The difficulty is that, in order to export successfully, American industry has to be efficient enough to
compete with experienced, aggressive exporting nations
such as Japan, West Germany, Taiwan, South Korea, and a
dozen more. The burdens we have imposed on our own industry make us less capable than ever of competing on an
equal footing with rival nations that do not share our political and cultural worries over big-scale technology.

Comparative advantage is the very basis of foreign trade.
Pakistan has a comparative advantage in the making of or-
namental rugs because the nation has highly skilled workers
who are willing to weave them by hand for low wages. In
the United States, you'd first have to find a skilled rug maker

who works by hand. Then you'd have to try and get him or her to accept something below the minimum wage. In the unlikely event that you can accomplish this, you could then compete with Pakistani rugs, though you'd still have a sizable disadvantage, in the eyes of customers, simply because you were offering imitation Pakistani rugs. You'd have to sell at prices well below those charged for genuine Pakistani rugs, even though you would have higher costs, for your labor is still much more expensive. No deal.

But not to worry; the United States has the overwhelming advantage in production of modern jet fighters. We have the technology and the mechanized assembly lines and the capital to make some of the best airplanes in the world. Our comparative advantage is solid. Now, if Pakistan exports rugs to the United States and we export jets to Pakistan, both our countries will be better off. Consumers in both nations will be getting these products at the lowest feasible cost, lower than if they could be produced at home. Of course, the case of jet fighters is special, since they are tools of national security. More than a few countries subsidize the production of home-grown fighters even at great expense. France, Israel, and Britain are examples. They do this not for economic reasons, clearly. It would be insane from a business viewpoint. They do it to make sure they have fighters no matter what happens, and maybe to preserve national pride.

Of course, comparative advantage changes like everything else. Not so long ago, the United States led many nations in exports because it was able to develop new technology faster than any other country was able to imitate that technology. We ruled the radio and television market and owned the computer market and sold a lot of industrial machinery, and of course we had abundant food to export. Now, in the early 1980s, the nation has lost most of its technological edge; technology is often imported into this country. A few years ago when Sony, the Japanese electronics manufacturer, bought a television plant in San Diego, it brought over its own technicians to teach the American assembly line workers how to operate the superior *Japanese* technology. A steel mill in Illinois joined in a venture with the Kyodo Shaft Company of Japan to install new, efficient steel-finishing machinery from Japan. This machinery was actually a cheaper Japanese imitation of German steel technology. For consolation, the United States is left with a large advantage in food production, simply because our farms are more capital-intensive, producing a higher yield per acre with far less human labor than is the case in any other nation.

Comparative advantage often dies hard. When an industry suddenly discovers that it is no longer the most efficient —for example, the lowest-cost producer of steel—it rushes to Washington for protection against dastardly foreign competition. Usually Congress responds favorably, invoking quotas for the import of steel, or high tariffs that make the steel just as expensive as domestic steel, or *ad valorem* taxes that require importers to pay a percentage of the value of their merchandise in taxes, or outright subsidies to the domestic steel industry. Businessmen make a heart-rending appeal to good old American patriotism, trying to convince us to "buy American" and support employment in the U.S. steel industry.

In the long run, none of this protection works, for the industry that has lost its comparative advantage will either change or die. In the meantime, its protection from foreign competition costs consumers hard cash because they are forced to buy goods made from steel that is artificially high in price, whether it is domestic steel or heavily taxed foreign steel. In recent years, steel, sugar, textiles, and TV sets have received protection from import competition, to our detriment. It is unfortunate when a factory has to close down because it has become too inefficient. But that's the way of the world. New industries are always arising, and we should let "old" ones die natural deaths, if that is the only solution to their ills that doesn't involve artificial government support of the industry's inefficiency.

Foreign exchange rates are directly affected by the balance of foreign trade and directly affect foreign trade in turn. Consider a hypothetical case of our balance of trade with Pakistan. Suppose that in 1981 Pakistan exported to the United States $10 million in rugs. We exported $100 million in jet fighters to Pakistan. Now we come to the crucial fact in understanding the workings of foreign trade. The Pakistanis must buy dollars to pay for our jet fighters, and we must buy rupees. That is, rug buyers must pay for the shipments they ordered in rupees, and the Pakistan government must pay dollars for the shipment of fighters. Let us for a moment isolate Pakistan and the United States, as if they were the only two countries in the world. As a result of the $100 million purchase of jet fighters versus the $10 million purchase of rugs, it seems that Pakistan needs a lot of U.S. currency. This means the demand for dollars will rise, and it follows that the price of dollars will rise. In other words, the increased demand for dollars will raise the rupee price of dollars, so the Pakistanis will have to pay more rupees per dollar than they did before. On the other hand, with only $10 million in rug imports, the United States won't need many rupees, certainly not enough to offset the dollars Pakistan needs. So the United States will not put pressure on the market for Pakistani currency. And what will the United States do with any excess rupees? Since American goods require payment in U.S. dollars, they can't be spent here. In fact, they can be spent only in Pakistan, or dumped on the foreign exchange market at distress prices. This will in fact happen because the United States doesn't need to buy any more than $10 million worth of rugs from Pakistan. Anything else the nation sells can be had cheaper or better from other sources. The extra rupees are dumped on the foreign exchange market, and they send the price of rupees plunging. In other words, the Pakistani deficit in trade has resulted in the depreciation of its currency against the dollar. Dollars are now very expensive to buy if you're a Pakistani. That means American exports are now expensive, since they must be paid for in dollars. But by the same mechanism, rupees are quite cheap in terms of dollars. And our advantage is that Pakistan's exports are bargains, since they must be paid for in rupees and since many rupees can be had for a dollar. Pakistani producers increase production for the American import market, which will soon be booming, because Americans will flock to stores that begin stocking Pakistani goods at their low prices. If the Pakistanis do a good job of it and have some luck, and if the United States refrains from import tariffs to make the Pakistani goods expensive again, then pretty soon we might be importing more of their goods—sugar, steel, and petrochemicals, in addition to rugs—than we are exporting. Then at last the foreign exchange situation will reverse. The dollar will be in the doghouse and rupees will appreciate in value because of our need to pay for Pakistan's goods in rupees.

Now, releasing ourselves from the silly confinements of our assumption, we extend this mechanism to all trading nations simultaneously, and this is how foreign trade works—almost. For there are also foreign investments to think about. Besides using excess rupees to pay for more Pakistani imports, or dumping them on the foreign exchange market, we could always invest the money in Pakistan itself. The quickest and easiest way would be to buy Pakistani short-term bonds, the equivalent of our T-bills. We could do that if their interest rates were attractively high. In fact, our hypothetical Pakistan with its huge trade deficit has worked to tighten its money supply, thus pulling its interest rates up and luring foreign money into its coffers to redress the trade imbalance. A lot of money in the world does indeed follow short-term interest rates to wherever they are highest.

Another investment alternative is in long-term bonds, but

do we really sufficiently trust the stability of Pakistan with
the demonstrated volatility of its government? If we did, we
might go further than merely buying bonds. Why not thus
build a factory in Pakistan to make products and sell them
in the Pakistani market? Labor costs are cheaper there anyhow. Corporations that sell everything from tractors to
razor blades have built manufacturing plants all over the
world, usually staffing them with foreign nationals. Going
multinational used to be the sexiest thing to do in American
business. That was in the days of glory, when the United
States stood at the helm of world events. But it all ended
when we gave in to floating exchange rates. By 1977 the dollar had floated downward in value as our trade deficit
soared to record levels. The multinational companies got hit
with large *foreign exchange translation losses,* as they're
called. When the multinationals changed pesos or francs
into depreciated dollars for use back at the home office, they
lost a lot of money in the translation. In the last few years,
opening plants in foreign lands, especially in increasingly
expensive Europe, has become decidedly less glamorous.

Really, the depreciation of the dollar against the other
major currencies has reversed the old order of things dramatically. Now it is foreign multinationals—companies ranging from Michelin Tires to Philips, the Dutch electrical manufacturer—that build plants in the United States. We should
be glad of it. Before 1970 we were the patrons of just about
every non-Communist nation in the world, investing money
in their economies and handing out millions in foreign aid to
their governments. And, of course, practically the whole
world was the American tourist's oyster, for the American
dollar bought fat quantities of any overseas currency one
might have wanted. Living in the beautiful countryside of
Colombia in the 1960s, working on Hollywood movie productions, I came across people who left their native Colombia for six months and went to work in Detroit. With the
pay they got in the automobile factories, they returned to

Colombia for the other six months and lived like kings. Then the exchange rate was about 17 pesos for every dollar. But inside Colombia, pesos were almost equivalent to dollars in buying power, in the sense that most Colombians earned perhaps 100 pesos a month, so obviously the necessities, and a good bit more, had to be priced within their range. For example, Piel Roja cigarettes then cost the equivalent in American money of a dime a pack. Now, though, it is foreign tourists who get the same kinds of bargains by shopping in the United States, for the same reasons. On any day in New York City you can hear French or British or Italian accents. The speakers are in New York to pick up on the "bargains" at Bloomingdale's and Gucci's. Yes, what most of us consider rather expensive items are cheap in comparison to the prices in Paris or Geneva. America has become the mecca for foreign tourists, now that the tables have turned.

But recall from our Pakistan example how a country with a depreciated currency is also able to export a lot because its goods are thus made cheaper compared to those sold inside foreign nations. This mechanism has worked for American business, but its effectiveness has been impaired because businessmen in this country remain steadfastly ignorant of the export business. This is a residue from the days when the dollar was supreme and there was little need to export; American goods were too expensive to export, anyway, because of the favorable exchange rate. So while the Japanese and West Germans became pros in the export business, we remain rank amateurs, unaccustomed to the intricacies of dealing with overseas markets. U.S. businessmen have little feel for the kinds of products foreign nations want. Jean-Jacques Servan-Schreiber, who in 1968 worried greatly over the specter of American hegemony, need have no fear. Back then he saw aggressive American multinational companies with sophisticated management outstripping the stodgy ways of European businessmen. America, it was feared, would soon own most of the businesses of any size and importance in Europe.

Traditional relationships in world leadership have turned around. The adjustment was inevitable, but the machinations of OPEC have brought it to serious proportions. Ever since World War II the United States took the lead in world commerce and statesmanship. While former powers were struggling to rebuild their countries, we surged ahead, growing in postwar prosperity, confident of our abilities and our lead in technology, especially the technology of nuclear bombs that gained us the seat at the head of the table in world affairs. Our political strength buttressed our economic strength and the value of the dollar remained high, under the old Bretton Woods system of fixed exchange rates (organized at Bretton Woods, New Hampshire, toward the end of World War II). It was in special demand because it had come to be the international trading currency, the coin of the world realm, a common denominator to make world trading a bit more efficient. American dollars were strong and would be accepted by any nation in lieu of their own currency. Money has long been a barometer of world leadership. When Britain ruled the seas, the pound sterling was in favor the world over. When France under Napoleon was in fullest flower, francs were the international currency. (Language, too, is a good indicator. In the eighteenth and nineteenth centuries, it was British English and French that were the standard second languages. Then during the twentieth century it came to be American English that was taught in classrooms overseas, even in Communist nations. The next "international" language could well be Arabic or Japanese.)

American dominance apparently reached its demise by 1970. The world monetary system was in deep trouble because there was a dollar "overhang" in Europe: too many dollars in European banks, because of the tremendous amount of importing our prosperous nation had been doing in the flush 1960s. Under the system of fixed exchange rates the dollar was greatly overvalued, and the strain began to show. President Nixon began a series of official devaluations, to try and bring the international price of the dollar more into line with the oversupply of dollars that bedeviled our trading partners. This oversupply was a special headache because it drained gold from the vaults of Fort Knox. The Bretton Woods system was based on gold to a limited degree, so that only the governments of foreign nations could cash in their dollars for gold bullion. They began to do so in the late 1960s, and as they possessed huge quantities of excess dollars, the transaction threatened to remove a substantial part of the dollar's "backing." The dollar "overhang" was hurting American exports, as well. In August 1971 Nixon blew apart the Bretton Woods system by setting the dollar free to "float" to its correct value. He removed the gold convertibility of the dollar. Immediately the dollar plunged in value, as well it should have; it was greatly in excess supply.

Currencies like the German mark and the Japanese yen appreciated against the dollar; the central bankers in these nations became worried that their currencies would go so high as to make their exports too expensive in America. This would be a calamity to these nations, since so large a portion of their Gross National Product, often a quarter or more, comes from foreign trade. So the monetary authorities of these countries from time to time intervene in the foreign exchange markets. They simply buy up dollars, to push the international price of dollars higher, which pulls their currency's value lower against the dollar, and therefore keeps the prices of their exports down. Given this intervention, practiced by the Japanese, the British, and even the United States, the present system of floating exchange rates has come to be called a "dirty float," as opposed to a "clean" one. In a clean float every currency could float to its proper relative value, depending on the demand and supply of that currency, which in turn depends on the

amount of trading and investment coming into the country
or going out of it. Nations with big balance of payments
deficits watch their currencies depreciate from an excess
supply owing to the countries' excess of imports over exports.

Alarmists predicted that the system of floating exchange
rates would send the entire world on an inflationary binge.
It hasn't happened. Trading nations have been unhooked
from the strict discipline of the fixed-rate standard, but their
currencies haven't fallen apart. Though throughout the
1970s the U.S. dollar depreciated against the currencies of
strong trading partners like Japan, West Germany, and
Switzerland, overall the dollar regained some of its former
strength. The classical international equilibrating mechanism works, though it does take a while for the effects to be
felt. By 1978 some trading nations were worrying over
whether the U.S. dollar had not gotten "too" strong.

18

A New Technology

EVERY SOLUTION begets problems. The large-scale technology that has given us a car in every garage also uses up hydrocarbon fuel, pollutes the environment, and leads us straight into bureaucratic socialism. On top of that, the world technological infrastructure becomes more vulnerable as it becomes more interdependent. A computer genius, surreptitiously communicating with computers built into underground bunkers in the American West or the Soviet wastelands, could conceivably trigger a shower of nuclear missiles. It would take no great intelligence to plug into CBS's television linkup and hijack the Evening News. The only surprise is that there hasn't been more technological terrorism than we've already seen. One could learn the basic principles by watching reruns of "Mission: Impossible."

A few years ago, one occasionally heard fuzzy-headed futurists calling for a world government that would end the chance of nuclear war, get rice to where it was needed, and manage the world's technology. The idea was that since technology had evolved to huge scale (in fact, the largest factories are now called "world-scale" plants), then people should lay down their petty nationalism and adapt to the new technology. But humans evolve much more slowly than machines. In the decade just past, we saw little proof that the people of the world felt they were living in any "global village." In the 1970s we witnessed tribal conflicts among Southeast Asians and Africans and religious conflicts among Middle Eastern peoples. If South Korea and Taiwan have plunged forward into modern technology, Iran attempted to move giant steps backward, to the mores of the thirteenth century. The natural instincts of the self and the group still override every rational design. Though 1984 is closing in on us, we have not yet changed into the sort of right-thinking, conformist robots who would be most amenable to world government. Such a government would perforce grow into an outrageous super-bureaucracy, regulating the world by trying to juggle a million variables at once: an impossible plan, to be sure, an ill-advised solution to the problems created by big-scale technology.

If going big is no longer any fun, then we could engineer a small-scale technology. Of course, it should also be fuel-efficient and nonpolluting. We could reach the desired smallness by moving backward to small scale or by moving forward to it. Moving backward, of course, is the most obvious way, and the one most beloved by ideologues still rummaging among the bones of the now-deceased counterculture. The high priest of technological nostalgia is E. F. Schumacher. In his gospel, *Small Is Beautiful*, Schumacher offers the sort of simplistic prescriptions that delight failed back-to-the-log-cabin Utopians who haven't sufficient ganglia in their cerebrums to think the thing out.

Schumacher confesses that he was once a slave to the outmoded notion of economies of scale as the justification for large enterprises. But in his meditations Schumacher came to hear the Muse of Small Scale, who advised him that the true worth of big technology could be gauged only by determining the degree to which we need economies of scale. And who is to determine how much we need them? Schumacher, of course. Guided by the wisdom of what he calls Buddhist Economics, he lays out an economic ethic of intentional parsimony. Thus enlightened, he postulates that people need both freedom and order—the freedom to operate small businesses independently, and the order that derives from large-scale enterprise. But Schumacher complains that people can never keep the conflicting needs straight, so we forget our true needs, as explained to us by Schumacher, and opt for the large-scale schemes. The truth is revealed: "Today, we suffer from an almost universal idolatry of giantism."

Schumacher speaks as if economies of large scale are merely a matter of choice, as if we voted for big-scale technology in some long-forgotten election. But these economies exist because the narrow, stubborn logic of technology has demanded them in the name of efficiency. And nontechnical economies of large scale follow from the logic of the large organization and big politics. It's hardly a matter of taste.

Armed with the precepts of Buddhist Economics, Schumacher delineates the idea of "appropriate-scale" technology rather than large-scale technology. To achieve the appropriate scale, we must, he says, revert to the old-fashioned hand-powered, water-powered, and wind-powered machines of earlier centuries. Yet how do we know what scale of technology is truly appropriate? Schumacher will tell us. The appropriate city, he says, would allow no more than 200,000 people (Schumacher is obviously a suburban Californian). The appropriate manufacturing plant would be housed in a toolshed. Transport would be courtesy of mule-drawn wagons. One wonders if Schumacher would insist that we give up the debaucheries of modern bathrooms and return to the outhouse. Clearly, the Schumacherian notions of reversion to small scale are extensions of the counterculture movement, in retreat from the modern world.

China in the 1960s, under the domain of Mao Tse-tung, experimented with what Schumacher might call "intermediate technology," and the results were anything but encouraging. The Chinese decided, as part of the "Great Leap Forward," to install steel furnaces in every backyard, so the people could manufacture steel in small proportions, thus making up for China's lack of large-scale steel capacity. The experiment didn't work because the tiny steel pots were amazingly inefficient.

More problematic even is Schumacher's demand that the underdeveloped nations of the world forever abandon their aspirations for large industrial enterprise of the modern variety. Instead, he lectures, the Third and Fourth worlds must accept the small scale of "intermediate technology," forgoing the possibility of domestically produced autos and TV sets and TV dinners. Instead, crude hand tools and ancient production methods of the labor-intensive variety must be employed locally to give unskilled work to the masses and to produce the old-fashioned artifacts of bygone eras.

Schumacher has overlooked what Third World leaders such as Fidel Castro and the Chinese high command understand all too well. To bring their nations into the twentieth century, they look first to improving agricultural productivity and later to building a modern industrial base of large-scale technology. Reading through some of Castro's speeches to the home audience, one finds exhortations to sugar cane workers to stop loafing as well as detailed and admiring descriptions of the marvels of some new, more efficient method of germinating seeds or weeding crops. The Chinese also have their eyes on new technology. Realizing that the most urgent need is to improve farm productivity so China can feed her own population—which happens to be over one fifth of the world's population—the leadership elevates productivity into a sacred goal. Chinese peasants are sent to pilgrimages at a model commune that employs clever farm production techniques and enjoys abundant harvests. In the meantime, China hopes to import new industrial machinery from the West. Schumacher's ideal of cottage-industry technology is too meager to propel underdeveloped nations to modern wealth. And if we say Third and Fourth world people shouldn't want modern large-scale technology because big is bad and because it upsets our aesthetic sensibility, that is merely an index of our own arrogance. The recommendations of Schumacher, in fact, are profoundly insulting to poor nations. Just as many people in underdeveloped countries saw American birth control programs in the 1960s as plots to keep those people subservient to the American Colossus, they will see "intermediate technology" as a codeword for technological genocide.

Even if Schumacher's prescriptions made sense for the modern world, how would we bring them to fruition? Do we precipitate the worst depression ever experienced by abandoning conventional technology and retooling for small-scale technology? Who will induce corporations to write off all their assets? Who will finance the investment in inefficient small scale? And how would we adapt hand-powered, wind-powered technology to the millions who live in large cities? Where will they put their solar reflectors? Of course, if we are to revert to truly old-fashioned technology, we would fuel it with coal. This, in fact, has been widely suggested, since the United States has huge reserves of coal. But scientists say a coal-burning world would be more interdependent than ever, for the heavy pollution of coal boilers would require careful international monitoring, and the heating of the earth's atmosphere by coal's carbon dioxide emissions would presage a potential dramatic change in the earth's climate, such that farmlands could turn to deserts and polar ice caps could melt.

Schumacher's visions, however, are irrelevant because we can glimpse at the beginning of a new technological wave that seems to promise the paradox of small scale wrought from large scale. The new electronic technology crams thousands of electronic circuits onto small slices of silicon. The scale of reduction is such that the entire text of the Bible can be transcribed onto a wafer that's one and a half inches square. Newer technology gets even more minute. As electronic circuits become smaller and cheaper, more of them can be used in a device. Whereas a decade ago it would have been unthinkable to construct a computer that could recognize human speech because the machine would require too many circuits, at present such a computer is under development. With advanced semiconductors and supercooled superconductors, more "intelligence" can be packed into smaller spaces.

This suggests it will be feasible to design computers that can monitor every possible function of every possible mechanism. For example, General Motors has spoken of cars equipped with small computers that could monitor all automotive functions, continuously solve differential equations, and adjust the carburetor 100 times a second, to squeeze out just the right amount of efficiency at the minimal level of pollution. Office buildings are beginning to be wired with computers that keep track simultaneously of air temperature and humidity and energy use; they are able to turn off lights when they aren't needed, turn back thermostats automatically, and feed extra warm or cool air into areas where it is needed. Already these crude computers save more than $100 million in fuel bills over five-year periods. It might turn out that sophisticated information technology will make control easier; it might make bureaucratic planning efficient through continuous monitoring. This is not what we have in mind, is it? We do not wish the wondrous new technology merely to hasten bureaucratic socialism.

Yet if we hypothesize that decentralized information could as well lead to decentralized, even small-scale human enterprise, then the possibilities are brighter. If we add up the new technology of highly integrated electronic circuit chips, advanced two-way 100-channel cable television systems, laser optics, and satellite communications, we begin to see the makings of an energy-efficient, quick information network, a new technology of information exchange. We can rightly ask if we have enough information to exchange; the scientific consensus is that we do not. But assuming for a time that we can develop it, then the potential of this technology stirs the imagination. Lewis Thomas, the biologist, wonders if humans are not, as social animals, linked into rudimentary circuits for the storage, processing, and retrieval of information. Thomas says, in *The Lives of a Cell*, that this information process "appears to be the most basic and universal of all human enterprises." Thomas attempts a metaphor of the world as one huge mind. The notion of numerous separate organisms joining to form a larger organism is one of his favorite devices, and in the context of the emerging information technology this may amount to something. Already European scientists speak of a coming "information economy."

While we are in full speculative flight, why not test the stratosphere? Thomas will be the pilot again. For he suggests that a lesson in what may be called biological economies of large scale may be learned from the lowly myxotricha, a protozoan pseudo-organism that turns out, on close examination, to be several smaller organisms working together. Thomas suggests that some underlying force drives together the several creatures comprising the myxotricha, and then drives the assembled "organism" into union with its termite host. Thomas says, "If we could understand this tendency, we would catch a glimpse of the process that brought single separate cells together for the construction of metazoans, culminating in the invention of roses, dolphins, and, of course, ourselves. It might turn out that the same tendency underlies the joining of organisms into communities, communities into ecosystems, and ecosystems into the biosphere." Thomas also points out that if it is in the nature of living creatures to pool resources, recognition of this would offer us a new way of accounting for the progressive enrichment and complexity of living things. Thomas is ruminating here on nothing less than a biotechnology of large scale.

Convergence theories are fashionable intellectual toys of the day. What if the new technology of sophisticated microelectronics were eventually to converge with a natural tendency for biological economies of large scale in information? We could then envision a world in which smallness would thrive side by side with bigness in an epoch of technology within the reach of everyone: pocket computers that do things we cannot even imagine today. This is a faint hope, yet a real one if we are willing to assume that technology can evolve in ways the human mind is unable to foresee.

The objection, of course, is the argument that no amount of electronic gadgetry can eliminate the need for large-scale basic industries of the most conventional sort. Electron beams can't conceivably replace the steel I-beams of building construction, can they? The objection, sound as it may be, is overstated. For the best hope is that a margin of safety would arise, a counterpoint to the more distressing qualities of the large-scale technology with which we so uneasily coexist. If alongside the traditional technology evolves a technology so sophisticated that it could tailor itself to human dimensions, it might also influence and alter the standard technology. Thus we would move toward smaller scale without regressing to Schumacher's "intermediate technology." We would then have moved closer to a compromise between biology and technology, chiefly because technology in its most advanced form bent to make peace with human nature.

Here one has to be cautious and at the same time daring. Advising caution in visions of technology's future, Dr. Louis Robinson, IBM's chief of research, warns that when one draws the outlines of what would seem a reasonable futurist scenario, one is sure to be on the wrong track. The reason is that if the scenario is conceivable today, then one has to ask why it isn't already in existence. Dr. Robinson adds that we can't really know how we will use the new information technology in the future, because in predicting the future uses of technology we are really predicting the course of social change. The real significance of automobile technology, after all, was in the way it changed our lives—creating suburbs and backseat sex, among other phenomena.

But just as extravagant speculation is bound to be faulty, smug caution errs in the other direction. History is littered with the now-absurd commentaries of shortsighted men who dismissed new technologies, men like those at Edison Electric who offered Henry Ford a cushy job if he would promise to give up his damned "useless" gasoline engine idea. If it is patently impossible to conjure up the shape of future technology, one can at least acknowledge the first faint shadows of a world that may be more dramatically different from today's than today's world is different from the pre-airplane, pre-automobile, pre-radio days of the mid-nineteenth century.

Whoever puts blind faith in technology should be prepared to receive plenty of dressing-downs from more practical and solid types who cling to the view that economic growth is no longer possible, that technology is forever frozen in its present mode, and that life fifty years from now will be identical to life in the present age. While our most popular savants are scoffing at technological potentialities and dreaming of log cabins, however, the savants of other nations are moving ahead quickly with the prospect for an *information economy*. By 1980 the governments of Canada, Japan, West Germany, France, and Britain, among others, had begun to study the impact of the microprocessor revolution on their economies and their life-styles. Of course, the impact of new microelectronic factories is bound to end up being almost trivial compared to the social and economic impact of the devices themselves. But at least some governments are preparing for the new wave of high technology. Characteristically, the United States Government isn't paying any attention—except for the unwanted attention paid to the electronics industry by meddling Washington regulators. Certainly the U. S. Government is at the opposite pole from the Japanese Government, which is financing advanced research in the new technology by private Japanese electronic corporations.

The brightest potential is for a technology that turns large-scale economies inside out and offers economies of miniaturization whereby the nation's infrastructure can recede to more human dimensions. The new technology would use less energy and remove the threat to the environment and alleviate the political fear of largeness. It would allow the first comfortable compromise between human and machine.

The question, then, is how we get from here to there. Today computers are still little more than glorified adding machines. We already have more technology than we know what to do with. We fear computers as the invaders of privacy, as the silent henchmen of an authoritarian state. In ten years or twenty, these machines, now relatively crude, might usher in a new long wave of growth, as we rebuild the technological infrastructure along cleaner, more pleasing lines. But getting from here to there is sure to send us past many political and economic pitfalls. Unable to discern the social meaning of a new technology now only in its infancy, and cynical of futurist prognostications, the human impulse will be to seek out the most obvious and vulnerable villains, on the theory that if we can banish them, the current evils will go with them and life will be restored to the seemingly more simple verities of past decades. This theory, put too zealously into practice, could wrench the nation with misguided upheavals. Instead, what is needed in these times is sophisticated understanding, some perspective, and a little patience.

A Skeptic's Guide to the
Main Economic Indicators

THE DAILY newspaper's front page gives high prominence these days to such things as the Consumer Price Index and the latest real Gross National Product growth rate. Many journalists, unaware of what these statistics really mean and how they are flawed, exaggerate their relevance. Every time the unemployment rate for black teenagers is announced to be, say, 25 percent, a reporter rushes up to Harlem or Watts to survey the tragedy. The situation *is* tragic, to be sure, but not in accord with the 25 percent figure, because the black teenage unemployment numbers are known to be wildly inaccurate. In the same manner, the President will huff and puff whenever the Producer Price Index climbs a half percentage point in a month. True, that's bad news, but what the President doesn't realize is that the Producer Price Indexes are also full of error and often exaggerate inflation.

By paying some attention here to what the statistics are all about we may learn to treat them with more detachment.

The Consumer Price Index—This is our major gauge of inflation, but it's quite a crude one and consistently exaggerates the amount of inflation in the country. The CPI is compiled by about five hundred off-duty schoolteachers and part-time housewives who go to local grocery and department stores to check the prices of items chosen for investigation by computers at the Department of Labor in Washington. The many items are supposed to represent the "market basket" of what the average American buys each month, though the basket sample excludes things bought by people living in rural parts. The Consumer Price Index exaggerates inflation because it fails to account adequately for changes in the quality of the goods we buy. Think of a color television set made in 1967, which sold for $300. Suppose that "same" TV set today sells for $375. The price has gone up 25 percent. But wait a minute. The quality of the set has vastly improved. The engineers have added more sophisticated circuits. The cabinet is made of a more attractive, durable plastic. If the truth be known, it's really an entirely different product from the one you bought in 1967. If you can properly account for the quality improvements that have gone into the set, you will find that actually the price has in some sense gone down. And practically speaking, the higher price represents not inflation but the higher costs of the improved product. Now, the Labor Department attempts to adjust for quality changes, but it can do so only when the quality changes are obvious and easy to evaluate; often they are not.

One prominent economist, Richard Ruggles of Yale, has said that if quality improvements are taken into account, then from 1949 to 1966 the inflation rate can be shown to have fallen, whereas the Consumer Price Index indicates that inflation was up by 36 percent during that period. This failure to take adequate account of quality change is perhaps the largest flaw of the CPI, though there are other technical defects.

The accuracy of the CPI is important because a change of 1 percent in the index can trigger a billion dollars' worth of money transfers affecting half the U.S. population. For example, all 32 million Social Security recipients have their benefit checks linked to the CPI by a cost-of-living escalator, as do nearly 3 million retired civil servants and military personnel. Then, too, changes in the index directly affect the food-stamp allotments for 20 million recipients, the subsidies for the 25 million children who are served food under the National School Lunch Act and the Child Nutrition Act, and benefits for millions more who partake of health and welfare programs with "poverty level" eligibility requirements.

The wages of nearly 10 million union workers are affected by movements in the Consumer Price Index, as are a quickly growing number of private contracts, covering everything from rent to child-support payments. This is called *indexing,* which ensures that the level of these payments keeps up with inflation as measured by the CPI. Some economists have recommended that everything be indexed, but such a step could lead to runaway inflation; there would be no incentive to stop raising prices. Brazil tried it in the 1960s, but the experiment was unsuccessful.

It may seem odd that the Consumer Price Index is issued by the Department of Labor. It is odd. The Labor Department's Bureau of Labor Statistics compiles the CPI because the index was first established, during the inflation of World War I, to adjust the wages of shipbuilding workers. Ever since then, organized labor has watched closely the way the CPI is calculated. It is in the interest of labor for inflation to be recorded as high as possible, so negotiators can easily justify their requests for higher wages.

When a television network anchorman announces that this month's inflation rate is up 0.9 percent, which translates to an annual inflation rate of 13.1 percent, you might wonder if he's done his arithmetic wrong. After all, 0.9 times 12 equals 10.8. The difference, however, is explained by the fact that, to find the annual rate, the monthly rate must be compounded over twelve months. The difference between the uncompounded and the compounded number is small, but the compounded figure is the correct one.

The Producer Price Indexes—These measure inflation in the prices of things consumers don't buy directly. One index measures the prices of industrial raw materials; another measures the prices of "intermediate" goods that need further processing before they're ready for sale. Still another records the prices of finished goods ready for shipment to retailers. This last index is given the most attention, because it is assumed to forecast consumer inflation three or four months in the future. If the manufacturer's price for new tires goes up, pretty soon the retail price of tires will go up, too; if retailers don't pass higher prices along to customers, they must accept a smaller profit.

But the Producer Price Indexes are even less accurate than the Consumer Price Index. Some serious scholars think these indexes ought to be scrapped entirely because they are so misleading. But they won't be discarded by the government, so we are forced to continue using them as predictors of inflation to come. To compile the Producer Price Indexes, the Labor Department's Bureau of Labor Statistics sends out forms each month to about three thousand companies in mining, manufacturing, and agriculture. They report their prices on about ten thousand items. But that covers only about 30 percent of the thousands of products made by all 550 major United States industries. And many of the price changes in the indexes are based on reports from only one or two companies. In other words, if the raw materials index goes up one month because of a rise in the price of iron ore, the index may have gauged iron ore prices at only two or three companies. It's possible that other iron ore producers haven't raised their prices.

Not only that, but the selection of the items to be priced is arbitrary and, frequently, out of date. For example, the BLS prices office machinery for the indexes but checks only old-fashioned items like adding machines. It excludes electronic computing equipment, and the prices of these computer office machines have dramatically dropped in price per computation. Whereas in 1952 it cost $1.26 to do 100,000 multiplications, they can now be done for a fraction of a penny. The Producer Price Indexes don't reflect this price decrease.

To compound the inaccuracy of the Producer Price Indexes, they measure only the list prices posted by companies. But anyone who buys or sells industrial products knows that list prices are almost always discounted, especially in slack business times. The only time list prices are accurate is during a boom when demand is strong. Even then, big buyers can negotiate discounts for bulk purchases.

The Labor Department is aware of these and other problems with the indexes. Officials of the department say that by the mid-1980s they might be corrected. Until they are, it's best to take the Producer Price Indexes with a huge grain of salt, no matter how solemnly network news anchormen proclaim their significance.

The Unemployment Rate—This statistic exaggerates America's unemployment so badly that back in 1978 the government set up a commission to try and figure out how to revise it. But old-line bureaucrats have resisted most of the changes recommended. The unemployment rate is based on information collected in monthly door-to-door surveys of random households. The problem lies in how the Labor Department classifies people as employed or unemployed. The government counts any civilian over the age of sixteen as unemployed if he or she has made even the most minimal effort to look for a few hours of work. Since more than 90 percent of all sixteen- and seventeen-year-olds are high school students, the minimum age ought to be raised to at least eighteen. The unemployment rate could also be made more realistic if the government included only those looking for twenty or more hours of work. As it is, even if you're looking for just an hour's work you're numbered among the unemployed.

Professor Kenneth Clarkson at the University of Miami has pointed out that changes in the welfare laws have also bloated the unemployment rate. This is because food-stamp and welfare recipients must register for work as long as they receive aid. And once they are counted as "looking for work" on paper, they are also counted as unemployed. Dr. Clarkson has calculated that this bias adds about 2 percentage points a year to the unemployment rate. In fact, Dr. Clarkson claims, the "welfare effect" is responsible for much of the increase in the unemployment rate that has occurred since 1973.

What's really wrong is that the unemployment rate is no longer the measure of human suffering that the news media paint it to be. Back in the 1950s the unemployment rate was a pretty accurate index of economic hardship. The labor force was made up mostly of males who were the sole breadwinners for their families. When they lost their jobs, there were no food stamps or extended unemployment compensation plans or welfare programs to cushion the blow. But in the 1960s and 1970s demographic change and the advent of generous social programs swelled the ranks of the unemployed with people who aren't suffering much hardship or trying very hard to find a job. A hefty portion of the "unemployed" that politicos fret over these days are bored housewives looking for pin money, and teenagers who are full-time students, and welfare mothers going through the bare motions of "looking for work" so they can get their benefits. At present more than half the unemployed live in families where the household head is working. Only 20 percent of the unemployed qualify as "poor" by the government's own definition.

There are actually seven unemployment rates compiled by the Labor Department, and if we look closely at them we find even more outrageous inaccuracies. For example, the much-touted unemployment rate for black teenagers, always reported to be very high—up to 40 percent—is wildly incorrect, because an inadequately small sample of black teenagers is included in the household surveys on which the unemployment rates are based. The unemployment rates for individual states and cities are so bad that they don't even meet the Labor Department's minimum standards for accuracy—not very exacting themselves. These state and local unemployment rates are figured by taking unemployment insurance claims and "inflating" them by a complex, poorly thought-out procedure. The procedure compounds error with almost every step. The inaccuracy of the figures costs everyone money, because these numbers are used to determine how billions of dollars in taxpayers' money will be allocated each year. When Congress required that appropriations under the Comprehensive Employment and Training Act (CETA), along with funds for public works and anti-recession aid, be distributed on the basis of state and local unemployment rates, it never stopped to ask if these statistics were any good.

The Bureau of Labor Statistics, realizing how inaccurate the state and local unemployment rates are, expanded its household survey in 1978 to try to calculate quarterly rates of unemployment for states and cities. But the national survey isn't nearly extensive enough to get a decent sample of unemployment in all the thousands of counties and municipalities in the country. About all the BLS does with its own state and local unemployment figures is create controversy. When the government readjusts the states' figures and they conflict with the original data, governors and mayors burn up the telephone lines to the BLS offices with complaints about shrunken state or local unemployment rates, which naturally mean fewer federal dollars flowing into their areas.

The Labor Department defends its unemployment statistics by saying they were never meant to carry the weight of social significance attributed to them, and that one must look at a range of data, not just "the" unemployment rate. After all, the BLS publishes tons of highly detailed figures each month in its journal, *Employment and Earnings*. But the fact remains that news commentators and politicians don't spend long hours burrowing through all the statistics.

Instead, they take the reported unemployment rate to be a God-given truth, the basis for quick action. They don't even wait for the Labor Department's frequent revisions to the rates. Many ill-advised, unnecessary policies are formulated on the basis of these faulty figures. One economist, Sar Levithan of George Washington University, points out that the unemployment figures tell us we're nearly twice as badly off as we were in the late 1960s—when the unemployment rate was low—but that just isn't true, he asserts. Levithan has called for replacing or complementing the present unemployment rate with a "hardship index" that would truly measure economic suffering. But the tradition-bound Labor Department isn't much interested.

The lesson is that here again is a government statistic that exaggerates our problems and fools government leaders and leads politicians to make unfounded charges and sends journalists off reporting heart-rending stories of how the whole nation is in the grip of dire poverty. You just have to take it with great skepticism. All the unemployment figures can do is to give some very general indication of the direction of unemployment—whether it's going up or not—and even then things like strikes can make that function misleading. These statistics are simply not to be trusted under any conditions. The importance attached to every decimal point in the unemployment rate by journalists and politicians is an index of their ignorance about what the figures really represent.

Gross National Product—Four times per annum, the government makes an heroic attempt to tote up in a single number —GNP—all the multifaceted movements of the American economy. The Gross National Product is relied upon as the principal index of national prosperity. But GNP can't really measure prosperity, for it ignores many of the things that make life worth while, such as sunsets and home cooking. On the other hand, it includes all manner of unpleasant things, like the costs of hurricanes and wars. Then, too, since the GNP figure is calculated from incompatible, incomplete data, it's riddled with error.

And it is eternally being revised. In fact, the Commerce Department figures that by the time its preliminary estimate of the after-inflation GNP growth rate in any quarter goes through its first annual revision, the figure might fall by as much as 1.9 percentage points or rise by 2 points. Suppose the first estimate presented on the evening news shows a healthy growth rate of 4 percent. By the time of the first annual revision, which takes place in July, that 4 percent may transform itself into an anemic 2.1 percent or even a robust 6 percent. And you can bet that the revision won't get as much media notice as the first figure did.

The Commerce Department's calculations say the −1.9 to +2 percent variation is valid nine tenths of the time, but for the other tenth the estimate might be revised even more drastically. Economist Arthur Okun, who was a chief economic adviser to President Lyndon Johnson, remembers one of the biggest miscalculations. The year was 1965 and the conflict in Vietnam was getting hot. During the last half of the year, businessmen, anticipating fat new orders from the Defense Department, began building up large inventories of raw materials. The Commerce Department missed the inventory accumulation and reported that real GNP had grown by 5.4 percent in the third quarter and 5.8 percent in the fourth. These numbers were eventually revised upward to 7.1 and 8.7 percent, and Okun later complained that, if the buildup had been caught, the Johnson administration would have seen how inflationary the war promised to be and might have increased taxes in 1965. Such an increase, according to this logic, might have choked off the long inflationary ferment that came to a head with Nixon's wage and price controls of the early 1970s.

Revisions are a way of life at the Commerce Department's Bureau of Economic Analysis, where the statistics for Gross National Product are turned out. The truth is that no GNP figure is ever final, for there are six routine revisions of each original estimate, and major revisions of the whole GNP series every few years. The main reason for all the tinkering is the immensity of the job. Gross National Product, which measures the market value of all final goods and services produced in the country over a period of time, is compiled from a motley array of sources, none of which was designed to make life easy for the technicians at the BEA. For example, the data on consumer spending come from the Census Bureau's monthly survey of retail stores plus a tally of car sales put out by the Motor Vehicle Manufacturers' Association. Export estimates come from customs declarations. Information about government purchases is taken from the *Monthly Treasury Statement.* Farm income is estimated by the Department of Agriculture. These sources don't always meet the standards of accuracy required by economists and prognosticators. Many of the numbers aren't even released in time for the quarterly estimates.

The BEA therefore keeps updating its estimates as new data flow into its offices high up in Washington's dowdy Tower Building. The very first GNP quarterly figure is an unpublished "guesstimate," known officially as a projection, which is given only to the President's Council of Economic Advisers, and some Cabinet officers, and the Federal Reserve Board. White House advisers use the GNP projections to divine whether a recession is near or if boom times are approaching. A real GNP growth rate that is zero or negative for three quarters in a row is supposed to signal recession dead ahead.

But that unpublished guesstimate is quite crude, and policy makers are better advised to wait for firmer figures. In fact the unpublished estimate, which is sent over to the White House fifteen days before the end of each quarter, becomes raw matter for a more refined version that is released to the public about fifteen days after a quarter's close. This is the one announced with much fanfare on the nightly network news shows. But it's only the beginning. The GNP is further revised in each of three successive Julys, when the bureau finally gets hold of comprehensive annual surveys, allowing use of data such as the yearly business profit sums reported on tax returns. After these July revisions come the intermittent large-scale revisions that the BEA calls "benchmarks" because they set new levels for the series by incorporating data from the Census Bureau's economic censuses. Often, in a benchmark revision, the BEA will change the way it defines or gauges some of the GNP components. The last benchmark revision, based on the 1972 economic census, was done in 1976, when the Gross National Product figures were revised all the way back to 1929, the year the series began. The next big benchmark revision will come after the 1980 economic census.

Every freshman economics student learns that GNP = C + I + G + X. Translated, that means Gross National Product is the sum of consumer expenditures (C), business spending on plants and machinery (I for investment, though not in the financial sense of the term), government purchases (G), and exports less imports (X). The curious thing about these components is that they include bad things as well as good ones. An oil spill actually increases GNP as companies and the government spend cash to clean up the mess. War is an absolute boon. But in contrast, the GNP categories don't include work done in the household, for which no money changes hands. Nor does the GNP compilation take account of the depletion of natural resources. It leaves out the value of increased human "capital," as when someone goes to college and raises his value in the marketplace. Neither does it count the value of organizational "capital." Illness and crime are ignored when the data are added up. In short, the Gross National Product doesn't say much about the quality of American life. A few analysts have tried their hand at GNP adjustments—adding in household production, for example, and subtracting for all sorts of social ills—to wind up with such constructs as "Net Economic Welfare," but these efforts remain curios of social science.

Jack Crimeans, at the BEA's Division of Environmental and Nonmarket Economics, explains the problem this way: "There is no consensus on what to add or what to subtract. Economists don't know how to measure well-being." He says when experts do try to correct the GNP's conceptual deficiencies, they often find that the depression years of 1932 and 1937, for instance, turn out to have been "great" years. During those bleak times, there was lots of household production, with so many out of work. And recession is the greatest thing in the world for slowing down pollution. With factories idle, the air turns clear and the rivers cleanse themselves of contaminating chemicals. All of this suggests the dimensions of the value judgments required to come up with any statistical measure of national well-being. Crimeans' office does publish figures on pollution abatement spending for anyone to subtract from the GNP if he wishes. And his department might in future years figure the value of household work and account for resource depletion. But like the pollution abatement numbers, these computations will be published separately from the GNP itself, so as not to tamper with the continuity of a series that goes back to 1929.

You'll notice that I keep referring to "real" Gross National Product—that is, after-inflation GNP—and it is by far the most meaningful version. After all, GNP is a big conglomeration of the dollar values of a wide variety of goods and services. The only common denominator between these apples and oranges is their price in dollars. So GNP can grow either because more things were sold or because the prices of the things went up. Usually both happen at the same time. So it is necessary to take out the price increases to measure how much the economy really grew, in terms of more products and services bought and sold. The Commerce Department figures real GNP by "deflating" each of the subcategories of the number after they have been compiled. In other words, the BEA divides the subtotals by price indexes that seem appropriate. For example, breakdowns of the Consumer Price Index are used to "deflate" consumer expenditures. The Producer Price Index breakdowns are used for business plant and equipment purchases. Special inflation indexes, such as the telephone-equipment price index provided by AT&T, are used to deflate special categories. Then the deflated categories are added up to get real Gross National Product. That tells how much the economy expanded. What business analysts and government economists examine most closely is the percentage change in real GNP—the so-called real GNP growth rate. Throughout the 1970s it was thought that a 4 percent real Gross National Product growth rate was about the right speed for the economy to grow. Any higher rate, it seemed, meant inflation would build up. In the 1980s we might have to get used to something more like a yearly average of 2 percent real growth. But whatever the rate, policy makers use the real GNP statistics as their guide in "fine-tuning" the economy and trying to engineer good times right before a presidential election. Maybe it would be a good thing if the policy makers paid a little less attention to every squiggle in the GNP graph, especially since the figures can change so drastically when they are revised.

When the Bureau of Economic Analysis "deflates" current-dollar GNP to arrive at real Gross National Product, what drops out of the calculation is known as the "implicit price deflator of the Gross National Product." It's a price index like the Consumer and Producer price indexes, but economists prefer it to the others because, since it's derived from the GNP, it covers all segments of the economy and thus should better reflect the true inflation in the economy. Not surprisingly, inflation as measured by the GNP deflator is always less than that shown by the Consumer Price Index and the Producer Price Indexes. However, since parts of the

CPI and the Producer Price Indexes are used to deflate Gross National Product, the GNP mirrors some of their already mentioned defects. Another problem with the GNP deflator price index is that it comes out only once every quarter. That's too slow for government fine-tuners who are under the illusion that they can engineer each month's progress of the national economy. It's also too slow for sundry Wall Street forecasters who love to scare the pants off investors and newspaper reporters by proclaiming a recession or wage and price controls every time the monthly inflation indexes move upward.

Besides Gross National Product and the GNP deflator, the Commerce Department breaks down the mass of data into various combinations, such as Net National Product (GNP minus an allowance for the depreciation of industrial machinery and plants). There is also Gross Domestic Product, which is GNP minus the export sector. In addition, the Commerce Department publishes the separate parts of GNP: consumer expenditures, business investment, and so on. In fact, the Commerce Department breaks the statistics down further, to categories like retail sales and inventories. If you want to see these items—and many businessmen do— you can find them in the department's monthly *Survey of Current Business*.

Productivity—This is the all-important link between wages and prices that was discussed in Chapter 14. The government measures it in terms of output per man-hour. This isn't really a conceptually valid way to gauge productivity, however. What counts is the combined productivity of workers, machines, energy, and even raw materials. This comprehensive measure is called *total-factor productivity*. A few academic economists calculate tables of total-factor productivity from time to time, but there are not yet any regular compilations of the numbers, because it's quite tough to do; one has immense difficulties with such technicalities as the fact that a machine bought ten years ago can't be compared with a machine bought today, and the fact that few firms keep good data on output per BTU of energy used.

The output per man-hour figures produced by the Labor Department are issued quarterly and annually. The quarterly output per man-hour figures jump around a great deal and are often revised later, so they can't be taken very seriously. Even if these quarterly figures were stable, they would hold little meaning, because productivity increases or decreases significantly only over the long haul. True, the productivity data vary with the business cycle, but these variations are not significant. They reflect only the tendency of businessmen to hold on to their employees though a recession has started. Thus, since output declines but man-hours stay the same, output per man-hour falls when a recession begins. It can also fall at the top of a business boom, because employers are adding extra workers who are less and less productive. Then, in the depths of a recession, when the economy is just starting to pull out, productivity goes up, because output rises a bit but businessmen aren't yet confident enough to hire new workers.

The most valuable way of looking at the output per man-hour figures is by watching their trend over a span of years, keeping in mind that these numbers directly reflect only the increases in human productivity. They can indirectly reflect the improvement in the productivity of machines to the extent that such machines allow a reduction in the number of man-hours. Most industries in the United States, however, are capital-intensive, which means they use more machines than workers; the output per man-hour figures are of dubious relevance to these industries. Take, for example, a chemical plant. What you have is a vast maze of tubes and stacks and pipes, operated by a handful of foremen and maintenance workers. Output per man-hour tells you little about productivity improvements in the refining industry. You need total-factor productivity data for that.

Consumers' Behavior—Several economic indicators, not widely reported outside the daily newspaper business pages, can be used to divine the prospect for consumer spending. This is important over the short term, since consumer spending accounts for more than 60 percent of the Gross National Product. When consumers spend money, boom times are all but inevitable; when they get tight-fisted, that means recession.

The increase in real, after-inflation personal income, as reported by the Commerce Department, suggests how much more money consumers have to spend. The personal-income figures, however, have to be weighed with other information, such as the indexes of consumer sentiment prepared by several research organizations. The best known is that produced by the University of Michigan, which conducts a quarterly national poll asking how people feel about the economy and whether they are buying now or holding off. The overall Index of Consumer Sentiment is the result of answers to such questions as "Would you say you and your family are better off or worse off financially than you were a year ago?" When the index goes down, it shows that the people surveyed tend to feel pessimistic about the economy. But the important question is what that pessimism means in terms of their buying behavior. It used to be assumed that when people felt gloomy over the state of the economy, they would retrench, stop spending, and thus make the economy truly gloomy, or gloomier than it would have been. But in recent years this has not been the case. Now when people see inflation continuing unabated, they go ahead and spend, figuring that prices will only be higher next year. This change comes out in people's answers to questions of whether they think the present is a good time to buy. In the late 1970s it became apparent that many Americans, accepting inflation as a fact of life, agreed on the cleverness of putting one's cash into durable items like cars and refrigerators and oil paintings rather than letting that money sit in a bank account. Therefore the queries about when people plan to buy have become much more closely watched.

But even these data need to be compared also with figures on consumer debt. The Federal Reserve Board publishes monthly estimates of how much we are using credit, including car loans and credit card revolving charge accounts, but not including home mortgage loans. The idea is that when the consumer debt numbers get too high, we're borrowing too much and will have to stop the spending spree to start paying back the credit. Analysts look at the Fed's data on consumer installment debt, but they also pay attention to the Fed's ratio of consumer debt to personal income.

Both figures, however, fooled a lot of analysts in 1978, when they saw consumer credit reach record levels. Many assumed that of course a recession would ensue by late 1978, because consumers would just have to devote more of their salaries to those Master Charge bills and bank payments. The analysts were fooled because they didn't notice that a lot of banks were extending two- and three-year car loans out to four years, so that each monthly payment took less of a bite and thus consumers could afford to borrow a bit more. Not only that, but in the late 1970s the war baby generation was coming into the twenty-five-to-thirty-four-year-old age group, when people use credit the most, to establish households and surround themselves with comforts they feel they are ready to afford. Finally, consumers began to realize that during inflation, if they use credit to finance their buy-in-advance-of-higher-prices behavior, they will pay back the loans in dollars that are less valuable than they were when the loans were taken out. So the consumer debt figures hit new records nearly every month in 1978, but no recession immediately followed.

Taking real personal income, consumer expenditures, consumer sentiment, and consumer debt and comparing the trends of these indexes, one might be able to learn something about what consumers are doing with their money.

This is very useful if you operate a boutique or sell cars, but using the data to predict a recession or boom times is foolhardy. The economy is too complex for that. One also has to see what the business sector is doing, and, of course, what the government is doing.

Business Behavior—As has been repeatedly pointed out in this book, the backbone of economic growth is business spending. But just a few pages ago I also said consumer spending can bring boom times or recession. Which is right? Both. Consumer spending is what makes the economy prosper. But where do consumers get their money? They get it by working for businesses, or for government organizations financed by taxes. Mostly they get their money from business, for doing work. So which comes first, the business spending that creates new jobs and puts money in the hands of people, or the consumer spending that puts money in the coffers of businesses and allows them to expand? In real life, both happen—or fail to happen—at once. But for the sake of clarity, we can say that business spending comes first.

When businessmen see profits to be made, when they feel optimistic about the economy, they invest money to build new plants or expand old ones. When they do that, they give employment to people who work in the construction trade. They also give work to those who manufacture the machines and equipment that are installed in the new facilities. When the new plant or the expanded one is ready, employees must be hired to operate it, to manage the workers, and to sell the extra products. That is, business investment creates jobs. And those jobs put money in people's hands; they spend it, which induces more businessmen to build new plants and create more jobs, which puts more money into more people's hands, which . . . and so it goes, at least in the ideal world, without all the impediments and conflicts present in the modern American economy.

The government and some private groups publish reports

of businessmen's plans for spending on new plants and equipment. The Conference Board, a business organization, puts out quarterly figures on "manufacturing capital appropriations." This measures the amount of money authorized for spending on new plants and equipment by the thousand largest manufacturing companies. The "contracts and orders for plant and equipment" data put out by the Commerce Department show the value of new contract awards for the building of commercial structures like banks, office buildings, factories, warehouses, garages, stores, and service stations. It includes the construction about to be started on public works such as highways and dams. A similar report is compiled by the F. W. Dodge Division of McGraw-Hill. Then the actual expenditures for new plant and equipment are published quarterly by the Commerce Department. The Census Bureau's tally of "housing starts" falls into this category; it measures the number of private homes that have just begun to be built each month.

To gauge how the business sector is already faring, rather than what it will do in the future, one can look at the industrial production figures of the Commerce Department. The index of industrial production takes into account the changes in the output of manufacturing, mining, and gas and electric utility businesses. But it excludes farm production, the construction industry, transportation, skilled trades, and service industries. What it tells us is whether industrial production is higher than it has been, or lower, or the same.

Another, more controversial statistic relating to the health of American business is the measure of capacity utilization. This purports to tell whether the nation's factories are going at full steam or whether there is room to speed up production before businessmen are pressured by consumer demand to expand their factories. Presumably, when business is operating at maximum capacity, then continued consumer demand will simply push up prices, because there's no way businesses can expand production overnight to meet the desires of the public; expansion takes time, especially with all the bureaucratic hoops a businessman has to jump through to get any expansion approved by the government. But there's a lot of argument about just how much capacity utilization is maximum. You'd think it would be 100 percent, but it doesn't seem to be, owing to imperfections in the capacity utilization measures. Some economists argue that, say, 90 percent is full capacity. Others say that since environmental laws have made a lot of manufacturing capacity inefficient and obsolete, 85 percent is more like it. Others point out that as energy costs go up, even more factory capacity is rendered useless, so maybe even 85 percent is too high a level and 80 percent represents full capacity. We'll leave the economists to their endless debates on the subject, but their disagreement suggests that we should be wary of any strict interpretations of the capacity utilization figures.

These numbers are calculated by the Commerce Department. But the Federal Reserve figures its own capacity utilization numbers, and so does the Wharton School of the University of Pennsylvania, among others. Heaven only knows which is the best. Like the wrangle over what percentage constitutes full capacity in the economy, this controversy is best left to the specialists. It gives them something to debate over lunch.

Corporate profits figures let us know how well business is doing in comparison to earlier periods. But before we look at the aggregate measure of all corporate profits, we should examine some curiosities about the reported profits of individual corporations. If we read in *The Wall Street Journal's* "digest of corporate earnings" that the New York Twisted Steel Corp. earned $5 million last year, but Ma's Fancy Outerspace Computers, Inc., made $10 billion, then clearly Ma's is a much more profitable business to be in, right? Not necessarily. The gauge of a business's profitability is not the absolute dollar value of profits—listed as "net income" in the financial statements. What matters is the amount of profits as a percentage of sales, and as a percentage of property (assets) used in the business. New York Twisted Steel may earn a 10 percent profit margin on its sales and a nice 20 percent return on its assets, its investment. Ma's might be making a piddling 3 percent profit margin and a 6 percent return on investment. It is just that Ma's is a big operation, selling a lot more in gross dollar terms than New York Twisted.

Beyond that, a corporation's profits can be artificially boosted for a year by the sale of a money-losing plant. Or they can be lifted by advantageous foreign currency transactions, if the company has overseas subsidiaries. Subsidiaries must convert their foreign money into dollars to send them to the home office; if the exchange rate is in the dollar's favor when this is done, then profits can soar. During inflation, a corporation's profits are more apt to be distorted by the defects of the standard accounting system. The first defect is found in the accounting of business inventories. The accounting system creates inventory profits, which businessmen often call "phantom profits." Suppose you operate a dressmaking business and you keep an inventory of wool cloth. Between the time you bought the stock of wool for your raw materials inventory and the time you write your financial statements, the price of wool rises a good bit. The amount it has risen gives you an artificial inventory profit because theoretically the value of your inventory has gone up. If it isn't clear why this is so, that's because one has to work through the accounting technicalities to see it. Any elementary accounting text will serve if you wish to go through the exercise.

Another problem with the traditional accounting system is that during inflation it fails to account fully for the replacement cost of the property used in the business; corporations therefore fail to set aside enough money, in the form of depreciation deductions, to replace the machines and equipment they own when these wear out. If proper account were taken of the cost of replacing the assets, these deductions would lower the business's profits to a more reasonable level.

Many corporations changed their inventory accounting system during the mid-1970s to lessen the effect of inventory profits, but as long as there is inflation, profits will still be artificially high because of inventory gains. As for underdepreciation, accountants have debated using "replacement cost accounting" but this method is very tricky and full of dubious assumptions. The government does require corporations to convert some of their figures to replacement rather than historical costs, but this is required only in the 10-k disclosure forms corporations have to send each March to the Securities and Exchange Commission. Even there in the 10-k, however, the replacement cost figures are so "soft" as to be pretty useless. And some analysts argue that historical accounting, which values assets at their original purchase price, is still appropriate. They say that if a corporation's assets are understated during inflation, this is balanced by the fact that its debts are overstated, since businesses, like consumers, will pay their debts back in cheaper dollars.

The Commerce Department comes out each quarter with corporate profit numbers for the American business sector. It reports the misleading "book" or accounting profits and it also reports profits after they are adjusted for inventory profits and underdepreciation. The trouble is that many a network correspondent or congressional demagogue will scream bloody murder about how "book" profits have increased, while ignoring the fact that corporate profits, correctly adjusted, have actually fallen.

Some of the best information on corporate profits is to be found in *Fortune* magazine's annual *"Fortune 500"* issue published each May. The data covers the 500 largest industrial corporations in the United States. *Fortune* also publishes a "Second 500" and a "Foreign 500."

Profits are important yardsticks by which to measure the

performance of corporations, but to measure a corporation's ability to make the kind of expenditures that really help the economy, one has to look at cash flow. This requires a bit of explanation. Recall that a business's profits, after taxes, can end up in either of two places. Some of the profits are distributed to stockholders in the form of stock dividends. The rest remain on the books, to increase the net worth of the business. These are called *retained earnings;* when added to the deductions made for plant and equipment depreciation, these make up cash flow. The amount of cash flow in turn reveals just how able a corporation is to spend money for expanded production. The Commerce Department publishes net cash flow figures, but they are rarely mentioned in the press. You'd have to read the *Survey of Current Business* to find them. But anyone who wants to know about cash flow usually has a particular company in mind, possibly as a potential common stock investment; in this case it is best to check the company's annual report and calculate some cash flow figures.

Business inventories reflect what happens between the production of goods and their sale—or, in other words, they reflect the discrepancy between demand and supply. In doing so, they are records of businessmen's judgments—and misjudgments—of what consumers will demand. Businessmen often refer to inventories as a "cushion" to protect them from the consequences of errors. If a producer keeps a little extra supply of gasoline, for example, then when demand unexpectedly surges he will have an extra margin to sell. His competitor down the road might not have kept much of an inventory on hand, and he will have to close down his service stations till he can buy more.

But nobody wants too much inventory. After all, it costs money to store goods on the shelf, and future sales don't put bread on the table today. In recent decades, modern "scientific" businessmen have adopted mathematical formulas and computer models to tell them how to pare inventories down to the minimum. Yet since the amount that can profitably be kept in inventory is dependent upon how much consumers will want to buy, errors are inevitably made. These errors can be broadly gauged from the statistics on business inventories published quarterly by the Commerce Department.

Interpreting the statistics can be tricky, though. For example, suppose the Commerce Department announces that inventories have declined for the past three months. Does that mean businessmen are cutting back because they see a recession around the corner? Or has a jump in consumer spending caught them by surprise? One must look at other figures, such as those for retail sales. In the same fashion, when inventories increase, one has to know whether this is happening because the economy is expanding and businesses are rebuilding their stocks for the next boom, or whether it's because people have stopped buying.

Economists place great significance on the behavior of business inventories. After all, when inventories decline, the next thing that will happen will be a fall in production, which means a rise in unemployment, a fall in people's income, a decline in their spending, a lowered Gross National Product (inventories are included in the "business investment" category of the GNP statistic), and, finally, recession. All of this follows unless the inventory decrease was due to a spurt in consumer demand that caught businesses off guard, a possibility that is less likely today with our careful husbandry of goods. In earlier years, a number of minor "inventory recessions" resulted in a lowered output because businesses misjudged the course of the economy.

As a rule of thumb, one can say that under normal circumstances an increasing accumulation of inventory augurs well for the health of the economy. A long decrease in additions to inventories spells lowered production and a likely downturn.

Government Receipts and Spending—If you want to know how much the government is currently confiscating in taxes, or the amount government bureaucrats are spending to buy their limousines and pay for junkets to Paris, the Commerce Department offers some statistics, although they won't give you breakdowns.

The federal government's receipt figures add up personal and corporate income taxes, sales taxes, excise taxes, and payments for Social Security. Expenditure statistics consist of the government's purchases of goods and services plus "transfer payments," which are the Social Security benefits, Workers' Compensation, hospital insurance, unemployment pay, food stamps, veterans' benefits, foreign aid, and a long list of government handouts. The expenditure figure also includes the amount of interest paid on the federal debt and subsidies paid out to businesses. This figure is measured in billions of dollars, at annual rates; it is state and local receipts and spending, however, that have ballooned the fastest over the last decade. The Commerce Department also publishes these figures, for those who enjoy reading bad news.

Obviously, then, when the government's expenditures exceed its receipts, that's what we call a government deficit. The last time there *wasn't* a government deficit, at the federal level, was in 1969. However, a few rich states such as Texas and California sometimes show budget surpluses.

Interest Rates—The most commonly reported of these is the "prime" interest rate, which is the interest rate banks charge their best corporate borrowing customers for short-term business loans. Naturally, the interest rate you pay for a car loan or a home improvement loan will be several points higher. The prime rate tends to be pretty stable; unlike other kinds of interest rates, it doesn't fluctuate freely. It is calculated by means of a formula, and the prime is raised or lowered in increments, when the banks feel the economic winds are changing. For instance, a major New York bank such as the Chase Manhattan will announce a quarter point increase in the prime rate when it feels inflation is getting worse, or after the Federal Reserve has cut back the supply of money. Most of the time, the other New York banks will follow. So will every other bank in the nation. When the prime rate is changed, the news gets around.

Other kinds of interest rates abound, but they are mostly of interest to bankers and Wall Street types. There is the Fed funds rate, which is the interest rate banks charge each other for overnight loans of millions of dollars of bank reserves. One bank may have surplus reserves for a night, so it will lend them to another bank that needs a few million for the next day to balance out its required reserves. All this is done on paper, by teletype, but the lending bank can make a nice little sum by charging the Fed funds rate, which is usually quite modest. One can also speak of the interest rate on three-month Treasury securities (bonds), the one on high-grade corporate bonds, the yield on home mortgages, and the interest rate on commercial paper, which is a form of loan made from one company to another—a corporate IOU. These interest rates move more or less in tandem. They can be found listed in *The Wall Street Journal*, in very small type.

The Dow Jones Industrials—We are now on the border between the economist's turf and the investor's speculative playground. But since the Dow Jones industrial average is daily reported in the press, we should briefly consider it. The Dow Jones industrials compilation is the average of the closing prices of thirty representative "blue chip" common stocks of big *Fortune* 500 corporations. There's also a Dow Jones average of fifteen public utility stocks and one for twenty transportation stocks, and a composite of all these separate averages.

When the Dow Jones industrials move upward or downward on any given day, that doesn't mean your stock has moved in the same direction. It may have done the opposite, or it may not have moved at all. Even when the Dow Jones industrials change abruptly, that will be significant only when trading volume on the New York Stock Exchange is high—that is, when the number of brokers buying or selling stocks approaches the proportions and fervor of a stampede.

Often newscasters and business editors attribute the day's movement of the Dow Jones averages to news of higher inflation or impending credit cutbacks or war in the Middle East. But this is merest conjecture. The movements can be random, without any logic, or they can be caused by the internal dynamics of the stock market. The market is now so dominated by institutional investors such as banks and mutual funds and union pension fund managers and insurance companies that often a slump in stock prices simply means the big institutions are fully invested in stocks and aren't ready to put more cash in the stock market.

Not surprisingly, business analysts often push for revisions of the Dow Jones industrials to reflect the changing makeup of American business. New companies are added to the Dow and old ones are removed every so often, though not often enough to satisfy all critics. For example, in 1959 four outmoded corporations were replaced by four new ones. In 1976 the Dow was again updated, this time by removing Anaconda, the copper company that had been bought by the Atlantic-Richfield oil company. In its place was put Minnesota Mining and Manufacturing. Even so, by 1979 the analysts were saying that the Industrials were weighted too heavily represented by the old-fashioned, mature manufacturing industries. There was little representation of the emerging semiconductor technology. None of the burgeoning mass media conglomerates showed up on the Dow, either. High technology didn't count enough. The result, if true, would obviously distort the performance of the stock market, with unpleasant consequences for investors and the companies whose stocks they misguidedly bought—or didn't buy. More than a few Wall Street gurus said that if the Dow Jones industrial average included the correct proportions of computer companies and other such denizens of fast growth, then the index would climb higher, thus attracting more investors, aiding more companies, and in the process making the economy more robust.

At present, the clamor is at least to put IBM in the index, and a few other modern corporations, shoving out older, declining industries, like steel and dime store retailing.

The Wall Street Journal, which administers the Dow Jones averages, has suggested it might soon make some substitutions to reflect the rise of the new technology.

Index